Build and Fly your own Plane

Build and Fly your own Plane

Robert Lowe

VAN NOSTRAND REINHOLD COMPANY
NEW YORK   CINCINNATI   TORONTO   LONDON   MELBOURNE

Printed in Great Britain

Published in 1980 by Van Nostrand Reinhold Company
A division of Litton Educational Publishing, Inc.
135 West 50th Street, New York, NY 10020, U.S.A.

First published in Great Britain 1980 by Granada Publishing – Technical
    Books Division
Frogmore, St Albans, Herts AL2 2NF
and
3 Upper James Street, London W1R 4BP

16 15 14 13 12 11 10 9 8 7 6 5 4 3 2 1

Library of Congress Cataloging in Publication Data

Lowe, Robert.
    Build and fly your own plane.

    Bibliography: p.
    Includes index.
    1. Airplanes, Home-built.   I. Title.
TL671.2.L64   629.133′343   79-27238
ISBN 0-442-21936-9

Granada ®
Granada Publishing ®

FRONTISPIECE: Heavens Above, *photo by Ken Burtt*

To
Michael Inskip
Alan Newnham
Bud Evans
and Sheila, my long-suffering wife,
who between them made it all come true.

Contents

List of illustrations

Foreword

Robert Lowe, a born again aviator following a lengthy boating hiatus, presents a new look at 'home-building' after a career of flying Hurricanes and Spitfires, engineering and mathematics and recently, to his eternal credit, building an Evans V.P.1. A builder himself, he presents in easy prose his experiences and a review of home-building for the practical aviator whose aerial adventures must fit into the economics of family living. Covering all aspects of selecting, building and flying a do-it-yourself aircraft, he offers his reader sound advice well seasoned with colourful anecdotes to emphasize his logic. Here is a book to encourage the wavering-to-start, provide guidance during the perilous first weeks, help with the multitude of how-best-to-do-it problems, be a friend during times of doubts, a source of encouragement during periods of remission, a silent companion through the months of progress, a source of guidance and courage as the first flight approaches and a friend forever as the thrill of flying one's own wings is added to life's accomplishments.

Bill Beatty, B.Ae.E.
Fellow V.P. Pilot

Acknowledgements

Parts of this book have appeared earlier as articles in *Popular Flying*, most of which were later reissued as a *Popular Flying* publication entitled *Enjoy the Sky*. They are now included here by kind permission of the Editors, to whom I am also indebted for permission to reproduce a number of photographs.

Thanks are also due to Macdonald and Jane's Publishers Ltd for permission to reproduce abstracts from *Jane's Pocket Book No. 14: Home-Built Aircraft*. These appear in the tables between pages 38 and 65.

Robert Lowe

Introduction

Building your own aircraft can be as easy or as difficult as you yourself choose to make it.

If you are capable of building one of the more complex designs you will need no advice from me. However, it is reliably estimated that well over sixty per cent of all home-built aircraft projects are sooner or later abandoned, so it would seem that a little guidance from someone who, with the minimum of manual skill, has actually built and flown his own little aeroplane could help to save a lot of wasted effort, expense and bitter disappointment.

Most hopeful home-builders are pilots and generally good pilots at that. Consequently they tend to select a design which promises outstanding performance and too often calls for skills in construction which they do not possess and can have little hope of acquiring.

In order to maximise the fun it is generally necessary to compromise and one of the purposes of this book is to suggest where, how and why these adjustments should be made.

There are national bodies that exist to help with advice and information and to further the interests of amateur aircraft builders and this they do very well especially in Great Britain, in France and in the U.S.A. The prospective builder would be well advised to join the appropriate association and pick their brains, for they alone have all the answers.

This is not a text-book on aeronautical engineering. Indeed, being the wrong sort of engineer, I am not qualified to write one. I am a mathematician by trade and am paid to sit in an office and think between tea-breaks.

In any case there are plenty of good text-books and most sets of plans are sold with building instructions, the best of which are as good as any text.

However there is a great deal more to the business of building an aircraft than is contained in any technical text-book and so I have tried to lead the reader through the trials, the frustrations, the paper work and the triumphs, looking under all the stones that the text-book writers leave unturned.

And it is precisely because I am no expert that I hope this book may be of value in persuading others that they can get themselves into the air at a cost within their slender means. 'What one fool can do another can' – to quote the great Professor Sylvanus P. Thompson in his delightful introduction to the calculus.

I built an Evans V.P.1 and so it is the building of this aircraft that I take as my model and try to talk the reader through, but the same principles apply to any wood and fabric aircraft.

Metal aircraft call for special skills and tooling. If you already have these skills you will need no technical assistance from me, though you may find much else of interest between these covers. But if you do not have them, be warned; they can take a long time to acquire.

So, if you are in a hurry to get into the air, set your sights lower and build in wood and fabric; in that medium this book may well give you some assistance.

When I started to build my little aircraft I scarcely believed that I would ever finish it. This, I think, was partly due to experience of Murphy's Law, that anything that can go wrong most assuredly will, and partly to the obvious scepticism of all my old friends. It seemed that it was only members of the Popular Flying Association (P.F.A.) who regarded me as a rational human being and not as a wild eccentric. I required constant reassurance, and this I could only find at the P.F.A. annual rally and at the monthly branch or 'Strut' meetings as they are called.

As completion drew near I was too busy to appreciate the fact, and it was not until after the first flight, when we had put 007 – yes, that is truly it's construction number – under wraps and lined up at the bar for a celebratory drink, that it suddenly hit me. I had actually done it. I had built an aeroplane – and it had flown.

I drove home in a golden glow of self-satisfaction. I imagined that this would wear off in time, but that does not seem to be the case. As time goes by it seems to me more and more remarkable that I, of all people, should have done this extraordinary thing. I cannot talk to a stranger for ten minutes without letting drop the fact that I have built an aeroplane and 'No, it's not a model, it's a real one and I fly in it.'

Whenever I realise that I am becoming a quite insufferable bore I remind myself that I am the least of all the amateur aircraft builders and that so many others have done so much better. I think of John Isaacs and his Fury and his even more beautiful Spitfire, both of which he designed as well as built; of Michael Vaisey's quite perfect Luton Minor and of Richard Husband's prize-winning V.P.1. Much as I love her I know that my 007 looks pretty dowdy in that company and I hang my head in shame – but not, I fear, for long.

Then I remind myself that I could not have done it without an enormous amount of help. Indeed, without the P.F.A. as a body it could never have been done at all.

So many people have chipped in with bits and pieces, with practical assistance and advice. There are, however, four people to whom I am

The Happy Home-builder, *Ken Burtt*

particularly indebted and who I can never adequately thank.

Firstly there is my inspector, Michael Inskip, who gently prodded me into it and thereafter kept me on the straight and very narrow path of acceptable workmanship. Even when he was rejecting my offerings he managed to make me feel grateful that he was doing it for my own good. He lent me tools, organised my bits of welding and spent many hours checking, measuring and testing my work. He hunted around for materials for me and his advice was always authoritative and sound. On the only two occasions when I was so presumptuous as to ignore his advice, he turned out to be perfectly right – and he never said 'I told you so.'

For everything to do with the engine I am indebted to Alan Newnham. The P.F.A. is full of people who give generously of their time and knowledge for the benefit of others, but there can be none more generous than Alan. Always cheerful, frequently profane, he can galvanise engines and people into sudden and productive effort. Without him I doubt that 007 would be flying yet.

Then there is Bud Evans, the designer of the V.P.s. Somehow he has managed to reduce aircraft building from a great and difficult art to something that anyone, even I, can do. Simplicity is said to be the hallmark of genius – any damn fool can produce a complex design – and by this standard Bud is certainly a genius. Big, gentle, friendly, he even

3

found time on one of his visits from the States to call on me and my little aeroplane, and give me his blessing and the benefit of his very valuable advice.

Finally there is Sheila, my ever-patient, uncomplaining wife, who has had to put up with wings in the dining room, ailerons, stabilator and rudder in the sitting room, plaster of paris on the polished floors, and most irregular meal times. Always ready to come out and help with holding wing-tips, reading scales, sewing fabric or assisting with the fuel flow test, she has even had to listen to aeroplane talk in bed. She accompanies me to rallies and to Strut meetings, ferries the car and helps in the hangar. And she does not even like flying. I cannot think what I can have done to be so blessed.

All I can say to the wife of a prospective aeroplane builder is that he is going to spend all his spare time close to home for several years and, while he is involved with his aircraft, he will have neither the time nor the money for the cigarettes, the whisky or the wild, wild women.

To the prospective builder himself, I would say 'Go right ahead'. If I can do it, so can you. You will have a lot of fun, meet some delightful people and find immense satisfaction at the end.

The occasion when your wheels leave the ground for the first time and you realise that you are flying on your very own wings is a moment that will live with you for the rest of your life.

Chapter 1

'There's one born every minute'

On a summer's evening in 1976 I taxied my little V.P.1 onto the grass runway at Goodwood in Sussex, opened the throttle all the way, pushed forward on the stick and felt the tail come up, and quite suddenly she was flying; clambering into the sky.

Over the end of the runway at 200 feet (60 m) I coaxed her into a gentle turn to avoid overflying Chichester. At 800 feet (240 m) I levelled off, eased the throttle back about a quarter of its travel and turned downwind.

Snug behind the windscreen I looked out at the white wings which I had built and were now, for the very first time, carrying me through the air.

This was the most exciting flying that I had ever known, more thrilling even than the Hurricanes, Spitfires and Mosquitos in which I once earned a precarious living, because this was the work of my own hands.

Opposite the downwind end of the runway I closed the throttle and let her settle into the glide. Instinctively I wheeled her into the curving, Spitfire approach, turning all the way down to the threshold, very conscious of the sensitivity of the controls, particularly in the pitching plane. A gentle flare and she bumped onto all three points.

I turned off the runway, pushed my goggles up and taxied back to the little crowd who had come to watch my aircraft's maiden flight.

In spite of all my 60 years I was grinning like a village idiot, still overcome by the intensity of this experience, hardly able to comprehend the fact that I had done it; I had actually built and flown this funny little aeroplane.

Of course the only really remarkable part of this exploit is the fact that I am almost totally lacking in any manual skills and the real credit belongs to the designer who made it possible for anyone, even so inept a carpenter as I, to build and fly his own aircraft.

Every year quite a number of amateur constructors take their little aeroplanes up on their maiden flights, but there would be many more if only they could be persuaded that it is not beyond their abilities and if only they knew where to go for advice and assistance.

Of recent years there has been a phenomenal increase in the number of people, men and women too, who have become interested in building their own aircraft. Indeed it now begins to look like the start of an avalanche.

5

There was a minor boom in amateur aircraft building in the late 1930s which produced some good and interesting designs, some of which are still being built to today, but this was brought to a sudden end by the Hitler war.

The aftermaths of both World Wars flooded the market with ex-military aircraft which kept the impecunious private pilots flying until the machines fell apart, and it was only when the supply of Avro 504s and Jennies and the later Tiger Moths, Magisters, Piper Cubs and Austers dried up that the poor pilots had to find another means of keeping airborne.

Fortunately the back-room designers and the small hardcore of people who just like building things had not been idle and there were designs specifically slanted at the home workshop ready and waiting for the frustrated pilots to work on.

The 1930s saw the Pietenpol Air Camper, the Long Longster, the Heath Parasol and the Corben Baby Ace, among others, take to the air in the United States, while in Britain the Luton Major and Minor, the Currie Wot and the Dart Kitten were the most popular of the successful types built and flown by amateurs.

From France came the notorious Pou du Ciel – the Flying Flea – which almost incredibly was afflicted with the inherent defect of an aft lifting surface which produced a mechanical couple which could overpower the control column, so that the Flea could not be pulled out of a dive once speed had built up.

It was unfortunate that, aerodynamically, the Flea failed to come up to its design specification as the idea behind it was sound and a number of successful variants of the same configuration have since been flown in France, but people still remember the Flea's reputation as a killer and fight shy of them.

After the Hitler war amateur design and construction were slow to get going again except in France where an imaginative government gave active encouragement to the building and flying of ultra-light aircraft, so that the French were first in the field with post-war designs, notably the Jodel D9 and D11, the Druine Turbulent and Turbi and the Piel Emeraude.

In Britain the inveterate constructors had to make do with the pre-war Lutons or the Currie Wot, or build to the new French designs until the advent of the Taylor Monoplane and the Tipsey Nipper. In 1963 John Isaacs unveiled his scaled down Hawker Fury, not unlike the Currie Wot in construction and so eminently suitable for amateur building; then, some twelve years later he followed this with his beautiful little Spitfire. About the same time Eric Clutton put his plans for 'Fred' on the market.

In the United States there appeared a steady stream of new designs, the Stitts Playboy, the Bowers Fly-Baby, the Stolp Starlet and Starduster, the Bedes, in particular the BD4, the Pazmanys, the Wittman Tailwind, the Smith Miniplane, the E.A.A. Biplane, and, perhaps most significantly, the

Evans V.P.1 and V.P.2, to name but a few.

We come to the building of our little aeroplanes by all sorts of ways and for many different reasons but, perhaps, we can be divided broadly into two camps.

Firstly, and most fortunate, are those who like making things with their hands, and aeroplanes in particular. They are blessed above all, but there are not many of them.

The great majority are pilots who are driven to it by the hard logic of economics. They must either give up flying or find a cheaper way to fly. And there can be no doubt but that it is by far the cheapest and, for most of us, the only way to fly.

At a time when one is hard put to it to find a Cessna 150 to hire for less than £18 per hour, my V.P.1 costs me less than £4 per hour inclusive of insurance and hangarage – less than 5 pence per mile; it costs more than twice as much as that to run a small car.

In addition to that I have a capital asset which has doubled in market value in the three years that I have been flying it.

This makes economic sense that even a bank manager should be able to appreciate.

There are, of course, less tangible bonuses that accrue, such as the delightful people that one comes to meet and the inexpressible pleasure of flying one's own creation.

The first step along this primrose path is to join the appropriate national association. In Britain it is absolutely essential since the Popular Flying Association is responsible for the certification of amateur built aircraft of less than 1750 lb (794 kg) all-up weight and under 125 hp (93 kW). You are not likely to build anything larger than that at a first attempt.

There was a time, just after the war, when amateur aircraft building was frowned upon in official circles in both Britain and America. The respective civil aviation authorities made things difficult for the poor home-builder with more and more onerous and restrictive legislation so that eventually the amateurs had to get together and form associations to set about the tedious business of winning concessions from their aviation authorities and opposing further restrictive legislation.

In view of the fact that amateur aircraft builders are, by nature, individualists these joint representations have been quite remarkably successful, to the extent that, in the United Kingdom, the Civil Aviation Authority has entrusted the whole of the inspection and certification of all home-built aircraft to the P.F.A.

This is a hard won and jealously guarded privilege, so that the P.F.A.'s inspectorate, though friendly and informal, tends to be searching and meticulous. Doubtful material or shoddy workmanship just will not get by.

In some ways things are easier in the U.S.A. The Experimental Aircraft Association (E.A.A.) has won a great many concessions from its

7

government and continues successfully to oppose restrictive legislation, but inspection and certification still remain in the hands of the Federal Aviation Administration (F.A.A.). Materials do not have to be released or inspected until they have been incorporated in the aircraft, there is no mandatory fuel flow test and there are no flight test requirements other than having to stay within a 25 mile (40 km) radius of base for the first 60 hours. There is no requirement for dual ignition and there are far fewer inspection stages than required by the P.F.A.

On the face of it it might seem that the amateur has an easier time of it in America but the British system has its compensations. To have one's inspector's expert advice always on tap is a very great boon.

The situation in France is altogether different. There, an enlightened government actively encourages its amateurs to design and build their own flying machines and goes so far as to reimburse to the constructor a large part of the cost as soon as his creation takes to the air. The benefit to France must be incalculable since, as a direct result of this policy, they now have the largest light aircraft industry outside the United States.

French designers are traditionally great innovators so that any rally held under the aegis of the Reseau du Sport de l'Air (R.S.A.) can be guaranteed to produce a crop of unusual and exciting little aircraft.

We can only be pleased at the good fortune of our friends across the Channel but, looking back to the great days of the De Havilland Moths, the Avro Avian and the Blackburn Bluebird, we must regret that Britain no longer has a significant light aircraft industry, especially in the knowledge that the requisite talent is still around and only stifled by an industrially inept and unimaginative government.

We can at least be grateful that, thanks to the Popular Flying Association, amateur aircraft building and the flying of home-built aircraft are once again flourishing under fair and reasonable conditions in Britain.

This rather loosely constituted, voluntary association of cheerful enthusiasts does a difficult job with an efficiency that is surely unequalled by most, if not all, more formally constituted bodies.

It disseminates a great deal of useful information, pertinent advertisements and entertaining reading through its bi-monthly magazine *Popular Flying*, probably the finest publication of its kind with the possible exception of the American E.A.A.'s *Sport Aviation* which, as one would expect, has far greater resources at its disposal.

More information and other practical assistance is passed around at the regular, informal, meetings of the P.F.A.'s local branches, or Struts as they are called, along with quite a lot of beer. I picked up nearly all my flight instruments at bargain prices as a result of a lucky encounter at a Strut meeting, and at another I found an engine and an expert to do the conversion for me.

It is only when one starts to build that one realises just how much these dedicated volunteers take upon themselves and how very well they do it.

Without the P.F.A. the way of the amateur constructor would be immensely more difficult, if not impossible. So the first thing that any would-be aircraft builder must do is to join the P.F.A. or, if living in America, the E.A.A. or, in France, the R.S.A. Better still, join all three. The addresses of these bodies are:

The Popular Flying Association,
Terminal Building,
Shoreham Airport,
Shoreham-by-Sea,
Sussex,
BN4 5FF.
Telephone: Shoreham-by-Sea 61616
Publication: *Popular Flying*, (bi-monthly).

The Experimental Aircraft Association,
P.O. Box 229,
Hales Corner,
Wisconsin 53130,
U.S.A.
Telephone: AC 414/425-4860
Publication: *Sport Aviation*, (monthly).

Le Reseau du Sport de l'Air,
39, rue Sauffroy,
75017, Paris,
France.
Telephone: 228.25.54
Publication: *Les Cahiers du R.S.A.*, (bi-monthly).

These bodies are the repositories of just about all the knowledge, experience and information on ultra-light and home-built aircraft that has been accumulated since flight began and this is readily available to their members. Their subscriptions are modest, since they rely heavily on unpaid, amateur assistance and they publish their own excellent magazines included in the subscription.

It would be a very foolish fellow who would forego so much assistance and so many benefits.

Undoubtedly the best way for the uninitiated to learn about home-built aircraft is to go to one of the rallies, preferably his national annual rally, though that of a local branch may prove less overpowering.

I learnt more in two days at the P.F.A. rally at Sywell than I could have picked up in years of reading books or magazines.

Sywell really opened my eyes. A grass airfield in the Midlands on a heavenly full summer day. So many little aeroplanes; Jodels, Nippers,

Lutons, Taylors, Betas, Turbulents, Condors, Currie Wots, Fabulous Fred, an Evans V.P.1 and many others, some of them built to a standard which would be uneconomic for a commercial builder to attempt, others with a finish which I felt that even I could achieve, but they flew.

This was the real stuff of flying. Here was the spirit that had powered the private flying movement of the 1920s and 30s and I had imagined was gone for ever. This was fun.

Walking around the paddock, looking a lot, taking photographs, talking to owner-builders, I acquired a great fund of information which provided material for thought and argument for weeks to come.

One's selection of a type to build is a deeply personal matter. There can be no 'best buy'; it depends so much upon individual circumstances, preferences and prejudices. This is probably the most agonising and crucial decision that the hopeful builder will have to make.

The field of choice is so enormously wide. At first sight they are all aeroplanes and to anyone unfamiliar with the complexities of an aircraft's structure the differences and the difficulties may not be apparent, so that the keen pilot may be induced to make his choice purely on the basis of performance. This could be an expensive and disheartening mistake.

It is a sad fact that most home-built aircraft projects are sooner or later abandoned. The majority of these are given up simply because they call for more skill and competence in the use of tools than is possessed by the ordinary, run-of-the-airfield pilot.

This is a pity because there are a number of aircraft designed specifically with simplicity of construction in mind. The best of them perform remarkably well and anyone with a pair of hands and two to four years of spare time could be certain of completing them.

So one's skill, or lack of it, should be one of the factors uppermost in one's mind when making the choice of an aircraft from the long list of designs on offer.

And what a catalogue it is, containing, among other less obviously glamourous offerings, scaled down fighters with dazzling performance figures, neat little two-seaters offering the comfort and equipment of the best store-bought products, fully aerobatic aircraft suitable for competition work and wickedly sleek little racing machines.

Most of them are good aircraft and will do all that their designers claim for them but many of them, so far as most of us are concerned, suffer from one serious defect that lies hidden under the enthusiastic descriptions of their merits, masked by their very creditable performance figures and almost obliterated by the mouth-watering photographs of the finished product in flight. They are not easy to build.

Many of them call for a skill in welding and forming metal which can take a long time and many hours in night school to acquire. Most of them require a purpose built aero engine, an indivisible cost which could be beyond the pockets of most home-builders.

It is true that some aircraft have been built in a remarkably short time by people whom one would never suspect of having the necessary skill or spare time. I know two doctors, one of whom built a Currie Wot and the other a Falconar F11, each in two years, but these are the exceptions.

I know of another Currie Wot nearing completion after ten years of effort and a Jodel D11 which has just flown after eleven years of patient work.

There are people who enjoy pottering along on a major project for year after year, for whom meticulous workmanship on every small component is an end in itself, but the great majority of us are short on manual skills and impatient to get flying.

Too many of us are beguiled by the glowing reports, the beautiful photographs and the fine performance figures of what is, undoubtedly, just the aircraft we have always dreamed of possessing, there, if not in the flesh, at least in the pages of *Sport Aviation* or *Popular Flying*. Perhaps we actually go to the P.F.A. or E.A.A. rallies and see our dream on the ground and in the air.

In a spate of enthusiasm we send for the plans and order up the materials. Then, little by little, the tedium of slow, meticulous work, made slower by lack of skill, begins to tell on us as we realise that the programme of work is stretching out for years ahead of us. Until, at last, we are forced to the conclusion that the whole project is beyond our ability or reserves of patience. Sadly we put our log-books away for ever and advertise the bits and pieces of our dream for sale. Every copy of *Popular Flying* or *Sport Aviation* carries such advertisements.

I have heard it said that most home-built aircraft have to pass through three pairs of hands before they fly. This may be an exaggeration but it is at least partly true.

So here is one way to reduce the building time and the frustration. Buy up somebody else's part completed project and finish it off yourself; but just make sure that the paper work is up to date and take your inspector along when you go to view your bargain. And some of them are real bargains.

Another way to limit the time in the workshop and by-pass the skill-demanding work is to buy a kit, but there are very few kits available – only the Tipsey Nipper and the Wittman Tailwind spring readily to mind – but for most of us the indivisible costs of this course are more than we can bear. The finished aircraft will still be a great deal cheaper than a factory built machine and you can still benefit from the great concession made to the amateur constructor, both by the C.A.A. in the United Kingdom and by the F.A.A. in the United States, that if you have built it yourself you may maintain it yourself. This represents a considerable saving in your annual operating costs.

So if your need for an aircraft is urgent and you have some savings under the mattress, a kit could be your best course.

But for those of us who have to build out of income the only way is to buy the plans, order up the materials as we need them or can afford them, and get down to work.

The choice of a type to build can be simplified if one first eliminates all those that will overstrain one's pocket or be beyond one's competence in the use of tools; one must be prepared to compromise on performance, equipment and comfort.

For a start a two-seater will cost about twice as much as a single-seater and take twice as long to build. An aero engine will cost up to ten times as much as a converted Volkswagen 'mill'. If, as in my own case, your resources are slender and your skill negligible you will, if you face the facts, finish up building a square-winged, Volkswagen-engined, open-cockpit single-seater and love every minute of it.

I built a V.P.1 and have never for a moment had cause to regret my choice. I was able to build it in a reasonable time – three years in fact – and it has turned out to be a lovely aeroplane to fly, reasonably fast with a good rate of climb and to have no vices at all.

The V.P.'s designer, Bud Evans of La Jolla, California, has managed to reduce what used to be a great and difficult art to something that anyone, even I, can do.

For most of us working in wood and fabric is easier than working in metal. We have all built cupboards, bookshelves, sledges and even boats. However crude our efforts we have some sort of feeling for wood. The building of a V.P.1 at least calls for no more skill than that; only a great deal of patience in meticulous setting out, checking every measurement before we cut and not forgetting to sharpen our tools before we go to work.

One valuable by-product of this last mechanical chore is that it compels a state of contemplation in which one can think calmly about the immediate job in hand; the best way to tackle it, how to set it out, any special priorities in assembly. The quiet rubbing of steel on stone concentrates the mind most powerfully. It is indeed a spiritual exercise without which your endeavours may well come to naught.

My own besetting faults are indolence and inertia. With any major project I have to talk myself into the situation where I must either get on with the job or be for ever shamed in the eyes of my friends.

In this particular enterprise I was fortunate in that John Dunford, who was charged by the Popular Flying Association with the responsibility for co-ordinating the efforts of V.P. builders in Britain, asked me to contribute, from time to time, a few notes on my progress for publication in *Popular Flying*.

Once having committed myself in writing I had no option but to carry the thing through to completion. Every two or three months I had to have done enough work to provide material for another article. It was shame and fear of ridicule that rode upon my back and drove the spurs into my sloth.

Vital Actions – Mag Check, *David Lolley*
Take-off from Popham, *David Lolley*

The Office – 007's instrumentation, *David Lolley*

This is not to say that I did not have a great deal of active encouragement from the P.F.A. as a body, from its officers and members as individuals and in particular from my inspector, Michael Inskip. Indeed one of the nicest things about building an aeroplane is the astonishing amount of help that is volunteered, often by total strangers, and the charming and friendly people that one comes to meet. One could not find oneself in better company.

Even for those who, like myself, do not much care for building anything, it can turn out to be the most tremendous fun. It can occupy every spare moment for two, three or four years, or more. There is a lot of hard work and much frustration but the end result is worth every minute of that labour.

And those of us who do, eventually, get our funny flying machines into the air find there a new joy in living and an unbounded sense of freedom which is given to nobody else at all. Others may fly higher or faster and make a rich living from the sky but we still take off into the golden light of the dawn of aviation and oh, how fortunate we are.

Chapter 2

Decisions, decisions

I could no more choose an aircraft for you to build than I could pick you a bride; but I can give you a few pointers from my own experience and observations that may help in making this difficult decision.

The brassy blonde could be marvellous for a honeymoon but the lady of less obvious charms could be the safer bet for a lifetime's companionship. And just as a pause for thought could save one from a disastrous entanglement so will a cold, objective consideration of all the factors affecting your choice of an aeroplane assure you of years of happy building and eventually flying your chosen project.

Without any doubt the most important factor affecting this decision is, for most of us, our own skill, or lack of it, and our powers of application.

A degree in aeronautics could qualify you to design your own aircraft and if your degree was followed by an apprenticeship in an aircraft building firm you would be capable of constructing even the most complex piece of high technology, always assuming that you could afford the special tools and dies. Regrettably very few of us are blessed with such a comprehensive education.

Once, in company with an old cabinet maker, I was admiring a coffee table made by a colonial customs officer to wile away the tedium of waiting for customers at a border post in the middle of Africa. It was a beautiful piece of work realised in iron-hard African redwood salvaged from an abandoned ox-waggon, so perfectly made and matched that none of the joints could be seen, even when we turned it over. Eventually the old man pronounced it perfect and went on to say 'You know there is nothing the professional can do that cannot be done just as well by an amateur – it just takes him a hell of a lot longer'.

This is the clue to it all – time. If you can see no end to your labour you will eventually tire of it and in the later stages of the work there is the risk of spoiling a large assembly that may have taken months, or even years, to build, simply through ignorance or plain ham-handedness.

If, like mine, your skill is negligible and what you have has been gained in very different fields, think hard before you embark on any but the very simplest of aircraft.

But do not let lack of skill put you off building at all. There are aircraft designed specifically to suit your level of skill, and some of them perform remarkably well.

As mentioned before the spectrum of choice is enormously wide. *Jane's Pocket Book of Home-Built Aircraft* lists some 130 different types and it is very far from being exhaustive.

At the end of this chapter you will find my own selection which runs to over ninety. I have omitted the amphibians which are beyond the scope of this book, the gyroplanes which frankly terrify me and, with regret, the freaks such as the Breezy, the Rail, the Birdman and the jet-propelled Bede which I find enormously attractive but not really very practical. I have also omitted all those aircraft which are well above the P.F.A. authorisation limits.

So, in order to find one's way through this jungle one must establish some criteria as guide-lines.

I would guess that for most of us a sober assessment of our own manual skills and capabilities will narrow the field most effectively, even more so than the consideration of cost.

In the matter of finance it must be obvious that the larger and more complex the aircraft the greater will be the final cost. On the other hand it could be argued that the more elaborate machine will take much longer to build so that the outgoings will be spread over a longer period and may even adjust to your cash-flow, though the extended building time may prove unacceptable and some of the indivisible costs – those that must be met in one payment such as a new Lycoming engine – may prove financially embarrasing.

If money and skill, or lack of either, are not factors of importance in making your choice, the first consideration must be the purpose for which you require the aircraft.

If it is to be for personal transport in all weathers it will need to be a two-seater cabin machine with a reasonably high cruising speed such as the Wittman Tailwind, the Pazmany PL-2, the Piel C.P. 750 or the Thorp T-18.

If your penchant is for aerobatics your choice will probably fall upon a short span, close coupled, high powered biplane like the Pitts Special, the Acro-Sport or the BA-4B, though having watched Bob Cole at work I would personally plump for the Isaacs Spitfire.

For pylon racing you would need a Taylor J.T.2 Titch, a Sonerai or a Rollason Beta.

You may hanker for the nostalgia of the 'War Birds' and wish to re-create an SE-5A, a D.H.2, a Hawker Fury or a Spitfire. Plans are available and they are not all that difficult to build.

On the assumptions that the Volkswagen is the cheapest reliable engine and that wood and fabric provides the cheapest and most easily built airframe, I have grouped my selection of aircraft under the following classifications:

(a) Single Seat; VW engine; Wood and Fabric wings and fuselage or Wooden Wings and Steel Tube fuselage structure, all fabric covered.

(b) Single Seat; VW engine; Sheet Metal wings and fuselage.

(c) Two Seats; VW engine. There are only five of these of which only one, the Evans V.P.2, is strictly wood and fabric.

(d) Single Seat; Aircraft Engine; Wood and Fabric wings and fuselage or Wooden Wings and Steel Tube fuselage structure, all fabric covered.

(e) Single Seat; Aircraft Engine; Sheet Metal wings and fuselage.

(f) Two Seats; Aircraft Engine; Wood and Fabric wings and fuselage or Wooden Wings and Steel Tube fuselage structure, all fabric covered.

(g) Two Seats; Aircraft Engine; Sheet Metal wings and fuselage.

One or two oddments have crept in such as the Colomban Cri-Cri with its two chain-saw engines which I just could not bring myself to leave out, so it slipped in with the V.W. engined, all metal single-seaters.

Mention of the Cri-Cri reminds me that before parting with good money for plans you should check with your particular approving authority – the P.F.A., the E.A.A. or the R.S.A. – that your preferred design has its approval or you may well find yourself with an aeroplane that no one will let you fly.

This is not just bureaucratic bloody-mindedness; each national body is required to check that a design accords in all respects with the criteria laid down by the civil aviation authority to which it is responsible, which means that they have to check all the design calculations and scrutinise the flight test data. This takes a great deal of time and if they were to skimp it they would soon lose their approval. The only sufferers would be the poor home-builders who would then have to deal directly with aviation authorities; heaven preserve us from that.

To the best of my knowledge the Cri-Cri is not yet approved in the U.K. by the P.F.A., but I would like to see our Engineering Committee's faces when they are asked to check it out. Like so many beautifully simple innovations the supporting calculations are probably extremely complex and can only be proved by extensive testing of the composite materials.

You will note that I have included with the all-wood classification those aircraft with steel tube framed fuselages. This is partly to avoid too many classifications but mainly because there is a certain amount of welding in all aircraft – the control column assembly, flying strut ends etc. – and most of us have to get that done by a certificated welder. That being the case, and as the overall cost seems to be comparable with an all wood fuselage, it seems reasonable to lump them together.

In several cases, the Nipper is one and the Wittman Tailwind another, it is possible to purchase a kit which includes the steel tube fuselage already welded up.

The word 'kit' seems to be pretty widely interpreted by some suppliers and often only means a few minor assemblies.

There are not, in any case, a great many kits available – by my reckoning three in the U.K. and eighteen in the U.S.A. and Canada. This is

17

not really surprising since over 70 per cent of all home-builts are of wooden construction and for this a kit is only of minimal assistance.

Anyway, if you are considering building from a kit, make quite sure of what the kit consists.

Engines are difficult to fit into my classification scheme since most aircraft can accept a variety of power-plants and there is a grey area between the upper end of the V.W. engines and the lower powered proprietary aero engines. I have shown the BA-4B in the V.W. engine classification since the plans provide for a V.W. conversion, though the two examples that I have seen have both been equipped with Rolls-Royce Continental 0-200A engines of 100 hp (74·5 kW).

This BA-4B is a most attractive little biplane. I was sitting at the holding point one evening, waiting to take off in my Evans V.P.1, with a BA-4B turning onto very short finals. As he passed me about twenty feet (6 m) up he rolled onto his back and flew down the runway and climbed away inverted. Let me say at once that it was out of hours so that the tower was not manned and the pilot was a very experienced and skilful professional. This practice is definitely not recommended but it certainly impressed the BA-4B on my memory.

That particular pilot is possessed of the same sort of impish sense of humour as my dear friend, the famous 'Stupe' Westinghouse, an American who flew with the R.A.F. with great distinction throughout the Hitler war. One day, flying a Spitfire, he found himself in clear air between two layers of cloud and some way behind a Tiger Moth, probably an E.F.T.S. pupil on solo and somewhat lost. Stupe rolled onto his back, overtook the Tiger and pushed up inverted into the cloud above. He completed the bunt to come out of cloud behind the Tiger Moth and observe, with huge delight, the crazy manoeuvering of the Tiger as the poor pilot tried to decide which way up he was.

The P.F.A. is only authorised to clear aircraft for the 'Special Category' Certificate of Airworthiness, Category 2. There are three categories of 'Special Category' Cs of A., of which numbers one and three do not concern us.

Category 2, which is issued on a P.F.A. recommendation, covers aircraft of an all-up weight not exceeding 1750 lb (793·8 kg), a stalling speed not exceeding 50 mph (80·5 km/h; 43·4 knots), a maximum engine power not exceeding 125 hp (93·3 kW) and 'whose design and construction and handling characteristics are of a standard acceptable to the Popular Flying Association'.

The Federal Aviation Administration in the U.S.A. does not place the same restrictions of all-up (gross) weight, stalling speed and power on the amateur builder. However it will be seen that the majority of American designs fall within these brackets anyway and where they exceed the British power limit there should not be a serious loss of performance in using a less powerful engine that satisfies the requirements of Category 2.

Most of the older designs, at least, have been flown with a great variety of engines. Take, for example, the Pietenpol Air Camper of 1931 vintage and still being built. The earliest examples used a converted Model A Ford water cooled engine complete with radiator, which developed 35 hp (26·1 kW) at 1600 rpm and 38 hp (28·4 kW) at full throttle and 2000 rpm. Post-war models are flying with the Continental A-65, the Lycoming 0-145 of 65 hp (48·5 kW) and the Franklin 65 hp (48·5 kW) engine. With the original engine a cruising speed of 70 mph was obtained so it would seem possible that a 1600 cc V.W. engine which would develop 46 hp (34·3 kW) at full throttle and 41 hp (30·6 kW) at cruising rpm could be employed. It is almost certain that the 1834 cc or 2180 cc V.W. engines could be used, especially if geared.

Another example is the Luton Minor of 1936 vintage which started out with a 35 hp (26·1 kW) Anzani engine and has since flown with a 40 hp (29·9 kW) Scorpion, the Aeronca J.A.P. of 37 hp (27·6 kW). The latest examples are using 1500 cc and 1600 cc V.W. engines with great success.

I am often asked to recommend aircraft for amateurs to build and this I will not do since any pilot's opinion of a particular aircraft is bound to be subjective and coloured by his own impressions and prejudices.

I loved the Hurricane and the Spitfire with equal fervour and would contend that in their proper roles each was at the top of its class. In spite of this I know plenty of pilots who detested and feared the Hurricane. This I could never understand. On the other hand I never met a pilot who did not drool over the Spitfire.

I disliked the Mosquito, probably because I came to it from the Spitfire and found that it would neither go high enough nor fast enough for my liking. This was on a photographic reconnaissance squadron – we were sometimes irreverently referred to as the Icarus All-Sorts because nobody flew nearer the sun than we did – and I had flown a Spitfire XI to 54,000 feet (16 500 m) but I could never get a Mosquito above 33,000 feet (10 100 m). This was still in range of the flak and the Me 109s. Another thing I did not like about it was the fact that the control column was slightly angled athwartships, so that when one went onto instruments one tried to square the spectacle control wheel with the column and correct the resulting turn with rudder so that all one's instruments went cross-eyed.

An ex-night-fighter friend of mine regards these criticisms as nothing less than slanderous sacrilege and evidence of my own incompetence. He worshipped the Mosquito to the point of idolatry but then he had graduated to it from Beaufighters.

So you will see how even experienced pilots' opinions on the same aircraft can differ wildly and one really has to make up one's own mind on the subject and not be over influenced by what others may say.

So any remarks that I, or any other pilot except perhaps a graduate of the R.A.F's test pilot course, may make about any particular type should be treated with some reserve and I can, of course, only comment on

Colibri, *Popular Flying Association*

aircraft of which I have personal knowledge.

Max Brugger comes to Sywell every year from Switzerland with a new model and they are all beautiful little machines. He must be one of the most prolific designer-builders currently in practice and production. I had a close look at the insides of a Colibri, which after running out of fuel had been damaged by a forced landing in a field that was a bit too short for it. It did not look particularly difficult to build.

My own aircraft is the Evans V.P.1 and I love it dearly. It performs quite remarkably well, even in the worst conditions and there could be nothing simpler or less expensive to build. This must be the minimum aeroplane in

Evans V.P.1, *Popular Flying Association*

everything except performance. The fuselage is 14 ft 8½ in (4·48 m) long without the engine and elevator, and the wings are 11 ft (3·35 m) long each, so it can be built in quite a small space. I built mine in a double garage and for most of the time I was building I got both cars in – one on either side of the aeroplane. It can be easily rigged and de-rigged – but this is not the same as 'folding'. It takes me about four hours to rig it for flight and two hours to de-rig it so once rigged I like to keep it that way, at least until it has to go home for its C. of A.

The Jodel D9, or D92 as the V.W. engined version is more properly called, is one of the earliest of the post-war French designs having made its first flight in January 1948, and is still one of the best. My only criticism of this aircraft, and the same applies to its big sister the D11 and variants and, indeed, to most other French designs, relates to the wing which is all in one piece with the ends cranked, tapered and washed-out. This wing is not easy to jig and building it would appear to take an inordinately long time. Because the wing is all in one piece the aircraft is not easy to transport to and from the airfield and it requires a big workshop in which to build it.

The Luton Minor originated in 1936. The performance figures which I quote are for the J.A.P. engined version. I have always regarded these as a trifle marginal. However the later models using 1500 cc and 1600 cc V.W. engines appear to climb and cruise very much better and I would regard this as a very good prospect for the home-builder. Apart from anything else I would regard the four cylinders of the V.W. engine as providing a better safety margin than the two cylinders of the J.A.P. since if you lose

Jodel D9, *Popular Flying Association*

Luton Minor, *Salisbury Times*

one cylinder out of two that is half your power gone and you can not stay up on that, as a distinguished member of the P.F.A. discovered when he had to force-land in the sea. The Luton's low stalling speed makes it a safe aircraft for the relatively inexperienced pilot – I cannot recall anybody getting hurt in a Luton Minor – and when fitted with a steerable tail-wheel and differential brakes it handles well on the ground. My only adverse comment would be on the difficulty of getting into it unless one is very agile. Perhaps one has to practise.

The Tipsey Nipper, when taxying, reminds me irresistably of the chickens doing their ridiculous dance in the opening scene of 'La Fille Mal

Tipsey Nipper, *Popular Flying Association*

Turbulent, *Popular Flying Association*

Gardèe', but it is, in fact, an extremely practical little machine. With its tricycle undercarriage the ground handling is impeccable, its flight performance and handling characteristics are good and with its snug little cabin it can be flown in all weathers. The steel tube fuselage structure might be rather beyond the capability of most amateurs but this can be obtained in kit form ready welded up.

The Turbulent is another pretty little machine from the French stable. It has a simpler wing than the Jodel but, like the Jodel, it is all in one piece and requires a sizeable shed in which to build it.

The Taylor Monoplane is deservedly one of the most popular of the

Taylor Monoplane, *W. J. Bushell*

Fred – ready to fly, *Eric Clutton*

British home-builts. The design and performance are excellent and it can be built in a small space. I have a friend who is building one in an 8 ft × 16 ft (2·4 × 4·9 m) garage.

Eric Clutton's Fred never ceases to delight me whenever I see it. It is such a cheeky little thing. It is no mini fighter but one could have an awful lot of fun with it and, what is more, it really can be folded up and towed away on its own wheels in very short order. This is one of the very few aircraft which can really be kept in one's garage, so saving on hangarage.

Fred – folded, *Eric Clutton*

24

Currie Wot, *Sunderland Echo*

The Currie Wot must be every small boy's dream of flying. This is another aircraft which has had a variety of prime movers including the 36 hp (26·9 kW) J.A.P., the Walter Mikron 3, a 55 hp (41·0 kW) Lycoming, a Continental A 65 and a Pobjoy R radial. I understand that it is fiddling but not difficult to build. There is a famous doctor who built one in two years and then wrote a delightful book about it called 'Birds and Fools Fly'.

The E.A.A. Biplane is quite a lot of aeroplane by home-builders' standards. I got friendly with one at Goodwood when I was test-flying my

E.A.A. Biplane, *Popular Flying Association*

Isaacs Fury, *John Isaacs*

V.P.1. It belonged to a professional pilot and had absolutely everything in the way of equipment. There was a great deal to admire both in the aircraft itself and in the way it was flown.

The Isaacs Fury is a 0·7 scale replica of the Hawker Fury. Its construction is very similar to the Currie Wot and so should not present any serious problems to the amateur builder. Its performance is sparkling and the example which I know best, built by Tony Francis commands attention and admiration wherever it appears.

The Isaacs Spitfire is a rather more sophisticated structure and not, I would think, for the relatively unskilled since the wing is all in one piece, tapered and washed-out at the tips. When I saw the prototype I thought it

Isaacs Spitfire, *Air Portraits*

Jurca Tempete, *Popular Flying Association*

was the most beautiful little aircraft that I had ever seen, and watching it perform in the hands of its test pilot, Bob Cole, I predicted out loud that it was sure to be adopted by the British aerobatic team. I have never seen aerobatics performed more precisely, in such a small space or so low down. It must be the perfect display aircraft.

The Jurca Tempete is quite a lot of aeroplane, though apparently not particularly difficult to build. It has certain flight characteristics which could startle an inexperienced pilot short on tailwheel time. It unsticks below the stalling speed because of ground effect on the rather low slung wing and must be held down until an excess over climbing speed has been obtained. On landing speed decays rapidly as soon as the throttle is closed, which can result in a hard landing. It needs to be handled with respect when near the ground but is otherwise a very pleasant and satisfying aircraft to fly.

The Pitts Special is the competition aerobatic aircraft par excellance and has held this position for quite a long time. It has been the choice of several

Pitts Special, *Popular Flying Association*

aerobatic display teams who could have chosen any aircraft they liked so this must say a great deal for the Pitts design. Apart from the welded steel fuselage there is nothing particularly difficult about its construction as witness the three hundred or so amateur-built Pitts that are known to be flying.

At Sywell '78 I found myself parked next to the first U.K. built SE-5A replica, and what a beautiful job it was. The Continental engine had been mocked-up with dummy plugs to look like the original V engine; there was even a dummy radiator shutter control to operate the dummy shutters. Weather conditions were as bad as they could be for demonstration purposes but it performed most impressively. It did not look especially difficult to build, indeed I believe the building time was about four years. It had

SE-5A Replica, *Air Portraits*

Cavalier, *Popular Flying Association*

appeared in part-built form at Sywell '77 and from what I saw of it in that state of undress I would surmise that it would present no more problems than a Currie Wot.

Turning to the two-seaters, I have always found the Minicab remarkably appealing. The Canadian modification, the Squaircraft Cavalier, with its tricycle undercarriage, looks more up-to-date, but then I am a dedicated tail-dragger. The wing, being in one piece, calls for a pretty big building shed but I am told that it is not difficult to jig.

Minicab, *Mike Jerram*

Druine Turbi, *Popular Flying Association*

The French do seem to go in for one-piece wings. The Druine Turbi attracts me because it is a tandem two-seater and open at that, though, in fact, the only Turbi I know personally has the cockpits enclosed under a single canopy. I have a preference for fresh-air planes and I do like to be able to see over both sides, especially when approaching to land.

The Jodel D11 and its variants, including the Canadian Falconar F11, is probably the most popular of all two-seat home-built aircraft, at least in

Jodel D11, *Popular Flying Association*

Falconar F11, *Popular Flying Association*

Europe, and this in spite of its cranked, tapered and washed-out one-piece wing. This must be because it handles so nicely in the air. It cannot be so very difficult to build, in spite of that wing, as I know a doctor who built a Falconar F11 in two years flat.

The Piel Emeraude is another deservedly popular French design. It has been around since 1953 and the factory built version was popular with flying schools so it must be pretty rugged.

Piel Emeraude, *Popular Flying Association*

Pietenpol Air Camper, *Popular Flying Association*

If ever I build a two-seater it will probably be the Pietenpol Air Camper. This delightful flying machine first appeared in 1931 and is still being built. Designed for the home-builder at a time when the best glues were only casein and the modern high-strength alloys were yet to come, it flew, in the words of its designer, like a home-sick angel. I would expect it to perform rather like the D.H.60 Moths in which I started flying.

On the other hand my final choice could well fall on the CUBy if I could afford a kit to get me over the welding problems. I have always had a soft spot for the Cub which I first flew back in 1938 when it was known as the

CUBy – Piper Cub, *Popular Flying Association*

Wittman Tailwind, *Popular Flying Association*

Taylor Cub and the enclosed cabin would save my wife from ruining her hair-do by having to wear a helmet. True, it is noisy and draughty, but it feels like a real aeroplane. For years I had nothing to fly but the Cessna 150. It was a good, safe, comfortable way of getting around by air but more like a levitating motor car than an aeroplane. Then, one day, a friend let me have a go in his J3 Piper Cub and I rediscovered the pure joy of flying.

Of all the two-seaters the Wittman Tailwind must be in a class by itself. Relatively simple to build, especially if you can afford a kit, it out-performs most, if not all, factory built aircraft in its bracket. I do not know

Thorp T-18, *Popular Flying Association*

how it does it, either a happy fluke or a stroke of genius – probably the latter. It is not, in my eyes, a very good-looking aeroplane on the ground but it looks right in the air and there is no doubt about its performance figures.

When Clive Canning arrived at Sywell in his Thorp T-18 in 1976, he had flown it from Australia, no less. He broke seven F.A.I. records and survived a shooting attack by four Syrian Migs by a bit of inspired tactical low-flying round the houses of Homs. He seemed to be rather surprised to be awarded the P.F.A.'s Roderick Turner Memorial Award and even more surprised when the Australians gave him their Oswald Watt Gold Medal. Nobody else was. If this conveys something of Clive's courage, guts, airmanship, modesty and wry sense of humour it must also say something about the Thorp T-18 which carried him through it and back to Australia. If you can cope with the metal work you could well wind up with an aircraft that has already carved its name in the annals of flight. A truly remarkable machine.

I have left till last the Evans V.P.2 since this is, without doubt, the poor man's two-seater and for sheer ingenuity it is unexampled. There are a great many currently being built in the U.K. but, at the time of writing, I have yet to see one flying. If it flies as well as the V.P.1, and reports say it does, a lot of people will build it for its own sake and not just because it is the cheapest and easiest two-seater to build.

I have made these few brief comments about aircraft of which I have first-hand knowledge. The fact that I have omitted the majority of the

Evans V.P.2, *Popular Flying Association*

aircraft in my list means only that I have had neither the opportunity of flying them nor of seeing them at close-quarters and talking to their constructors.

So long as an aircraft has received the approval of its own national authority it must be a good machine in its own class and provided it has the approval of your own national authority you will be perfectly safe in building it.

Two of the problems of getting first-hand information about any particular home-built aircraft are, firstly, that when a person has spent years building it, he or she, will be very reluctant to allow anyone else to fly it and secondly, every builder considers that his own aircraft is immeasurably superior in every way to anybody else's. These, of course, are only in the nature of things and I fear that my reactions are no different from other home-builders, but they do present problems to the earnest researcher.

It is almost impossible to arrive at the full and true cost of building since one receives an enormous and surprising amount of help.

One's inspector will invariably have useful contacts within the industry through which many odd items can be obtained either at cost or recovered from the scrap dump for nothing.

My colleagues at work kept producing various parts which they thought might be useful and very often they were; my magneto switches and tail-wheel came this way. But the most fruitful source will prove to be the regular P.F.A. Strut meetings. Just mention your need to one of the chaps at the bar and in no time at all the word has gone round and someone will appear at your elbow either with the very thing you want or with information as to where to get it.

The fact that I had a lot of help in this and other ways need not invalidate my costings since it is fair to assume that any other builder will be able to count on just as much assistance. Even so I find that the total outlay on my Evans V.P.1, as near as I can make it, came to:

Aircraft	£1040
Plans, Books etc.	£22
Insurance for first year's flying	£85
Registration and Certificate of Airworthiness	£29
Total	£1176

This expenditure was spread over three years and ten months between October 1972 when I first sent for the plans and August 1976, say four years at £294 per year.

Actual building time from first cutting wood to first flight was three years and two months.

I would guess that to arrive at present costs for a V.P.1 it would be necessary to increase the above figures by 12% per annum from 1974 to your building start time. Thus a V.P.1 to be started in 1980 could be expected to cost about £2321 in the U.K.

Undoubtedly the best way to temper the cost to the individual and simultaneously reduce the building time is to find a compatible partner or partners. This makes sense because an aircraft in single ownership is grossly under-used.

However this is a counsel of perfection which is not easily realised since, leaving aside the personality problems which are always the most difficult to resolve, your partner must obviously hold a pilot's licence and live within easy travelling distance of you, a pretty rare combination of qualifications. A little selective drinking at Strut meetings would seem to be the best way to explore the possibility of such an arrangement.

Building and flying your own aircraft is a long term project, so take your time over deciding what to build. You may find, as I did, that the big decisions are the easiest to make. It only took me three months to reduce my list to three aircraft but another five months to bring it down to one.

Once you have cut your first bit of wood it is too late to change your mind.

(a) SINGLE SEAT; V.W. ENGINE; ALL WOODEN CONSTRUCTION OR STEEL

Make and model	Power	Length ft, inch (m)	Span ft, inch (m)	Wing area sq. ft (sq, m)	Empty weight lb (kg)	Gross weight lb (kg)	Cruising speed knots (mph) (km/h)
Brugger Colibri	1600 cc	15′ 9″ (4·80)	19′ 8¼″ (6·00) low wing	88·25 (8·20)	474 (215)	727 (330)	86 (99) (160)
Corby CJ-1 Starlet	1600 cc	14′ 9″ (4·5)	18′ 6″ (5·64) low wing	68·5 (6·36)	420 (190)	650 (295)	107 (123) (198)
Evans V.P.1	1500 cc or 1600 cc	18′ 0″ (5·49)	24′ 0″ (7·32) low wing	100 (9·29)	482 (218·6)	750 (340)	72 (83) (134)
Flaglor Scooter	1500 cc	15′ 8″ (4·78)	28′ 0″ (8·64) high wing	115 (10·68)	390 (177)	650 (295)	69 (80) (129)
Gatard Stratoplan AG 02 Poussin	1200 cc	14′ 10½″ (4·53)	21′ 0″ (6·4) low wing	66·2 (6·15)	375 (170)	617 (280)	69 (80) (130)
Jodel D 92	1200 cc to 1600 cc	17′ 10½″ (5·45)	22′ 11″ (7·0) low wing	96·8 (9·0)	420 (190)	705 (320)	74 (85) (137)
Lobet-de-Rouvray Ganagobie 05	1200 cc to 1600 cc	16′ 1¾″ (4·92)	24′ 3¼″ (7·4) high wing	92·25 (8·57)	630 (285)	800 (362)	87 (100) (161)
Luton LA.4A Minor	1500 cc or 1600 cc	20′ 9″ (6·32)	25′ 0″ (7·62) high wing	125 (11·6)	390 (177)	750 (340)	60 (69) (111)
Nipper	1500 cc or 1600 cc	15′ 0″ (4·56)	19′ 8″ (6·0) mid wing	80·7 (7·5)	465 (210)	750 (340)	81 (93) (150)
Turbulent	1500 cc or 1600 cc	17′ 6″ (5·33)	21′ 7″ (6·58) low wing	77·5 (7·2)	395 (179)	620 (281)	87 (100) (161)
Taylor Monoplane	1500 cc or 1600 cc	15′ 0″ (4·57)	21′ 0″ (6·40) low wing	76 (7·06)	410 (186)	610 (276)	78 (90) (145)

TUBE AND FABRIC FUSELAGE, AND WOOD AND FABRIC WINGS

onstruction	Open or cabin	Landing gear	Rate of climb ft/min (m/min)	Remarks
y & fabric ng covers	Cabin	Tail wheel	590 (180)	Plans from 1751 Villarsel-le-Gibloux, Fribourg, Switzerland
& fabric	Optional	Tail wheel	800 (200)	Plans from 86 Eton St., Sutherland, N.S.W. 2232. Australia
y & fabric	Open	Tail wheel	600 (183)	Plans from Evans Aircraft, P.O. Box 744, La Jolla, California 92037 – and from P.F.A. England
y & fabric	Open	Tail wheel	600 (183)	Plans from Ace Aircraft, 106 Arthur Road, Asheville, N. Carolina 28806. U.S.A.
& fabric	Cabin	Tail wheel	435 (132)	Plans from 52 Route de Jonzac, 17130 Montendre, France
& fabric	Open	Tail wheel	590 (180)	Plans from 36 Route de Seurre, 21 Beaune, France
& fabric	Cabin	Tail wheel	—	Plans from Suite 7/506, Miller Street, 2062 Cammeray, New South Wales 2062, Australia
& fabric	Open	Tail wheel	250 (76)	Plans from P.F.A. Terminal Building, Shoreham Airport, Shoreham-by-Sea, Sussex. U.K.
el tube & fabric elage, wood & ric wing	Cabin	Tricycle	650 (198)	Plans & kit from Nipper Kits & Components Ltd., 1 Ridgeway Drive, Bromley, Kent BR1 5DG. U.K.
& fabric	Open	Tail wheel	450 (137)	Plans from P.F.A. Terminal Building, Shoreham Airport, Shoreham-by-Sea, Sussex. U.K.
& fabric	Open or canopy	Tail wheel	1000 (305)	Plans from 25, Chesterfield Crescent, Leigh-on-Sea, Essex, SS9 5PD. U.K.

Make and model	Power	Length ft, inch (m)	Span ft, inch (m)	Wing area sq. ft (sq. m)	Empty weight lb (kg)	Gross weight lb (kg)	Cruising speed knots (mph) (km/h)
Clutton 'Fred'	1600 cc	16' 0" (4·88)	22' 3" (6·78) high wing	110 (10·2)	560 (254)	773 (351)	62 (71) (114)
Stewart JD1 Headwind	1500 cc or 1600 cc	17' 9" (5·41)	28' 3" (8·61) high wing	110·95 (10·3)	437 (198)	700 (317)	65 (75) (121)
E.A.A. Pober Pixie	1600 cc or 1700 cc Limbach	17' 3" (5·26)	29' 10" (9·09) high wing	134·25 (12·47)	543 (246)	900 (408)	74 (85) (137)
Croses EAC-3 Pouplume	1200 cc to 1600 cc	9' 10" (3·0)	25' 7" (7·8) biplane	172 (16·0)	310 (140)	573 (260)	38 (43·5) (70)
Rollason Beta	1600 cc or 50 hp (37·3 kW) Ardem or Continental C90	16' 8" (5·04)	20' 5" (6·31) low wing		550 (250)	850 (386)	133 (153) (245)
Rand Robinson KR-1	1200 cc to 1600 cc	12' 6" (3·81)	17' 2" (5·23) low wing	64 (5·95)	340 (154)	600 (272)	130 (150) (241)

onstruction	Open or cabin	Landing gear	Rate of climb ft/min (m/min)	Remarks
›ruce ply & ‹bric	Open	Tail wheel	400 (120)	Plans from Eric Clutton, 92 Newlands St, Shelton, Stoke-on-Trent, Staffs. U.K.
‹eel tube & fabric ‹selage, wood & ‹bric wing	Open or enclosed	Tail wheel	400 (122)	Plans from 11420 Route 165, Salem, Ohio, 44460. U.S.A.
‹eel tube & fabric ‹selage, wood & ‹bric wing	Open	Tail wheel	500 (152)	Plans from E.A.A. P.O. Box 229, Hales Corners, Wisconsin 53130. U.S.A.
‹y & fabric	Open	Tail wheel		Development of Pou du Ciel Plans from M. Emilien Croses, Route de Davayé, 71 Charnay les Macon, France
›ruce & ply	Cabin	Tail wheel	—	Racer Plans from Rollason Aircraft Ltd., Redhill Aerodrome, Surrey. U.K.
‹uce, ply, ‹rofoam ‹Dynel epoxy ‹vered	Cabin	Tail wheel – retract-able	600 (182)	Plans & kits from 5842K McFadden Avenue, Huntington Beach California 92649. U.S.A.

(b) SINGLE SEAT; V.W. ENGINES; SHEET METAL CONSTRUCTION

Make and model	Power	Length ft, inch (m)	Span ft, inch (m)	Wing area sq. ft (sq, m)	Empty weight lb (kg)	Gross weight lb (kg)	Cruising speed knots (mph) (km/h)
Aerosport Quail	1600 cc	15′ 11″ (4·85)	24′ 0″ (7·32) high wing	84 (7·8)	534 (242)	792 (359)	100 (115) (185)
Aerosport Scamp	1600 cc 1834 cc or 2100 cc	14′ 0″ (4·27)	17′ 6″ (5·33) biplane	102·5 (9·52)	520 (236)	768 (348)	74 (85) (137)
Andreasson BA-4B	2100 cc	15′ 0″ (4·6)	17′ 7″ (5·34) biplane	90 (8·3)		827 (375)	104 (120) (193)
Besneux P. 70B & Pottier P.70S	1600 cc	16′ 4¾″ (5·00)	19′ 4½″ (5·90) midwing	77·5 (7·20)	397 (180)	639 (290)	89 (103) (165)
MacDonald S-21	1500 cc	18′ 6″ (5·64)	25′ 0″ (7·62) low wing	94 (8·73)	456 (206)	720 (326)	78 (90) (145)
Tiger Hawk	1831 cc	13′ 3″ (4·04)	18′ 0″ (5·49) low wing	57 (5·30)	525 (238)	800 (362)	139 (160) (257)
Monnett Sonerai I Formula V Racer	1600 cc	16′ 8″ (5·08)	16′ 8″ (5·08) midwing	75 (6·97)	440 (199)	700 (317)	130 (241) (150)
Parker Teenie Two (Jeanie's Teenie)	1500 cc or 1600 cc	12′ 10″ (3·91)	18′ 0″ (5·49) low wing		310 (140)	590 (267)	95·5 (110) (177)
Pazmany PL-4A	1600 cc	16′ 6½″ (5·04)	26′ 8″ (8·13)	89 (8·27)	578 (262)	850 (385)	85 (98) (158)
Rekcub	1500 cc Porsche or 1600 cc V.W.		biplane				
Colomban MC10 Cri-Cri	2 × 8 hp (6·0 kW) Rowena Chainsaw engines		low wing		139		103

nstruction	Open or cabin	Landing gear	Rate of climb ft/min (m/min)	Remarks
ni- nocoque	Cabin	Tricycle	850 (259)	Plans & kits from Box 278, Holly Springs, N. Carolina 27540. U.S.A.
ced metal	Open	Tricycle		Plans & kits – as above
ced metal	Open	Tail wheel	2000 (600)	Aerobatic Plans & kits from Crosby Aviation Ltd., Leicester Road, Knutsford, Cheshire.
metal	Cabin	P.70B Tail wheel, P.70S Tricycle	985 (300)	Plans from 4 Rue Emilio Castelar, 75012 – Paris. France
metal	Open	Tail Wheel	850 (259)	Plans from 1282 Fowler Creek Road, Sonoma, California 95476. U.S.A.
metal	Cabin	Tricycle	900 (274)	Plans & kits from 1930 Stewart Street, Santa Monica, California 90404. U.S.A.
elage steel e & fabric, tal wing	Cabin	Tail wheel		Plans & component kits from 955 Grace, Elgin, Illinois 60120. U.S.A.
metal	Open	Tricycle	800 (240)	Plans & kits from P.O. Box 181, Dragoon, Arizona 85609. U.S.A.
metal	Cabin	Tail wheel	650 (198)	Plans & kits from Box 8005, San Diego, California, 92138. U.S.A.
		Tail wheel		
metal	Cabin	Tricycle		

(c) TWO SEAT; V.W. ENGINES

Make and model	Power	Length ft, inch (m)	Span ft, inch (m)	Wing area sq. ft (sq, m)	Empty weight lb (kg)	Gross weight lb (kg)	Cruis speed knots (mph) (km/h
Evans V.P.2	1834 cc or 2180 cc	19′ 3″ (5·87)	27′ 0″ (8·23) low wing	130 (12·08)	700 (317·5)	1040 (471·7)	65 (75) (121)
Larkin Skylark	1600 cc (Pusher)	19′ 6″ (5·94)	26′ 6″ (8·08) midwing	114 (10·59)	790 (358)	1246 (565)	91 (105) (169)
Monnett Sonerai II	1700 cc	18′ 10″ (5·74)	18′ 8″ (5·69) midwing	84 (7·80)	506 (230)	925 (419)	122 (140) (225)
Rand Robinson KR-2	1600 cc to 2200 cc	Slightly enlarged KR-1 to accommodate two se					
Rutan VariEze (Canard)	1600 cc to 1834 cc	12′ 5″ (3·79)	22′ 4″ (6·81) low/mid wing	53·6 (4·98)	490 (222)	980 (444)	126 (145) (233)

44

onstruction	Open or cabin	Landing gear	Rate of climb ft/min (m/min)	Remarks
y & fabric	Open	Tail wheel	*1834 cc* 400 2 up 450 1 up *2180 cc* 122 2 up 137 1 up	Plans from Evans Aircraft, P.O. Box 744, La Jolla, California 92037 U.S.A. and from P.F.A. England
eet metal wings, bular fuselage, oy tail booms	Cabin	Tricycle	550 (168)	Plans and kits from P.O. Box 66899, Scotts Valley, California 95066, U.S.A.
selage steel tube fabric, metal ng	Cabin	Tail wheel	750 (229)	Plans and kits from 955 Grace, Elgin, Illinois 60120, U.S.A.
				Plans and kits from 955 Grace, McFadden Avenue, Huntington Beach, California 92649 U.S.A.
.P & foam dwich	Cabin	Tricycle – nosewheel retracts		Plans & component kits from P.O. Box 656, Mojave Airport, Mojave, California 93501, U.S.A.

Make and model	Power	Length ft, inch (m)	Span ft, inch (m)	Wing area sq. ft (sq, m)	Empty weight lb (kg)	Gross weight lb (kg)	Cruisi speed knots (mph) (km/h
Ace Baby Ace Model D	Continental A65	17′ 8¾″ (5·40)	26′ 5″ (8·05) high wing	112·3 (10·43)	575 (261)	950 (431)	87 (100) (160)
Bowers Fly-Baby 1-A	Continental C75	18′ 6″ (5·64)	28′ 0″ (8·53) low wing		605 (274)	924 (419)	96 (110) (177)
Cassutt Special 1	Continental C85-8F	16′ 0″ (4·88)	14′ 11″ (4·54) mid wing	66 (6·13)	516 (234)	730 (331)	165 (190) (306)
Chasle YC-12 Tourbillon	Continental C 90 90 hp (67·2 kW)	19′ 2¼″ (5·85)	22′ 0″ (6·70) low wing	80·7 (7·50)	690 (313)	1015 (460)	129 (149) (240)
Currie Wot	Walter Mikron 62	18′ 9″ (5·72)	22′ 1″ (6·73) biplane	146 (13·6)	530 (240)	790 (358)	69·5 (80) (129)
E.A.A. Acro-Sport	Continental 0-200	17′ 6″ (5·33)	19′ 7″ (5·97) biplane	115·5 (10·73)	733 (332)	1350 (612)	113 (130) (209)
E.A.A. Biplane	Continental C-85-8	17′ 0″ (5·18)	20′ 0″ (6·10) biplane	108 (10·03)	710 (322)	1150 (522)	96 (110) (177)
Isaacs Fury	Lycoming 0-290, 125 hp (93·3 kW)	19′ 3″ (5·87)	21′ 0″ (6·40) biplane	123·8 (11·50)	710 (322)	1000 (450)	100 (115) (185)
Isaacs Spitfire	Continental 0·200, 100 hp (74·6 kW)	19′ 3″ (5·88)	22′ 1½″ (6·75) low wing	87 (8·08)	805 (366)	1100 (499)	116 (134) (215)

onstruction	Open or cabin	Landing gear	Rate of climb ft/min (m/min)	Remarks
ood & fabric wing, el tube fuselage	Open	Tail wheel	1200 (365)	Developed from Corben Baby Ace Plans & kits from 106 Arthur Road, Ashville, North Carolina 28806, U.S.A.
ruce ply & fabric	Open	Tail wheel	1100 (335)	Wings fold Plans from 10458, 16th Avenue South, Seattle Washington
ood & ply wing, el tube selage	Cabin	Tail wheel	2000 (610)	Racer Plans from 11718 Persuasion Drive, San Antonio, Texas 78216, U.S.A.
/ & fabric	Cabin	Tail wheel	1380 (420)	Plans from Le Goya, Rue de Traynes, 65 Tarbes, France
ood & ric	Open	Tail wheel	700 (213)	Aerobatic Plans from P.F.A., Terminal Building, Shoreham Airport, Shoreham-by-Sea, Sussex, BN4 5FF. U.K.
ood & fabric wings, el tube & fabric selage	Open	Tail wheel	3500 (1067)	Aerobatic – competition Plans from E.A.A., P.O. Box 229, Hales Corners, Wisconsin 53130 U.S.A.
ood & fabric wings, el tube & fabric selage	Open	Tail wheel	1000 (305)	Plans from E.A.A., P.O. Box 229, Hales Corners, Wisconsin 53130. U.S.A.
ood ply & fabric	Open	Tail wheel	1600 (488)	0·7 scale replica, aerobatic Plans from Mr J. Isaacs, 23 Linden Grove, Chandlers Ford, Southampton, U.K.
ruce &	Cabin	Tail wheel	1100 (336)	0·6 scale replica, aerobatic Plans from Mr J. Isaacs, 23 Linden Grove, Chandlers Ford, Southampton, U.K.

Make and model	Power	Length ft, inch (m)	Span ft, inch (m)	Wing area sq. ft (sq. m)	Empty weight lb (kg)	Gross weight lb (kg)	Cruis speed knots (mph (km/h)
Jurca Tempete M.J.2.	Continental A.65 65 hp (48·5 kW)	19′ 2½″ (5·855)	19′ 8″ (6·0) low wing	85·90 (7·98)	639 (290)	950 (430)	89 (102) (165)
Keleher Lark-1B	Continental A-65 65 hp (48·5 kW)	17′ 0″ (5·18)	23′ 0″ (7·01) mid wing	80·5 (7·48)	550 (249)	855 (387)	103 (119) (192)
Lefebvre MP.205 Busard	Continental 90 hp (67·2 kW)	17′ 6¾″ (5·35)	19′ 8¼″ (6·0) low wing	64·6 (6·0)	527 (239)	760 (345)	113 (130) (210)
Mason D.H.2. Replica	Le Blond 5F Radial 90 hp (67·2 kW)	22′ 0″ (6·71)	25′ 0″ (7·62) biplane		762 (345)	1222 (554)	57 (65) (105)
Miller WM-2	Continental 65 hp (48·5 kW)	20′ 0″ (6·10)	40′ 0″ (12·19) low wing	144 (13·38)	775 (351)	1050 (476)	109 (126) (203)
Payne Knight Twister KT-85	Lycoming 0-320-B 160 hp (119 kW)	14′ 0″ (4·27)	15′ 0″ (4·57) biplane	60 (5·57)	535 (243)	960 (435)	122 (140) (225)
Piel C.P.80/Zef	Continental C.90	17′ 4¾″ (5·30)	19′ 8¼″ (6·0) low wing	66·7 (6·20)	573 (260)	837 (380)	151 (174) (280)
Pitts S-1D Special	Lycoming 10-360-B4A 180 hp (134 kW)		17′ 4″ (5·28) biplane	98·5 (9·15)	720 (326)	1150 (521)	122 (141) (227)

nstruction	Open or cabin	Landing gear	Rate of climb ft/min (m/min)	Remarks
uce ply abric	Cabin	Tail wheel	555 (170)	Aerobatic Plans from 2, Rue des Champs Phillippe, 92 La Garenne, Colombes, Seine, France or 581 Helen Street, Mt. Morris, Michigan 48458 U.S.A.
ced wood wing, l tube fuselage, ic cover	Cabin	Tail wheel	900 (274)	Plans from 4321 Ogden Drive, Fremont, California 94538, U.S.A.
uce ply abric	Cabin	Tail wheel		Racer Plans from CESA, Camus, rue Adeline, 76100 Rouen, France
od & braced steel e, fabric covers	Open	Tail wheel		0·8 scale replica Try E.A.A. for details
& fabric	Cabin	Tail wheel – single main wheel retracts	890 271	Powered glider Details from Box 570, R.R.1. Furlong, Pennsylvania 18925. U.S.A.
l tube & fabric lage, wood & ic wings	Open	Tail wheel	900 (275)	Plans from Route No. 4, P.O.B. 319M, Escondido, California 92025, U.S.A.
ice & ply	Cabin	Tail wheel	2360 (720)	Racer Plans from 104 Cote de Beulle, 78580 – Maule, France.
den wing, steel fuselage, fabric r	Open	Tail wheel	2675 (816)	Aerobatic – competition Plans from P.O. Box 548, Homestead, Florida 33030. U.S.A.

Make and model	Power	Length ft, inch (m)	Span ft, inch (m)	Wing area sq. ft. (sq. m)	Empty weight lb (kg)	Gross weight lb (kg)	Cruise speed knots (mph (km/h)
Replica Plans SE-5A Replica	Conti-nental C.85 85 hp (63·4 kW)		22′ 10″ (6·96) biplane	140 (13·01)	790 (358)	1100 (499)	74 (85) (137)
Sindlinger HH-1 Hawker Hurricane	Lycom-ing 0-320 150 hp (112 kW)	19′ 8″ (5·99)	25′ 0″ (7·62) low wing	101 (9·38)	1005 (456)	1375 (624)	143 (165) (265)
Smith DSA-1 Miniplane	Lycom-ing 0-235-C 108 hp (80·6 kW)	15′ 3″ (4·65)	17′ 0″ (4·80) biplane	100 (9·29)	616 (279)	1000 (454)	102 (118) (190)
Stephens Akro	Lycom-ing A10-360-A1A. 180 hp (134 kW)	19′ 1″ (5·82)	24′ 6″ (7·47) mid wing	94 (8·73)	850 (385)	1200 (544)	139 (160 (257
Stewart JD2FF Foo Fighter	Franklin 4 125 hp (93·3 kW)	18′ 9″ (5·72)	20′ 8″ (6·30) biplane	140 (13·0)	725 (328)	1100 (499)	100 (115 (185
Stolp SA-500 Starlet	Lycom-ing 0-235-C 108 hp (80·6 kW)	17′ 0″ (5·18)	25′ 0″ (7·62) high wing	83 (7·71)	766 (347)	1100 (499)	103 (119 (192
Stolp SA-700 Acroduster	Lycom-ing 180 hp (134 kW)	15′ 9″ (4·80)	19′ 0″ (5·79) biplane	105 (9·75)	740 (335)	1190 (539)	143 (165 (266

nstruction	Open or cabin	Landing gear	Rate of climb ft/min (m/min)	Remarks
ruce ply & fabric	Open	Tail wheel	500 (152)	Plans from 953 Kirkmond Crescent, Richmond, B.C. Canada
ruce ply & fabric	Cabin	Tail wheel – main wheels retract	1850 (564)	$\frac{5}{8}$ scale replica Plans from 5923 9th Street N.W. Puyallup, Washington 98371, U.S.A.
ced wooden wing, el tube fuselage	Open	Tail wheel	1250 (380)	Aerobatic Plans from Mrs F. W. Smith, 3502 Sunny Hills Drive, Norco, California 91760, U.S.A.
oden wings, steel e fuselage, fabric er	Cabin	Tail wheel	4000 (1220)	Aerobatic Plans from P.O. Box 3171, Rubidoux, California 92509, U.S.A.
od & fabric wings, l tube & fabric elage	Open	Tail wheel	1200 (366)	Plans from 11420 Route 165, Salem, Ohio 44460, U.S.A.
od & fabric wing, l tube & fabric lage	Open	Tail wheel	1325 (404)	Plans & kits from 4301 Twining, Riverside, California 92509, U.S.A.
od & fabric wings, netal fuselage	Open	Tail wheel	3000 (914)	Aerobatic Plans & kits from 4301 Twining, Riverside, California 92509, U.S.A.

Make and model	Power	Length ft, inch (m)	Span ft, inch (m)	Wing area sq. ft. (sq. m)	Empty weight lb (kg)	Gross weight lb (kg)	Cruising speed knots (mph) (km/h)
Taylor J.T.2 Titch	Continental C.85 85 hp (63·4 kW)	16′ 1½″ (4·91)	18′ 9″ (5·72) low wing	68 (6·32)	500 (227)	745 (338)	135 (155) (250)
War Aircraft Replicas Focke-Wulf 190	Continental 0-200 100 hp (74·6 kW)	16′ 7″ (5·05)	20′ 0″ (6·10) low wing	70 (6·50)	630 (286)	900 (408)	126 (145) (233)
White W.W.1 Der Jäger D.IX	Lycoming 0-235-C1 115 hp (85·8 kW)	17′ 0″ (5·18)	20′ 0″ (6·10) biplane	115 (10·68)	534 (242)	888 (403)	116 (133) (214)
Baby Great Lakes	Continental 65 hp (48·5 kW)	13′ 9″ (4·19)	16′ 8″ (5·08) biplane	86 (8·0)	475 (215)	850 (385)	100 (118) (190)
Jungster-1	Lycoming 0-235 100 hp (74·6 kW)	16′ 0″ (4·88)	16′ 8″ (5·08) biplane	80 (7·43)	606 (275)	Aerobatic 850 (386) Max. 1000 (253)	109 (125) (201)

nstruction	Open or cabin	Landing gear	Rate of climb ft/min (m/min)	Remarks
ʹuce ply & fabric	Cabin	Tail wheel	1100 (335)	Racer Plans from Mrs J. F. Taylor, 25 Chesterfield Crescent, Leigh-on-Sea, Essex, SS9 5PD U.K.
uce ply & epoxy ʹered foam	Cabin	Tail wheel	100 (305)	Half Scale replica Plans from 348 South Eighth Street, Santa Paula, California 93060, U.S.A.
ʹod wings, steel ʹe & fabric fuselage	Open	Tail wheel	2400 (732)	Plans from Meadowlark Airport, 5141 Warner Avenue, Huntington Beach, California 92649, U.S.A.
ʹod wings, steel ʹe & fabric fuselage	Open	Tail wheel	2000 (610)	Plans from Barney Oldfield Aircraft Co. P.O. Box 5974, Cleveland, Ohio 44101, U.S.A.
ʹuce ply & fabric	Open	Tail wheel	1500 (457)	Replica of Bucker BO 133 Jungmeister, aerobatic Plans from K & S Aircraft Supply, 4623 Fortune Road S.E., Calgary, Alberta, Canada.

(e) SINGLE SEAT; AIRCRAFT ENGINE; SHEET METAL OR PLASTIC

Make and model	Power	Length ft, inch (m)	Span ft, inch (m)	Wing area sq. ft (sq, m)	Empty weight lb (kg)	Gross weight lb (kg)	Cruise speed knots (mph (km/h
Bede BD-5G	Xenoah 70 hp (52·2 kW)	13′ 3½″ (4·05)	17′ 0″ (5·18) low wing	38 (3·53)	410 (186)	850 (385)	182 (210) (338)
Bede BD-6	Hirth 55 hp (41·0 kW)	16′ 9″ (5·11)	21′ 6″ (6·55) high wing	55·5 (5·16)	375 (170)	650 (295)	122 (140) (225)
Bushby/Long MM-1 Midget Mustang	Lycoming 0-290-D2 135 hp (101 kW)	16′ 5″ (5·00)	18′ 6″ (5·64) low wing	68 (6·32)	590 (268)	900 (408)	187 (215) (346)
Davis DA-5A	Continental A65 65 hp (48·5 kW)	15′ 9″ (4·80)	15′ 7¼″ (4·76) low wing	57.2 (5·31)	460 (208)	775 (351)	122 (140) (225)
DSK Airmotive DSK-1 Hawk	Lycoming 0-145-B2 65 hp (48·5 kW)	15′ 0″ (4·57)	20′ 4½″ (6·21) low wing	64 (5·95)	525 (238)	893 (405)	114 (131) (211)
Jameson RJJ-1 Gypsy Hawk	Continental A65 65 hp (48·5 kW)	16′ 1″ (4·90)	18′ 8″ (5·69) low wing		520 (236)	820 (372)	100 (115 (185
Van's RV-3	Lycoming 0-290-6 125 hp (93·3 kW)	19′ 0″ (5·79)	19′ 11″ (6·07) low wing	90 (8·36)	695 (315)	1050 (476)	161 (185 (298

nstruction	Open or cabin	Landing gear	Rate of climb ft/min (m/min)	Remarks
ht alloy	Cabin	Tricycle – retract- able	1750 (533)	Aerobatic Plans from Bede Aircraft, Newton Municipal Airport, P.O. Box 706, Newton, Kansas 67114, U.S.A.
ht alloy G.R.P.	Cabin	Tricycle	900 (274)	Plans from Bede Aircraft, Newton Municipal Airport, P.O. Box 706, Newton, Kansas 67114, U.S.A.
metal	Cabin	Tail wheel	2200 (670)	Plans from Mr Robert Bushby, Route 1, P.O. Box 13B, Minooka, Illinois 60447, U.S.A.
metal	Cabin	Tricycle	800 (244)	Plans from P.O. Box 207, 405 North St. Paul, Stanton, Texas 79782, U.S.A.
metal – surplus p tank may be d	Cabin	Tricycle	1500 (457)	Plans from 126 Georgia Place, Fort Walton Beach, Florida 32548, U.S.A.
metal	Cabin	Tricycle	900 (274)	Plans from 124 – C North Stanford Ave., Fullerton, California 92631, U.S.A.
metal	Cabin	Tail wheel	1900 (579)	Plans from 22730 S.W. Francis, Beaverton, Oregon 97005, U.S.A.

(f) TWO SEAT; AIRCRAFT ENGINE; WOODEN CONSTRUCTION OR STEEL T|

Make and model	Power	Length ft, inch (m)	Span ft, inch (m)	Wing area sq. ft (sq, m)	Empty weight lb (kg)	Gross weight lb (kg)	Cruis speed knots (mph (km/l
Aerosport Woody Pusher	Continental 75 hp 60·0 kW	20' 5" (6·22)	29' 0" (8·84) high wing	130 (12·07)	630 (285)	1150 (522)	76 (87) (140)
AM-69 Georges Payre	Continental C90-14F 90 hp (67·2 kW)	25' 11" (7·90)	29' 4" (8·94) low wing	120·5 (11·20)	1155 (524)	1605 (728)	86 (99) (160)
Bakeng Duce	Lycoming 0-290-6 125 hp (93·3 kW)	20' 9" (6·32)	30' 4" (9·25) high wing	138 (12·8)	898 (407)	1500 (680)	122 (140) (225)
Bearn G.Y.20 Minicab & Squaircraft 'Cavalier'	Continental A65-8 65 hp (48·5 kW) & others	17' 10½" (5·45)	24' 11" (7·59) low wing	107·6 (9·99)	595 (270)	1069 (484·9)	97 (112) (180)
Druine Turbi	Beaussier 4B02 45 hp (33·6 kW) & others	22' 6" (6·86)	28' 6" (8·69) low wing	139 (12·91)	610 (277)	1090 (494)	74 (85) (137
Croses EC-6 Criquet	Continental 90 hp (67·2 kW)	15' 3" (4·65)	25' 7" (7·80) staggered biplane	172 (16·0)	639 (290)	1213 (550)	92 (106 (170

nstruction	Open or cabin	Landing gear	Rate of climb ft/min (m/min)	Remarks
oden wing, steel e fuselage, fabric er	Open, tandem	Tail wheel	600 (183)	Plans from Box 278, Holly Springs, North Carolina 27540, U.S.A.
uce & ply	Cabin, tandem	Tail wheel	590 (180)	Plans from R.S.A., 39 Rue Sauffroy, 75017 – Paris, France.
oden wing, steel e fuselage, fabric er	Open, tandem	Tail wheel	2000 (610)	Plans from 19025, 92nd W, Edmonds, Washington, 98020 U.S.A.
uce ply & fabric	Cabin, side by side	Minicab, Tail wheel Cavalier, Tricycle	590 (180)	Minicab: Plans from A. W. J. G. Ord-Hume, 14 Elmwood Road, Chiswick, London W.4. Cavalier: K & S Aircraft Supply, 4623 Fortune Road S.E. Calgary, Alberta, Canada.
uce, ply bric	Open, tandem	Tail wheel	500 (152)	
uce &	Cabin, side by side	Tail wheel	320 (98)	Similar configuration to the Pou du Ciel Plans from M. Croses, Route de Davayé, 71 Charnay les Macon, France

Make and model	Power	Length ft, inch (m)	Span ft, inch (m)	Wing area sq. ft (sq. m)	Empty weight lb (kg)	Gross weight lb (kg)	Cruis speed knots (mph) (km/h
Cvjetkovic CA-65	Lycoming 0-290-6 125 hp (93·3 kW)	19' 0" (5·79)	25' 0" (7·62) low wing	108 (10·03)	900 (408)	1500 (680)	117 (135) (217)
EAA Nesmith Cougar	Lycoming 0-235 115 hp (85·8 kW)	18' 11" (5·76)	20' 6" (6·25) high wing	82·5 (7·66)	624 (283)	1250 (567)	144 (166) (267)
Fike Model 'E'	Continental C85-8 85 hp (63·4 kW)	19' 2" (5·84)	22' 4½" (6·82) high wing	143·1 (13·29)	690 (313)	1100 (499)	83 (95) (153)
Hatz CB-1 Biplane	Lycoming 0-320 150 hp (112 kW)	18' 6" 5·64	26' 0" (7·92) biplane	190 (17·65)	966 (438)	1600 (726)	87 (100) (161)
Jodel D.11 & D.119	Continental A65-8 65 hp (48·5 kW)	20' 7" (6·27)	27' 0" (8·23) low wing	136·6 (12·68)	750 (340)	1240 (562)	86 (100) (161)
Jurca M.J.5 Sirocco	Lycoming 0-235-C2B 115 hp (85·8 kW)	20' 2" (6·15)	23' 0" (7·0) low wing	107·64 (10·0)	947 (430)	1499 (680)	116 (134) (215)

nstruction	Open or cabin	Landing gear	Rate of climb ft/min (m/min)	Remarks
uce ply abric	Cabin, side by side	Tail wheel – retractable	1000 (305)	Plans from 624 Fowler Avenue, P.O. Box 323, Newbury Park, California 91320, U.S.A.
oden wing, steel e fuselage, fabric ered	Cabin, side by side	Tail wheel	1300 (395)	Plans from E.A.A. P.O. Box 229, Hales Corners, Wisconsin 53130, U.S.A.
oden geodetic g, steel tube lage, fabric cover	Cabin, tandem	Tail wheel	1000 (305)	Plans from P.O.B. 683, Anchorage, Alaska 99510, U.S.A.
oden wings, steel e fuselage, fabric ers	Open, tandem	Tail wheel	1200 (366)	Plans from Merrill Airways, Municipal Airport, Merrill, Wisconsin 54452, U.S.A.
ice ply, GRP & ic	Cabin, side by side	Tail wheel	500 (152)	Plans from 36, Route de Seurre, 21-Beaune, France
ice ply & fabric	Cabin, tandem	Tail wheel. – main wheels retractable	820 (250)	Plans from 2, Rue des Champs, Phillippe, 92-La Garenne-Colombes, Seine, France.

Make and model	Power	Length ft, inch (m)	Span ft, inch (m)	Wing area sq. ft (sq. m)	Empty weight lb (kg)	Gross weight lb (kg)	Cruis. speed knots (mph) (km/h
Lederlin 380-L	Continental C90-14F 90 hp (67·2 kW)	15′ 7¾″ (4·77)	26′ 0″ (7·92) staggered biplane	186·8 (17·35)	794 (360)	1323 (600)	97 (112) (180)
Piel C.P. 750 Beryl	Lycoming 0-320-ELA 150 hp (112 kW)	22′ 7¾″ (6·90)	26′ 4½″ (8·04) low wing	118 (11·00)	1058 (480)	1675 (760)	143 (165) (265)
Piel Emeraude	Continental C90-12F	20′ 8″ (6·3)	26′ 4½″ (8·04) low wing	116·7 (10·85)	838 (380)	1433 (650)	108 (124) (200)
Pietenpol Air Camper	Franklin 65 hp (48·5 kW)	17′ 8″ (5·38)	28′ 2″ (8·60) high wing	140 (13·0)	630 (286)	1050 (476)	82 (95) (153
Powell P-70 Acey Deucy	Continental A65 65 hp (48·5 kW)	20′ 9″ (6·32)	32′ 6″ (9·91) high wing	155 (14·4)	750 (340)	1275 (578)	72 (83) (134
Rutan VariViggen	Lycoming 0-320-A2A 150 hp (112 kW)	19′ 0″ (5·79)	19′ 0″ (5·79) low wing	119 (11·06)	950 (431)	1700 (771)	130 (15((24)
Shober Willie II	Lycoming 0-360-A3A 180 hp (134 kW)	19′ 0″ (5·79)	20′ 0″ (6·10) biplane	148 (13·75)	856 (388)	1350 (612)	130 (15((24)

nstruction	Open or cabin	Landing gear	Rate of climb ft/min (m/min)	Remarks
ooden wings, steel ɔe fuselage, fabric vers	Cabin, side by side	Tail wheel	900 (275)	Similar configuration to the Pou du Ciel Plans from 2 rue Charles Peguy, 38-Grenoble, France
ɔoden wings, steel ɔe fuselage, fabric ers	Cabin, tandem	Tail wheel	1280 (390)	Aerobatic Plans 104 Cote de Beulle, 78580 – Maule, France
ruce, ply & fabric	Cabin, side by side	Tail wheel	551 (168)	Plans from 104 Cote de Beulle, 78580 – Maule, France
ruce, ply & fabric	Open, tandem	Tail wheel		For plans J. W. Grega, 355 Grand Boulevard, Bedford, Ohio 44014, U.S.A. Original Plans in 1931 & '32 'Flying & Glider Manual' re-issued by E.A.A.
nposite wing, steel e fuselage, fabric ers	Open, tandem	Tail wheel	400 (122)	Plans from 4 Donald Drive, Middleton, Rhode Island 02840, U.S.A.
uce, ply & fabric. er wing panels of al	Cabin, tandem	Tricycle – retract-able	1200 (366)	Stall-proof canard Plans from P.O. Box 656, Mojave Airport, Mojave, California 93501, U.S.A.
oden wings, steel e fuselage, fabric ers	Open, tandem	Tail wheel	3000 (915)	Aerobatic Plans from P.O. Box 111, Gaithersburg, Maryland 20760, U.S.A.

Make and model	Power	Length ft, inch (m)	Span ft, inch (m)	Wing area sq. ft (sq. m)	Empty weight lb (kg)	Gross weight lb (kg)	Cruis speed knots (mph) (km/h
Spezio DAL-1 Tuholer	Lycoming 0-320 150 hp (112 kW)	18′ 3″ (5·56)	24′ 9″ (7·55) low wing	120·7 (11·21)	900 (408)	1500 (680)	109 (125) (201)
Steen Skybolt	Lycoming 180 hp (134 kW)	19′ 0″ (5·79)	24′ 0″ (7·32) biplane	152·7 (14·2)	1080 (490)	1680 (762)	113 (130) (209)
Stolp SA-300 Starduster Too	Warner Super Scarab 165 hp (123 kW)	20′ 0″ (6·10)	24′ 0″ (7·32) biplane		1105 (501)	1650 (748)	104 (120) (193)
Turner T-40	Lycoming 150 hp (112 kW)	20′ 1″ (6·12)	28′ 0″ (8·53) low wing	102 (9·48)	828 (376)	1650 (748)	152 (175) (282)
Wag-Aero CUBy	Continental or Lycoming 65 hp (48·5 kW) to 125 hp (93·3 kW)	22′ 4½″ (6·82)	35′ 2½″ (10·73) high wing		692 (314)	1340 (608)	82 (94) (151)
Wittman Tailwind	Continental 100 hp (74·6 kW)	19′ 3″ (5·87)	22′ 6″ (6·86) high wing	90 (8·36)	700 (318)	1300 (590)	139 (160) (257)

onstruction	Open or cabin	Landing gear	Rate of climb ft/min (m/min)	Remarks
ooden wing, steel be fuselage, fabric vers	Open, tandem	Tail wheel	2400 (732)	Wings fold Plans from 25 Madison Avenue, Northampton, Massachusetts 01060, U.S.A.
ooden wings, steel be fuselage, fabric vers	Open, tandem	Tail wheel	2500 (762)	Aerobatic Plans from 3218 Cherry Street, Denver, Colorado 80222, U.S.A.
ooden wings, steel be fuselage, fabric vers	Open, tandem	Tail wheel	2600 (792)	Plans from 4301 Twining, Riverside, California 92509, U.S.A.
ruce & ply	Cabin, side by side	Tricycle – retracts	1500 (457)	Wings fold Plans from P.O. Box 425, Stratford, Connecticut 06497, U.S.A.
ooden wing, steel be fuselage, fabric ver	Cabin, tandem	Tail wheel	490 (149)	Updated Piper Cub Plans & kits from Box 181, 1216 North Road, Lyons, Wisconsin 53148, U.S.A.
ooden wings, steel e fuselage, fabric ver	Cabin, side by side	Tail wheel	900 (275)	Plans & kits from P.O. Box 276, Oshkosh, Wisconsin 54901, U.S.A. or AJEP Developments, The Lodge, Marden Hill Farm, Hertford SG14 2NE. U.K.

Make and model	Power	Length ft, inch (m)	Span ft, inch (m)	Wing area sq. ft (sq, m)	Empty weight lb (kg)	Gross weight lb (kg)	Cruisi speed knots (mph) (km/h
Bede BD-4	Lycoming 0-235-Cl 108 hp (80·6 kW)	21′ 4½″ (6·52)	25′ 7″ (7·80) high wing	102·33 (9·51)	960 (435)	1600 (725)	126 (145) (233)
Bushby M-11 Mustang 11	Lycoming 0-320 160 hp (119 kW)	19′ 6″ (5·94)	24′ 2″ (7·37) low wing	97·12 (9·02)	927 (420)	1500 (680)	175 (201) (323)
Davis DA-2A	Continental A65-8 65 hp (48·5 kW)	17′ 10¼″ (5·44)	19′ 2¾″ (5·86) low wing	82·5 (7·66)	610 (277)	1125 (510)	100 (115) (185)
Pazmany PL-2	Lycoming 0-290-6 125 hp (93·3 kW)	19′ 3½″ (5·90)	28′ 0″ (8·53) low wing	116 (10·78)	900 (408)	1445 (655)	111 (128) (206)
Smyth Model 'S' Sidewinder	Lycoming 0-290-G 125 hp (93·3 kW)	19′ 4″ (5·89)	24′ 10″ (7·57) low wing	96 (8·92)	867 (393)	1450 (657)	139 (160) (257)
Thorp T-18 Tiger	Lycoming 180 hp (134 kW)	18′ 2″ (5·54)	20′ 10″ (6·35) low wing	86 (8·0)	900 (408)	1506 (683)	152 (175) (282)
Zenair (Heintz) Zenith	Continental 0-200-A 100 hp (74·6 kW)	20′ 8″ (6·30)	22′ 11¾″ (7·0) low wing	105·9 (9·80)	881 (400)	1499 (680)	116 (134) (215)

onstruction	Open or cabin	Landing gear	Rate of climb ft/min (m/min)	Remarks
etal & GRP mposite	Cabin, side by side	Tricycle	900 (274)	Plans & kits from Bede Aircraft, Newton Municipal Airport, P.O. Box 706 Newton, Kansas 67114, U.S.A.
l metal	Cabin, side by side	Tail wheel – retractable	1400 (425)	Plans from Route 1, P.O. Box 13B, Minooka, Illinois 60447, U.S.A.
l metal	Cabin, side by side	Tricycle		Vee-tail Plans from P.O. Box 207, 405 North St. Paul, Stanton, Texas 79782, U.S.A.
l metal	Cabin, side by side	Tricycle	1500 (457)	Plans from Box 80051, San Diego, California 92138, U.S.A.
l metal	Cabin, side by side	Tricycle	1200 (366)	Plans from P.O. Box 308, Huntington, Indiana 46750, U.S.A.
metal	Cabin, side by side	Tail wheel	2000 (610)	Plans from P.O. Box 516, Sun Valley, California 91352, U.S.A.
metal	Cabin, side by side	Tricycle	787 (240)	Plans & kits from 236 Richmond Street, Richmond Hill L4C 3YB, Ontario, Canada.

Chapter 3

Getting started

It is just possible that the workshop facilities that you possess may have been a factor in your choice of an aircraft to build. It certainly coloured my thinking during the decision making stage. But if you have not up to now considered this aspect you may have to build a suitable workshop.

A friend of mine, on deciding to build a Jodel D11, designed and built a workshop 33 feet long by 12 feet wide (10 m by 3·7 m). Right down the middle he erected a vertical jig to take the 27 ft (8·2 m) long wing and, in the centre of one side, he had double doors so that when he was ready to marry the fuselage to the wing he could lay out the wing on trestles and then introduce the fuselage through the double doors and lower it into place on top of the wing. Having done this, he then enclosed the rear end of the fuselage, which was sticking out of the side of the shed, with a temporary shelter.

To me this demonstrated a most remarkable and enviable confidence in his ability to carry the project through to completion since the workshop must have cost as much as the aeroplane itself and he was not a rich man.

Alas, I had no such faith in my own skill and pertinacity, indeed every time I wrote a cheque for materials I felt that I was giving hostages to fortune. I was lucky enough to have a double garage 24 ft wide by 21 ft deep (7·3 m by 6·4 m) and, for most of the time I was building, it accommodated two cars, two bicycles, my daughter's moped and the motor mower as well as the growing aeroplane.

My jig table was 2 ft wide by 16 ft long (0·6 m by 4·9 m) with racks for sawn timber underneath, and this was positioned down the centre of the garage between the two doors. It was only during the wing-building period that one of the cars (mine) had to stay outside.

Once the airframe was finished I made and fitted the special transport gear for stowing the wings vertically on either side of the fuselage, dismantled the jig table and put the airframe in its place. And there it stayed all through the winter with the cars on either side while I installed the engine.

I doubt that there are many aircraft other than the V.P.s, Fred and the Taylor Monoplane that can be so easily and inexpensively accommodated.

You will need room for a good solid bench with a decent vice positioned so that it can take the longest single component that may have to be

66

shaped – in my case it was the leading edge spars, each 11 ft (3·4 m) long which I had to turn end for end while working them – and you will need space to set up your drill press. You must also find room for timber racks – I built mine under my jig table.

A surprising number of constructors have built their aeroplanes in their sitting rooms or bedrooms. It is a wonderful wife who will permit this but it is a fact that there are such remarkable women. The only thing to check and make sure of is that you can get the completed airframe out of the room when you have finished it. I have been caught this way myself.

I once built a boat in my pantry. It was only a dinghy but I checked carefully to see that it would fit through the door. Then, in course of construction, I introduced one or two modifications and it was only on completion that I found it had grown by about two inches (50 mm) in beam and three (75 mm) in moulded depth. I had to take out the window frame and hack away some of the brickwork in order to extract it.

There was also the well known builder of a Currie Wot whose workshop was a basement flat in London. He, too, checked on all the dimensions but he reckoned without the London County Council who installed a lamp standard opposite his exit. I understand that they were very co-operative, however, and temporarily removed the lamp-post while he got his aeroplane out into the road.

So you must either make the aircraft fit the building space or make the workshop fit the aircraft.

Your workshop must be well lit since you will be doing much of the work at night – at least I did – and it is important that you should be able to heat it and maintain a reasonable, steady temperature for quite long periods. This is not just for your own comfort but because temperature can be critical when gluing wood or working in glass reinforced plastics and especially when doping fabric.

Power tools will require 15 ampere outlets with a 13 ampere fuse on the plug and all power tools, even inspection lamps on wander leads, must be earthed. I had two 15 ampere outlets but both were on the same wall, near my bench. I could have done with another two outlets on the side wall which would have obviated the long wander leads lying all over the floor. And never try to run a power tool off a light socket.

Now, having settled what you are going to build and where you are going to build it, you must find an inspector. For the next many months he has got to be your best friend so, if you have any choice in the matter, it is as well to find someone with whom you can get along.

The P.F.A. supplies a list of all their inspectors throughout the country so you are bound to find that there is one within a reasonable distance. The inspectors give their services free but you are expected to reimburse their travelling expenses.

I was fortunate in that my inspector lived in the same short road and fortunate too in that he, as an ex-de Havilland apprentice, knew just about everything there was to know about wooden aeroplanes. He was also a quite extraordinarily nice person.

Remember always that your life is in your inspector's hands and he, at least, is always conscious of this; so never take it amiss if and when he occasionally rejects your offerings and you have to buckle down and do a job again – and do it properly. His jurisdiction is all-embracing and extends to materials as well as workmanship.

I remember a chap sounding off about the iniquity of his unspeakable inspector who had rejected a pile of spruce, for which he had paid quite a lot of money, in spite of the release notes which he had brandished under his inspector's nose. I rather suspect that he had left his timber lying in a heap on his garage floor, instead of racking it properly, so that it had warped and twisted, and he really had no one to blame but himself.

I once had a parcel of spruce rejected because, in spite of the warning notices on the wrappings, British Rail had left it lying out in the rain during transit so that it had distorted. Fortunately my wife noticed its sodden condition on arrival and recorded the fact on the carriage note that she was asked to sign.

I notified the suppliers who replaced the entire order immediately, claimed on British Rail or their insurers and asked me to hold the material for British Rail's inspection and collection. I put it in my lowest timber rack and six months later, not having heard a murmur from British Rail, I was about to throw it out to make room for more material when I found that it had straightened itself out. On re-inspection Mike agreed that it was now acceptable and could be used.

The morals of this story are:

(a) Check all consignments of materials before signing for them.
(b) Rack your timber properly so that it lies straight and can breathe.
(c) Your inspector is concerned just as much with what he can see as with what appears on the release notes.

My inspector scrutinised all my materials as they arrived, even advised me on which way round to build them into the structure and marked them accordingly when there was any doubt. Although I am a chartered engineer I had never before appreciated the importance of grain, not only in timber where it is fairly obvious, but also in steel and alloy where it is not.

I have a suspicion that half the troubles which amateur builders experience both in building and, later, in operating their aircraft arise through not making the maximum use of the immense and detailed knowledge which their inspectors possess about materials and stresses in aircraft structures. I learnt an immense amount from my chap.

You can generally meet a number of inspectors at your local P.F.A. Strut meetings and come to an arrangement with one of them over a glass or two of ale. All the inspectors that I know are remarkably nice people – they must be or they would never have taken the job on, for it is a labour of love and no sinecure.

I suppose that most people use a project like this as an excuse to rush out and buy all the tools they have ever coveted.

I had a couple of boxes of assorted tools left over from my boat building days, a bag of household repair tools and an electric drill. I turned them all out on the floor of the garage and surveyed them with dismay. The saws were rusty and blunt, the chisels and plane irons were rusty and nicked. There were a few serviceable drill bits in sizes one would never want to use and one or two peculiar 'specials' like the riffler for cleaning out the ports in the head of the Meadows engine that had powered my 'chain-gang' Frazer Nash forty years ago.

Over the years in which I had neglected the tool boxes my children had taken their toll. I set to work with Plus-gas, paraffin and emery paper to salvage what I could from the wreckage, compiling a list of replacements as I went along.

Looking back to my boat building days the one power tool that had been most used, apart from the drill, had been a portable band-saw that I had been able to borrow. Of course boats have heavier scantlings than aeroplanes so it seemed to me that a jig-saw attachment for the drill would probably serve equally well. In practice this proved so useful that I tended to use the hand-drill to save dismantling the jig-saw. If I were starting again I would get a proper electric jig-saw – our American cousins call it a sabre-saw – which is more robust than the drill attachment and would leave the drill always available.

For cutting plywood I came to use a metal cutting blade which was slow but did not tear the face laminations of the thin plywood as the coarser blade did. This slow speed of cutting can be an advantage to a ham-handed worker like me since one has a chance to see and correct one's errors before they become serious.

Bud Evans, the designer of the V.P.s, recommends the purchase of a 'Karbo-Grit' sanding wheel. I found that Woolworths supplied a very good equivalent and took it home eager to try it out. I found that it had to be used with extreme caution and kept moving all the time, never being allowed to dwell for long on one spot. It tears away unwanted wood at a most satisfactory speed so that one can easily remove too much and, waving it around in tight corners, one can readily remove wood from places from which it should not be removed. It also takes skin off knuckles and noses.

After the electric drill itself, the one essential tool is a drill-press stand. Whatever holes are drilled must be truly perpendicular to the surfaces they penetrate and without the drill-press stand this is impossible to guarantee. The centres of all holes should be started with a bradawl on wood and a centre-punch on metal to ensure that the drill finds the right centre.

During the many months of construction I acquired a horizontal bench stand and a grinding wheel attachment; both very useful but by no means essential.

Prior to starting on aeroplane building I had never realised to what close limits you need to proportion your hammer weight to the size of nail or brad to be driven. I knew I would need a small hammer for the little brass brads and bought the smallest one in the shop. Mike, my inspector, picked it up from my bench and asked 'Are you planning to drive a few piles?' He then fetched his own which was about a quarter the weight of mine. Trying them one against the other on the smallest brads I found that Mike's hammer would drive nineteen out of twenty while my own would buckle three out of four. So you will need a *very* light hammer.

Apart from the usual household tools – chisels, planes, saws, screwdrivers, bradawl, centre-punch, hand drill, pincers, pliers etc. – the only other common tools you are likely to need are a small, fine-toothed back-saw (the kind known as a gentleman is the most appropriate) and a Stanley knife.

The cheap spring steel type of hole-saw will not last long on our sort of work and it will pay to buy the heavy bell-type saws. Incidentally I found that my $\frac{3}{8}$ inch (9·5 mm) chuck drill was not man enough for these and the motor burnt out in the course of drilling the lightening holes in the wing ribs, so I swapped it for the larger two speed model with the $\frac{1}{2}$ inch (12·7 mm) chuck and this has proved entirely adequate.

One essential piece of equipment is an engineer's sliding, adjustable square and bevel. My inspector produced his when he found me using a carpenter's bevel and thereafter it always seemed to be in use.

You will also require a steel tape measure at least as long as the aircraft, a steel straight edge not less than four feet (1·2 m) long and a T-square. These two latter items are expensive and are not likely to be required again so perhaps one should try to borrow them.

You cannot have enough clamps, especially the small ones of about two inch (50 mm) opening. I managed with only nine, seven of my own varying between two and four inch (50 mm and 100 mm) opening and two tiny ones lent to me by my ever helpful inspector. You are never likely to need so many clamps again so borrow all you can. I could have done with at least twenty, especially when building wings.

You will also require two bar or sash cramps. I managed to pick up a pair of things called picture frame cramps for £1 each which did the job admirably. Our local ironmonger dug them out from under a pile of old stock but one would normally expect to pay very much more for clamps of this size.

So it may be seen that the building of a small, wood and fabric aeroplane does not call for a great array of expensive tools, though there are some who will try to persuade you to the contrary. The Evans V.P.1 requires eight small alloy bushes which our local machine shop turned up for me.

out of bar, which I supplied, for a total cost of £2 the lot.

Yet I know one builder who spent £600 on a most beautiful little lathe and defended his purchase tooth and nail. I can only think that he wanted the lathe anyway and was prepared to grasp at any straw to justify his extravagance.

I would not say that he was dishonest, because I am married to a Scot who employs the same zany system of accounting.

She is totally addicted to sailing and justifies the cost of her lovely little cutter on the grounds of the money that it saves us. Whenever we arrive in a port she makes for the plushiest hotel and enquires their charges. She then takes the price of their most expensive suite and full board, deducts the cost of a couple of tins of beans, some croissants and a bottle of vin ordinaire, and that is how much the boat is saving us per day.

Somehow we have never managed to stay long in the Channel Islands because we save so much more money in France. Her great ambition, soon I fear to be realised, is to tie up at the Pont Alexandre 3me in the middle of Paris, so that she can use the Meurice as her yardstick. We will be saving so much money that we will never be able to afford to leave.

The acquisition of materials will very likely present you with your greatest problems.

It is absolutely vital to use only materials of the correct specification, and in many if not most cases this will call for 'released' materials. These are materials which have been inspected and approved by manufacturers or suppliers who have the C.A.A.'s approval, suitably stamped and provided with 'release notes' – bits of official paper saying that they do indeed meet the appropriate specification in all respects.

In cases where 'released' aircraft materials are not called for you must be sure to get a certificate of conformity with the designer's specification from the supplier. The V.P.1 specifications call for a fair amount of 'marine ply' and the British Specification for this is *B.S.1088* which will be stamped on each full sheet. You should, none the less, get a certificate from the supplier to the effect that it is indeed *B.S.1088* marine ply. My inspector was satisfied with the invoices on which this was stated.

Aircraft spruce is expensive but you can save a lot of money by shopping around. I got all mine from a well known firm in Yorkshire who not only quoted the lowest price but also gave very prompt delivery and replaced material damaged in transit with the minimum of cor-respondence and delay. Consequently I bought as many of the other materials – A.G.S. nuts, bolts and washers, brads, glue etc – from them as they could supply.

Most aircraft require some special alloys, both of steel and aluminium, and some of these can present problems. I never imagined for a moment that I would have any difficulty in obtaining steel sheet and so I did not order it until it was needed. But I had to wait for more than six months for a little bit of S514 sheet steel for my wing roots and flying strut ends.

Eventually I sent a cri de cœur to the General Manager of the Special Steels Division of British Steel.

It seems that the stuff is only rolled about once every eighteen months and the whole stock is taken up very quickly. My plea worked because I found myself on the list for a sheet from their nearest stockist as soon as the next rolling was delivered.

I did not need anything like a whole sheet but the surplus came in handy when I was able to give it to the engineer at the airfield where I did my test flying as a small return for the immense amount of help that was so cheerfully and freely given by him and his staff on that momentous occasion. Having not long returned from overseas he was as surprised as I to find that some essential materials were so hard to obtain in the U.K.

If you are building to an American design you will find that you will have to use the nearest British equivalents to the American specifications. This could, in itself, present some difficulty except that the P.F.A., bless them, provide a list of approved alternatives; these can all be found in the *P.F.A. Handbook.*

It is strongly advised, therefore, that as soon as you receive the plans of your chosen aircraft, you go carefully through them and take out the quantities of all special steel and aluminium alloys that you will require and place them on order. Make a list of all special components such as fuel cocks, strainers, wheels, axles, brake parts, tail wheel, streamline section tube etc. and set about obtaining them. Some will come easy but others most certainly will not.

The supply situation varies from month to month and what is scarce today will be plentiful next year. I was delayed for lack of S514 steel and two years later a friend building a V.P.2 had no trouble whatever.

At an early stage it is as well to have your instruments available, or at least those for which holes may have to be cut in bulkheads, as it is so much easier to cut a hole to fit the instrument while the bulkhead is lying flat on the table than after it is built into the fuselage.

So right at the beginning you should decide on your instrumentation. The published plans of the V.P.1 provide only for the minimum – rev-counter, air-speed indicator (A.S.I.), altimeter, and oil pressure and temperature gauges.

The V.P.1's range is something over 200 miles (322 km) so one will obviously need a compass, especially in a country with a confusing plethora of landmarks, such as southern Britain or France, and it would be nice to have a little blind flying capability just in case one gets caught out.

An E2A compass weighs next to nothing and mine is attached to the underside of the roll-over bar – what one might call a 'head-up display'. This is not the best place from the point of view of the compass itself as the proximity of the steel tube gives it a hefty deviation on certain headings but so long as you swing the compass and fix the deviation card in the cockpit this is no great disadvantage.

I found it possible to enlarge the instrument panel to take one more instrument so I was faced with the agonising decision as to what to choose and what to leave out. My own favourite instruments are the gyro direction indicator and the artificial horizon. I also like to refer constantly to the climb and dive indicator. However, having to rely on one and only one gyro instrument I felt that it would have to be the turn-and-slip indicator.

I noticed at Sywell that many other people, faced with the same problem, had made the same choice and I think it is the right one.

The artificial horizon and the direction indicator (D.I.) can topple – the venturi driven instruments are particularly prone to this – so it is as well to get used to not having them. Over-reliance on the D.I. nearly killed me once over Turkey. I did a very steep diving turn into cloud at about 22,000 feet (6 700 m) to dodge an excessively attentive 109 and, thinking that I was going back on the reciprocal and could descend through the cloud over the flat lands of the Meander plain, I went on down until I broke cloud at about 4000 feet (1220 m) in a valley that led down to the Gulf of Kerme, between mountains whose tops were over 7000 feet (2130 m). How I missed them I will never know but it cured me of my infatuation with the D.I.

Do not try to cram in too many instruments; your tiny panel will not accept them and there is no point in placing instruments where you cannot read them.

When you reach the covering stage you will have the choice of Egyptian cotton or Dacron. I tried both, cotton on the empennage and 'Ceconite' (dacron) on the wings. As a result of this experience I personally would never again use anything but Ceconite which is readily obtainable from an exceedingly friendly and helpful firm based at Shoreham.

My V.P.1 normally lives in a corner of a little black hangar at the end of a private strip on a very remote farm. One night a fox came through the window and jumped down onto my cotton covered elevator, putting a permanent and unsightly dent into it which had to be cut out and patched with a square of doped-on cotton cloth. On the other hand once, when attending an air show at Bournemouth, I caught a small boy walking over my Ceconite covered wing. I lifted him off pretty smartly but to my surprise he had not even marked it. He was a very small boy but he must have weighed a lot more than a fox.

Quite apart from its performance in service, which is really the deciding factor in its favour, I found Ceconite easier to apply than cotton.

It is almost inevitable that when building to an American design in the U.K., and possibly to a British or French design in the U.S.A., one will find that certain components are unobtainable or very difficult to locate. I was reduced to designing my own axles and having them machined up from 52 ton/sq in (3·4 MPa) steel. This was because, when I found that I could not obtain the old type Cessna axles specified, I decided to use wheel hubs which incorporated roller bearings and called for a smaller diameter of axle.

This brings me to the problem of modifications. The lighter the aircraft the more stark will be the design. Lightness is all important and the smaller the aircraft the more vital does it become. Nearly all amateurs' modifications and 'improvements' add weight. Add enough and the aircraft will not come off the ground.

Some additions may be highly desirable – a compass for instance – and some modifications may be necessary but on no account do anything without first consulting your inspector and, if possible, the designer. Every part of an aircraft has been designed for a purpose and to fit in with other parts. This may not be obvious to the constructor who has got his nose close to the work and can lose sight of the overall intention.

There are well documented cases where an 'improvement' has affected the structural integrity of the airframe with disastrous results.

Above all watch the weight, especially aft. My inspector was so conscious of this that he would only allow me one coat of primer and one of white paint inside the box fuselage. I thought that he was being unnecessarily fussy at the time but in the event it turned out that he was entirely justified. Just consider for a moment the weight of a gallon can of paint and then think of it as a percentage of the empty weight of the finished aircraft.

Problems of weight and centre of gravity are too easily overlooked by simple pilots like me when in fact we should always keep them at the back of our minds. Twice, during my professional flying career, I nearly came to grief through neglect of them.

The first time was in a grossly overloaded Blenheim. I had used up most of the runway when I realised that she was not going to unstick. It was too late to stop so I shoved the throttles through the gate, bounced her over the fence at the end of the overshoot and found a sheer drop of 200 feet (60 m) beyond. I stuffed the nose down and just got her flying before we hit the bottom of the valley.

That was distinctly hairy and I really should have learnt that lesson once and for all but eighteen months later, when the war was over, I did it again.

In mitigation I can only say that I had done most of my service flying in Hurricanes, Spitfires and Mosquitos in which the problem did not arise or, if it did, it was someone else's business to sort it out.

That second sin of omission could have been very unpleasant but in the event it provided the most hilarious moments of my whole service career.

Not long before the end of the war I had taken the air navigators' course and had consequently been sent to run the navigation flight at a training school in southern England.

Just after VJ Day I was approached by an aged warrant officer who asked if he could fly with me the next time I was going up. It appeared that he had been due to retire from the service in 1939 but had been retained for the duration of the war and now that it was over he was definitely due for final discharge.

Rather diffidently he told me that in the whole of his service career he had never been up in the air and what would his grandchildren think if he had to confess to that? He had, he said, studied the form among the pilots on the station and concluded that he would be safer with me than with anyone else. How sadly he had misjudged the situation. Anyway I agreed to take him up when next I was flying and promptly forgot all about it.

Some days later I had put myself down for a night cross-country detail and when we emerged from the briefing room into the darkness on the tarmac we were confronted by a bulky figure wearing a flying helmet and a Sidcot suit with a pilot type parachute banging against the backs of his knees as he walked. It was our warrant officer come for his joy ride.

I could hardly go back on my word, so I told him to get into the Anson and tuck himself down out of the way. The crew consisted of a staff pilot, myself, three pupils and now the W.O.1.

Because I was inclined to suffer from air-sickness unless I was in the pilot's seat I was in the habit of doing the flying myself while the staff pilot attended to the pupils.

And so we took off into a lovely moonlit night. We flew down to a turning point in Dorset, then east along the south coast of England to turn on the Ford 'pundit' beacon and set course on the last leg for base.

Some time after we had left Ford the starboard engine began to run rough and the oil pressure dropped to the bottom of the gauge.

This did not worry me particularly as I had done plenty of asymmetric flying on Mosquitos, which seemed to go just as well on one as on two engines, so I shut down the starboard engine, opened up the port one and kept on going.

It was some minutes before I realised that we were losing height at an uncomfortable rate and nothing I could do would stop it. We would obviously not reach base so I turned back for Ford but it soon became clear that we would not make Ford either, so I diverted to Thorney Island.

We tried to raise Thorney on the radio but they were having a night off. I was still not worried as I could perfectly well get down without a flare-path by using the landing lights, but when I tested them they would not come on. It was the starboard engine that drove the generator.

Rather than attempt a night landing with an overloaded aircraft on a black runway without lights I decided to ditch in Chichester Harbour and accordingly briefed the crew on ditching procedures.

At this the poor W.O.1 suddenly realised that on his first and only flight he was going to crash and imagined that he would probably not even be around to tell his grandchildren about his great aerial adventure. The poor chap panicked and the staff pilot and the pupils had their hands full suppressing him for the short time remaining in the air.

Now I had spent much of my boyhood sailing in Chichester Harbour and knew it very well so that when I considered the best places for a ditching I realised that wherever we went down we would probably have to wade ashore through thigh-deep, glutinous mud.

I therefore decided to stretch my approach as far as possible to alight along the Wittering shore outside the harbour mouth where we could land on a sandy beach. So with the staff pilot in the right hand seat and the rest of the crew on the floor as near midships as possible, we made our approach.

It was a perfect night for it. There was a slight ripple on the sea and the moonlight reflected from it gave us a good landing path. The groynes on the beach showed up well and I aimed to touch down just outside the line of the groyne ends, giving us perhaps fifty feet (15 m) to go to dry land.

I warned the crew that the landing would be hard and deceleration sudden. In the event the arrival was noisy but we ran on much further than I had expected.

As soon as we stopped I went out through the crash exit in the roof and stood on the wing to supervise the embarkation into the dinghy. The rest of the crew were supposed to jettison the door, throw out the dinghy which would automatically inflate and then embark themselves before taking me on board from the wing.

It almost happened like that except that when I arrived on the wing I found that the tide was out and we had landed in no more than six inches of water, which explained our landing run since the Anson's wheels, when retracted, still projected a little way below the engine nacelles.

I saw the door fall away. But instead of the dinghy pack flying out like a rugger ball from the scrum, a great rubbery bulge appeared in the doorway. The clowns had managed to inflate it inside the aircraft.

Panic reigned supreme. The dinghy bulged and recoiled again and again. Orders were shouted and countermanded or ignored and over it all I could hear the W.O.1 wail 'We're sinking'.

I stood there ankle deep in water and laughed till I ached all over and had to sit on the wing, so weak I was with laughter.

At last they managed to get a corner of the dinghy out through the top of the door and the rest followed, slowly at first and then in a rush with the crew piling out one on top of the other.

The ungrateful lot, including the W.O.1, were exceedingly rude to me and only my relatively superior rank saved me from physical assault. Some people are short on a sense of humour.

But the point of all this is that it is the easiest thing in the world to overload an aircraft to the point where it is dangerous to fly it and every pound that you add in 'improvements' is cutting into your factor of safety and raising your stalling speed.

My own modifications added 14 lb (6·4 kg) to the empty weight of the aircraft and I hoped to sweat it off my own weight. The pay-load of the

V.P.1 is 170 lb (77·1 kg) and when I started building I weighed just that without any clothes on. This promised pretty chilly aviating but by the time of first flight I had managed to slim down so that the all up weight was just three pounds (1·4 kg) under the maximum. A near thing involving immense sacrifices since I like to eat well.

If you get your plans directly from the P.F.A. they will automatically register the project, allocate a construction number and send you all the relevant papers. My construction number was 7007, so that from then onwards the little aeroplane was referred to in the family as 007.

If you get your plans from any other source, such as the designer himself or from someone who having bought the plans has taken fright and decided to go no further, you must immediately advise the P.F.A. and ask for registration and documentation.

Not to do this is to deprive yourself of all the help and guidance that you are certain to need and it may land you with an aircraft that no inspector will certify. It is just not worth the risk.

The papers you will receive are: Notes on Building; a List of P.F.A. Approved Inspectors; a List of Approved Materials; a List of Suppliers of Aircraft Materials; and, most important of all, the little green Log-Book of Inspection Schedules.

Each inspection stage is duplicated in the log-book and your inspector signs both halves at each stage. You then tear out the duplicate and send it to the P.F.A. office.

The objects of this are that the office can maintain a record of the progress of construction and, if you sell the aircraft in an incomplete state, the buyer can check the inspection stages with the office and be assured that all inspections are up to date and he is not inheriting a rogue. It also means that if you lose the original log-book the office can issue a duplicate with the completed stages certified as having been inspected.

When all is finished you send the completed log-book together with the weighing sheet from which the centres of gravity are determined and the engine inspection sheet to the P.F.A. office with your application for a Certificate of Airworthiness (C. of A.).

If all is in order you will receive a permit to test-fly the aircraft together with a schedule of air tests to be carried out and recorded. When this schedule has been completed you will receive the coveted C. of A. – the Freedom of the Skies.

First flight is still as yet a long way off – the ultimate goal. But so long as we keep it in sight we are bound, eventually, to reach it.

Once one has sent for the plans and registered the project with the P.F.A. the real work begins.

The first essential step is a concentrated study of the plans, the building instructions and any notified modifications.

In the case of the V.P.1 the drawings are very fully detailed and generally well cross-referenced. They are in fact the best I have seen to date. They arrived stapled together into a large, floppy book. After the first couple of evenings of turning the sheets backwards and forwards, following the cross referencing of various items, I pulled out the staples and punched the sheets for a ring binder. I could now take out all the sheets on which any one item appeared and lay them side by side for study.

As a chartered engineer I know from experience just how essential is this careful study and annotation of the plans so that one has a clear idea of the designer's intention and absolute certainty about how one is going to carry it out.

Bud Evans is a fine engineer and his drawings are beautifully clear and well detailed but it is possible for anyone unfamiliar with the conventions of a different discipline to mis-read even the best of drawings. An example is Bud's detail of the aft spar bulkhead on which the direction of view of the elevation is not stated. This should have been obvious but I marked my wood for drilling and it was only on the final check that I found that I had marked one hole on the wrong side of the centre-line through reading the drawing back to front.

So study the drawings, check your observations and make your own notes in red ink. You cannot afford to waste material and labour through silly mistakes – not with the price of spruce quoted in pence per cubic inch.

From the plans one has to abstract the quantities for ordering materials. In order to spread the cost you will probably want to order only enough material for each stage in turn. On the other hand you will not want to be delayed waiting for some minor fitting or special alloy which turns out to be on six or more months delivery.

It would be as well, therefore, to consult with your inspector when you have made out your list and decide what must be ordered immediately and what can be left until later.

From my own experience I would say that spruce, plywood, fabric, glue, brads and most nuts, bolts and washers will not present any problems, but that special alloys such as the S514 steel for the wing roots and flying strut fork ends, the flying struts themselves and the extruded aluminium plate for the undercarriage may be harder to obtain and should be placed on order right at the start.

Certain items may have to be obtained from America – the $\frac{3}{8}$ inch (9·53 mm) eyebolts for the stabilator hinge are a case in point – and these may be had through a well known and extremely helpful and courteous firm based at Bicester, Oxon, who import all American aircraft components. They will be just as prompt and friendly about the minute order for your V.P.1 as they would be if you were ordering a complete new undercarriage assembly for a Boeing, but remember that, with air-freight and duty, any parts obtained from the States will be pretty pricey. I know two builders who have made their own eyebolts but they are much better machinists than I could ever hope to be.

It is a sad fact that, in the U.K. at least, there are a number of firms who are loftily disinterested in business and just do not bother to reply to letters. How they continue to function without the ability to read and write is beyond my simple comprehension. I would almost go so far as to say that they are in the majority and one, at least, is a sizeable concern.

It is not for me to blow other people's trumpets but of the two firms that I found to be efficient, prompt and very helpful, one is near York and the other at Shoreham. They can both read and write and get their sums right. Long may they prosper for we could not do without them.

The advertisement pages of *Sport Aviation* must cause every non-American builder to commit the deadly sin of envy. There seems to be nothing that is not available on demand and at reasonable prices in America. Indeed if one were planning to build something really complex it might almost be worth emigrating for a couple of years just to solve the supply problem.

There will be quite a lot of items that you will have to pick up as and when the opportunity occurs. SR4 magnetoes and engine and flying instruments will come into this bracket. Watch the advertisements in *Popular Flying* and carry a list of your needs to every Strut meeting.

Even the engine itself could be considered in this way – that is how I got mine. The building of little aeroplanes seems to produce in the nicest people the ghoulish propensities of eighteenth century Cornish wreckers, so that they are forever on the lookout for Volkswagens of low mileage that have run head-on into brick walls.

I must confess that I was reluctant to spend money on an engine and other equipment until I was quite sure that I would have an airframe in which to install it, so slight was my faith in my own competence.

It took me a long time to wake up to the fact that that gentle genius, Bud Evans, had designed all or most of the hard to acquire skills out of the V.P.1 and the few that remained were in components which one could get made out by experts or specialist firms.

The mention of workmanship brings us back to the burden of our song. Do not take on anything that is going to be beyond the limits of your skill. Of course you can expect to learn quite a lot as you go along and you can expect that your basic skills will improve with practice but remember that right from the start your work has got to pass the scrutiny of your inspector.

The poor chap may wince at your finish but he is not going to worry too much about that provided that the work is structurally sound and not over-weight. He may pull you up for failing to wipe off surplus glue that has squeezed out of joints and insist that you remove the hardened globules with a chisel but it is less the appearance of the work that he is concerned with so much as the excess, unnecessary weight that you will be carrying. This may seem to you like nit-picking, as it did to me at first, but he knows very well that half an ounce here added to half an ounce somewhere else adds up to pounds in the end.

My inspector insisted on seeing my scarfed joints before I glued them together and, after rejecting the first three outright and seeing that I was in danger of running out of wood, he demonstrated how it should be done using a very fine toothed saw then sanding the faces very lightly with only finger-tip pressure so that in the end there was full contact over the whole of both surfaces. We then glued them and forced them together in the jig.

He also required me to make test pieces using the off-cuts from each scarfe and when they had set up to full strength he put them in the vice and broke them with a heavy hammer in two directions to see that they broke through the wood and not through the joint.

This is the sort of scrutiny that your work will have to withstand. The simple wood and fabric aircraft call for no great skill in the use of tools, only a great deal of care.

It is, I think, important not to look too far ahead. Treat each little job as an end in itself, even if it is only the making and fitting of a piece of quarter-round to a cockpit gusset. That way the work will be better done and one will continually surprise and delight oneself when a lot of little jobs suddenly add up to one big one – like a fuselage.

Before I start on any major project I like to read up all I can about it. I am a sucker for second-hand book shops and the older and more arcane the book the more I am attracted to it. I even have on my shelves a delightful and very serious tome entitled *Aeriel Navigation of Today* dated 1910 by one Charles Turner who had only ever flown a balloon. I am therefore probably the least reliable compiler of a selective bibliography.

Reading, they say, maketh a full man. It can also make him very confused since so many eminent authorities disagree profoundly on matters of the greatest importance. It is therefore, I think, as well to restrict one's reading to the essentials, at least in the early stages.

If one is building one of the V.P.s the building instructions that come with the plans are quite excellent, though very condensed. Follow them in the order given and to the letter and you can hardly go wrong.

The *P.F.A. Handbook* is essential to all who are building in the U.K. since it details the inspection, certification and registration procedures, lists the U.K. alternatives to American specifications and has excellent explanatory notes on woodwork, glues, fabric, metal work, Volkswagen engine conversion and much else besides.

The American equivalent is the *E.A.A.'s Aircraft Builder's Handbook* which besides giving details of American and Canadian licensing procedures goes into great detail over centre of gravity determination and test flying procedures.

Even at this early stage it is as well to get hold of the pilot's notes for your aircraft if they exist, or failing this get a reprint or a copy of any flight test reports that may have been published in *Popular Flying*, *Sport Aviation* or *Les Cahiers du R.S.A.* and make them your bedside reading until you know them by heart.

Anyone who was in the war-time R.A.F. will recall the importance that was placed upon the thorough understanding of the pilot's notes for the types upon which one was supposed to be currently in practice. The last page of *Tee Emm*, the monthly issue of training memoranda, always carried a popular advertisement suitably slanted such as 'Pilots Notes – Prevent That Thinking Feeling' or 'Have You Macread Your Pilots Notes Today?'

I was in a squadron in a fairly remote theatre of the war when we were re-equipped with a very different type of aircraft to the one we had been flying. They sent us the aeroplanes but no pilot's notes and not even an instructor to give us a bit of dual. It cost us one experienced pilot and one valuable aircraft for the lack of ten bob's worth of pilot's notes.

If you have built a single-seater your first take-off will be in a type that is new to you; there will be no chance of any dual. The pilot's notes will save you from finishing up in a heap.

In the case of the Evans' aircraft the pilot's notes are *Flying the Evans V.P.* by Bill Beatty who test flew the prototypes. They are a model of what the pilot's notes should be.

As soon as you acquire your engine, and this can happen at any stage of the project, you will get a set of conversion plans and instructions but you should also obtain the workshop manual applicable to your engine. In the case of the Volkswagen there seem to be several different publications. I have two and they differ wildly. I found the most reliable source to be *The Owner's Workshop Manual for the Volkswagen 1500 and 1600 Type 3* by J. H. Haynes.

Finally you must have something to turn to for inspiration and reassurance. I used Dr John Urmston's lovely book *Birds and Fools Fly* about the building of a Currie Wot. Once you have started to build and the inevitable doubts and fits of indecision set in, a quiet evening with John Urmston will rekindle your enthusiasm and get you going again. I must have read this book at least four times in course of building 007. It is such a comfort to know that someone else has been there before you, has faced the problems and discouragements and has won through in the end to fly his own handiwork.

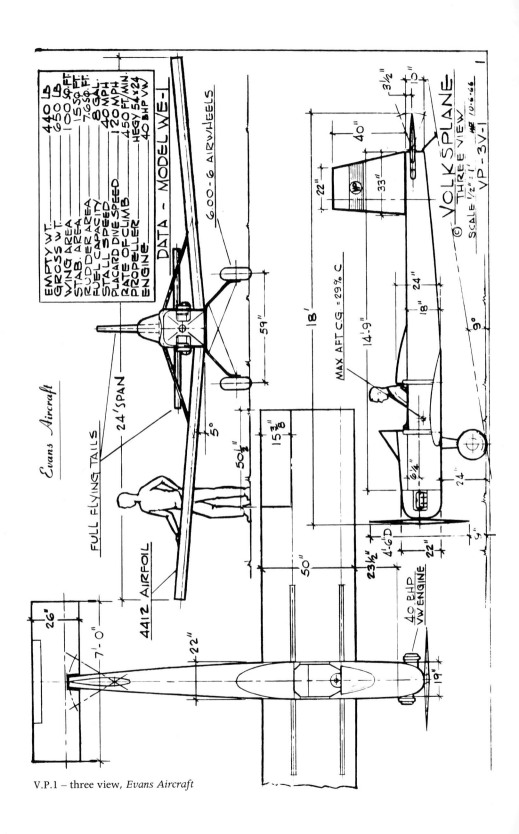

V.P.1 – three view, *Evans Aircraft*

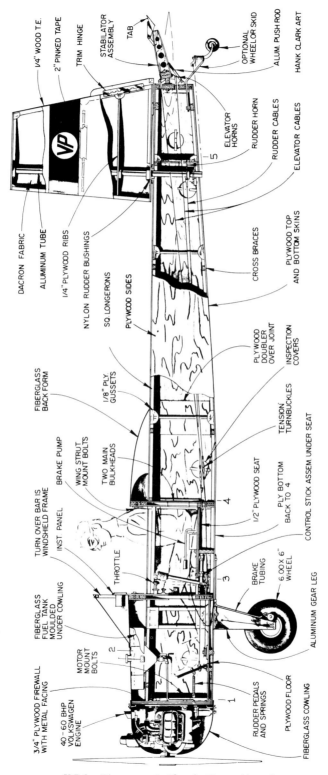

V.P.1 – Diagrammatic Sketch, *Evans Aircraft*

1/4" WOOD T.E.

2" PINKED TAPE

TRIM HINGE

STABILATOR ASSEMBLY

TAB

OPTIONAL WHEELOR SKID

ALUM. PUSH ROD

HANK CLARK ART

ELEVATOR HORNS

RUDDER HORN

RUDDER CABLES

ELEVATOR CABLES

5

DACRON FABRIC

ALUMINUM TUBE

1/4" PLYWOOD RIBS

NYLON RUDDER BUSHINGS

SQ LONGERONS

PLYWOOD SIDES

CROSS BRACES

PLYWOOD TOP AND BOTTOM SKINS

FIBERGLASS BACK FORM

1/8" PLY GUSSETS

PLYWOOD DOUBLER OVER JOINT

INSPECTION COVERS

TURN OVER BAR IS WINDSHIELD FRAME

INST PANEL

BRAKE PUMP

WING STRUT MOUNT BOLTS

TWO MAIN BULKHEADS

TENSION TURNBUCKLES

1/2" PLYWOOD SEAT

PLY BOTTOM BACK TO 4

CONTROL STICK ASSEM UNDER SEAT

4

THROTTLE

BRAKE TUBING

6.00 x 6" WHEEL

ALUMINUM GEAR LEG

3

FIBERGLASS FUEL TANK MOULDED UNDER COWLING

MOTOR MOUNT BOLTS

2

3/4" PLYWOOD FIREWALL WITH METAL FACING

40 - 60 BHP VOLKSWAGEN ENGINE

RUDDER PEDALS AND SPRINGS

PLYWOOD FLOOR

FIBERGLASS COWLING

1

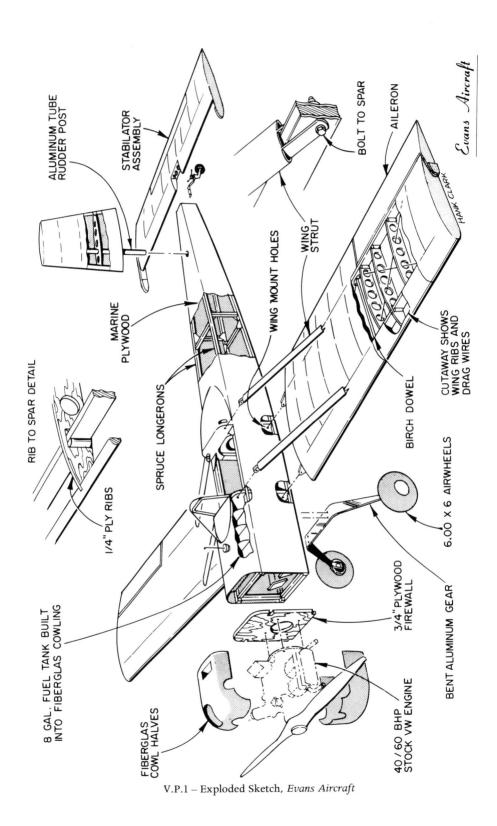

ALUMINUM TUBE
RUDDER POST

STABILATOR
ASSEMBLY

BOLT TO SPAR

AILERON

Evans Aircraft

HANK CLARK

WING MOUNT HOLES

WING STRUT

MARINE
PLYWOOD

RIB TO SPAR DETAIL

SPRUCE LONGERONS

CUTAWAY SHOWS
WING RIBS AND
DRAG WIRES

BIRCH DOWEL

1/4" PLY RIBS

6.00 x 6 AIRWHEELS

8 GAL. FUEL TANK BUILT
INTO FIBERGLAS COWLING

3/4" PLYWOOD
FIREWALL

BENT ALUMINUM GEAR

FIBERGLAS
COWL HALVES

40/60 BHP
STOCK VW ENGINE

V.P.1 – Exploded Sketch, *Evans Aircraft*

Chapter 4

The fuselage

Many people, unsure of their skills, make a start by building a small component such as a rudder or an elevator so that they can get their hands in without risking too much. This is fine in theory except that a rudder or an elevator, with its compound curves, is not the easiest part of an aeroplane to build.

Knowing nothing whatever about building aeroplanes I blindly followed the building instructions that came with the V.P.1 plans.

Bud Evans starts his instructions with the fuselage but, being a man of remarkably few words, he does not say why one should start by building the biggest single component. The reason does not become apparent until one comes to assemble the other bits and pieces when one discovers that the fuselage is needed to try them on in the course of construction. In a sense the fuselage then becomes the assembly jig.

So be bold and start with the fuselage. After all that only consists of a lot of smaller bits and you can get your hand in on those.

It has a further advantage in that once you have a darn great fuselage half filling your garage it seems that you already have most of the aeroplane and you have the feeling that you have gone too far to give up.

The first thing that you will require is the building table. This is the major jig and so it needs to be absolutely firm.

I built the carcase of mine out of 'Terlan' perforated steel angle, 15 feet long overall by 20 inches wide (4·6 m by 0·5 m) over the uprights. The top rails consisted of angles with the top flanges projecting outwards. The top consisted of a single 8 ft by 4 ft (2·4 m by 1·2 m) sheet of $\frac{1}{2}$ inch (13 mm) blockboard ripped down the middle and bolted to the top rails to give a table top 16 ft long by 2 ft wide (4·9 m by 0·6 m). It will thus be seen that the top overhung the carcase by 2 inches (50 mm) on each side and 6 inches (150 mm) at the ends. This was so that clamps could be applied anywhere around the table.

The feet of the angle uprights sat on 20 inch (0·5 m) long transverse angles to which they were bolted and which in turn were screwed down to the floor which was drilled and plugged.

The hardest part was levelling the table both transversely and longitudinally since, like most garage floors, the surface undulated somewhat. This was achieved with penny washers under the transverse angles around the screws that held the feet to the floor. It sounds easy but it took hours because every time I tightened up on a screw the bubble in the level would creep off centre.

Having, at last, levelled the table I struck the centre-line with a chalked string. It then appeared that the middle of the table was off-centre by $\frac{3}{4}$ inch (19 mm) and I had to slacken off the floor screws, tap the middle legs across and go through the whole levelling process all over again. An expert would have checked the centre-line before he started to level up, but then, as I have said before, I an no expert – at least I was not one then.

Having re-levelled the table I struck the centre-line again and cut it into the table-top using a chisel and the steel straight-edge.

It is important to level your work table and ensure a permanent centre-line since any inaccuracy here will re-appear in the finished fuselage. I once had to fly a Spitfire whose fuselage was twisted an inch (25 mm) out of true as a result of a wheels-up landing on a beach. The poor thing could not be trimmed in any plane and had to be flown very carefully all the time. Very tiring, especially on instruments and not what I would want in my own aeroplane.

Having erected the building table we can make a start by building the main bulkheads. Draw them out full size on the table top using a thin, hard pencil and then nail 1 inch (25 mm) square strips of deal round the outside pencil lines. This is your first jig.

The two main bulkheads of the V.P.1 are both 24 inches by 22 inches (0·61 m by 0·56 m) outside dimensions so both can be built in the same jig.

Cut the component parts of the carcase with great care so that they are not under-size (remember that a saw blade has thickness); cut to the outside of the marking out pencil line so that the parts are a tight fit when assembled in the jig.

Having checked the assembly remove the parts from the jig and line it with Melinex. This is a thin plastic film to which glue will not adhere and its purpose is to prevent the glued assembly being stuck to the table or the jig.

Most disasters have happened to me, but not this one. I was warned against it by a melancholy individual, at a Strut meeting, who had just been caught out in this way. His vivid account of the consequences so impressed itself on my mind that on two occasions when I had glued assemblies setting in the garage I awoke in the night and, unable to recall whether or not I had remembered to line the jig, I got up and went downstairs to check.

There are two resin glues specially recommended for use in aircraft construction. For those who like technical terms these are 'Urea-Formaldehyde Resin' and 'Resorcinal-Formaldehyde Resin'. The most easily obtained commercial formulations are 'Aerolite 306' and 'Aerodux 185' respectively.

Aerolite 306, the urea-formaldehyde resin glue, is recommended for the V.P.1 and appears to be the more suitable for the amateur builder because it has a much longer shelf life, up to two years under good conditions – I kept mine in a cupboard in my study – and, when mixed, a shelf life of ten to fourteen days. Its setting is also less affected by temperature.

It consists of a white powder which is mixed with warm water in the proportions of four parts of powder to one of water, well stirred until it forms a milky white liquid with the consistency of a thinnish honey and then left to stand for half an hour so that all the air bubbles can get out. The powder should be measured into a clean, dry container such as a jam jar. The water should then be added slowly while stirring with a wooden stick.

The instructions actually tell one to dissolve a hundred parts by weight of powder with forty-five parts by weight of water but it is much easier to do it by volume rather than by weight and it seems to work just as well. I mixed mine up in batches of four egg cups full of powder to one egg cup full of water. The mixture can be kept in a jar with a screw-on lid for ten to fourteen days and probably much longer but I did not like to take any chances and discarded any residue after that time.

The application is simplicity itself. One merely applies the glue to one side of the joint, using a spatula of thin ply as a spreader, and the hardener to the other side by brush before bringing them together and clamping them or otherwise ensuring that they are in close contact as in a jig.

The hardener is a thin liquid with an acrid smell and comes in three strengths marked GBQ which is fast setting, GBP for medium setting and GBM for slow setting. At a temperature of 21°C (70°F), the 'shuffling' times within which the joint must be made and clamped are respectively 5 minutes for GBQ, 10 minutes for GBP and 15 minutes for GBM. You will have slightly more time at a lower temperature but I would not count on it.

The hardener can be had either colourless or colour-coded brown for GBQ, green for GBP or mauve for GBM. For your own satisfaction I would strongly recommend that you have it coloured. Your inspector will probably require this as evidence that the hardener has, in fact, been applied to the joint.

The hardener stains the wood around the joint which is of no consequence if one is painting but would look unsightly under varnish. Hence, presumably, the colourless hardener.

The instructions tell one to sand the surfaces to be glued before applying the glue but de Havilland practice was to score them with a criss-cross pattern using the corner of a chisel and my inspector would accept nothing less.

When gluing plywood to sawn timber one is advised to apply the glue to the timber and the hardener to the plywood surface. I am not sure of the reason for this but I did it religiously.

The joint must remain clamped while the glue is setting and appropriate times in hours are given as:

| | Temperature | | | |
Hardener	10°C (50°F)	16°C (60°F)	21°C (70°F)	27°C (80°F)
GBQ	6	$2\frac{1}{2}$	2	$1\frac{1}{2}$
GBP	7	3	2	$1\frac{1}{2}$
GBM	12	5	$3\frac{1}{2}$	$2\frac{1}{2}$

I never left any of my joints clamped for less than 12 hours but this was because of my working habits and for no other reason.

There are, of course, many places where it is impractical to use clamps as, for instance, when gluing large sheets of ply to the skeleton timber framework of the fuselage. This is where the little brass brads come in. They should be spaced about an inch apart and it pays to start them in the ply before applying the glue to the joint. You then have a reasonable chance of getting the glued surfaces nailed tightly together within the permissible 'shuffling' time.

I was worried at first because, I think, of something I had read, that the brads would have to be withdrawn in areas that had to be sanded down later (for example, from the overlap of the torsion box ply on the leading edge spar), but I found, in the event, that the brads sanded down as easily as the ply so I left them all in.

I was concerned to see that the temperature in the garage was always over 10°C (50°F) when gluing was in progress and maintained at that level through the setting time, even in the winter. I doubt that my inspector would have allowed anything less but I was told by a reliable witness that he had seen gluing with Aerolite 306 being undertaken by a well known and reputable firm in an open hangar with snow on the ground outside. It must be remarkably tolerant to temperature though I would not tempt providence to this extent on my own aeroplane.

It is most important not to allow the hardener, or even the fumes of the hardener, anywhere near the glue pot or a surface spread with glue until you are ready to make the joint. Even the fumes of the hardener can set the glue off.

The resorcinal-formaldehyde glue – Aerodux 185 – is generally preferred by the commercial firms but remember that they are working in a temperature and humidity controlled environment and generally on larger assemblies where the longer 'shuffling' time is a decided advantage.

The glue is a dark brown liquid to which the HRP 150 powder hardener is added in the proportions of one part by weight of hardener to five parts by weight of glue, the mixture then being stirred until smooth.

The method of application is to coat both surfaces evenly with the mixed glue, allow them to stand for five minutes or so and then bring them together and clamp them lightly.

The critical times are given as:

Temperature	Shuffling Time (hours)	Clamping Time (hours)
17°C (62°F)	$1\frac{1}{2}$	$4\frac{1}{2}$
21°C (70°F)	1	$3\frac{1}{2}$
25°C (77°F)	$\frac{1}{2}$	$2\frac{1}{2}$

It is really a matter of personal preference and circumstance as to which glue you use. For garage building I would personally choose the urea-formaldehyde glue but if in doubt a chat with your inspector should resolve the matter.

The bulkheads of the V.P.1 are faced with marine ply on both sides and the ply can be glued to one side at least while the carcase is still in the jig.

Once the bulkheads have been faced with ply on both sides the top corners can be rounded and the notches to receive the longerons can be carefully cut out. Then one should drill all the holes that are required using the drill-press stand. These will be the holes for the bushes that take the bolts at wing root and flying strut ends, control cables, harness attachment, fairlead attachment, instrument panel and roll-over bar attachment and engine instruments.

It is therefore as well to have the bushes and the oil pressure and temperature gauges handy to be sure of a perfect fit. My oil pressure gauge was of the rectangular type – it came out of an Anson – and not the normal round variety, so it was fortunate that I had it to hand as it called for a very odd shaped hole which would have been difficult to cut had the bulkhead not been flat on the bench.

The firewall is cut out from a sheet of $\frac{3}{4}$ inch (19 mm) thick marine ply and the sternpost consists of a core of $\frac{3}{4}$ inch (19 mm) thick Douglas fir faced with $\frac{1}{8}$ inch (3 mm) marine ply. No problems here. At this stage one also cuts out the plywood seat from $\frac{1}{2}$ inch (13 mm) thick marine ply and the seat support from $\frac{3}{4}$ inch (19 mm) thick spruce.

Now we can clear the building table ready for building the fuselage sides.

I was unable to get $\frac{3}{4}$ inch (19 mm) square spruce in lengths long enough to make a longeron without jointing two pieces together. This required a scarfed joint at 1 in 12 or 9 inches (228 mm) long. To do this I first made a jig by nailing a 2 ft (0·6 m) length of 1 inch (25 mm) square deal to the table, laying the $\frac{3}{4}$ inch (19 mm) square longeron against it and nailing another piece of 1 inch (25 mm) square deal hard up against its other side. I then sawed out the scarfe with the two ends to be joined laid side by side and the saw running across both at once. Then, when my inspector had approved of the dry joint, I lined the jig with Melinex, applied glue and hardener to the two faces of the joint and drove them hard together in the jig. The off-cuts of the scarfe were used for making test pieces.

Building Table – with
longerons laid out

Now I could draw out the fuselage side panels on the table. All round the outside lines I nailed $\frac{1}{2}$ inch (13 mm) ply blocks to hold the longerons in place, taking care to see that there was a block opposite each end of each upright stiffener. The ends of the uprights are merely butted and glued against the longerons but the joint is strengthened by the presence of the plywood skin on the one side and a plywood gusset, or biscuit as it is sometimes called, on the other side.

When all the members have been assembled dry in the jig they are removed, the jig lined with Melinex by every joint, the members put back in the jig and glued. Finally the gussets are glued and nailed in place over every joint.

When the glue has set the assembly can be prized out of the jig and, in due course, the plywood skin can be glued onto the frame on the side opposite the gussets.

The other side is assembled in the same jig but, instead of gluing the gussets over the joints, one attaches the side skin of ply and applies the gussets to the joints when the panel has been removed from the jig.

All very cunning but not at all difficult when an expert like Bud Evans is leading you by the hand.

I had pottered along for weeks cutting out flat pieces of ply, making up bulkheads, firewall and sternpost and laying out and making fuselage sides.

Friends who came to see the 'aeroplane' seemed quite unimpressed with my piles of flat ply; even the fuselage sides with stiffeners neatly gusseted to the longerons failed to arouse more than polite applause.

To entertain my public
– instrument panel
bolted to main
bulkhead

In order to entertain my public I even went so far as to make up the instrument panel complete with most of the instruments, bolt it to the bulkhead and stick it in the vice where they could see and admire it.

Then, one evening, I came home to find that my wife had gone out baby-sitting for the grandchildren. The previous evening I had finished work on the second fuselage side so, after tea, I lifted it out of the jig and began prizing the jig blocks off the table.

I cleared and cleaned the table and went on to check the centre-line and mark out the positions for the 4 in by 2 in (100 mm by 50 mm) blocks to which the bulkheads have to be clamped for assembly.

For once everything went right. The four-by-two was to hand and only needed a touch of the plane to square it up – always check everything for squareness; I have learnt by bitter experience that it very seldom is square. I had decided to bolt rather than spike the four-by-two to the table and surprisingly I found a hoard of quarter inch (6·35 mm) bolts 5 in (127 mm) long left over from rebuilding a garage fourteen years before.

In no time at all I had the blocks set up. I clamped the bulkheads and the firewall to the blocks. The seat and its support dropped into place. I looked at it all and wondered, would the sides fit after all this? Might as well try.

The first side slipped into place, a nice tight fit at all points. The second followed. A bar cramp just ahead of the main bulkhead and a couple of one inch (25 mm) blocks tacked to the table on either side to prevent any disasters. I pulled the tail ends in and lashed them to the sternpost with a length of cord, and stood back.

Miraculously it looked like an aeroplane. I walked all round it, admiring it. I got the step-ladder and climbed gingerly into the cockpit. Just as gingerly I climbed out and went in search of cushions.

A neighbour, walking his dog, realised that something was up and came in to investigate. We both tried the cockpit for size and were standing back admiring the three dimensional aeroplane over a few cans of beer when my wife arrived.

From somewhere she unearthed a flat cap and I had to get back in the cockpit with the cap on back to front doing an Orville Wright.

Having to take it all apart next morning to start gluing was a terrible anti-climax. It was a whole week-end before it was once again more or less three dimensional.

At this point it looked as though the fuselage was nearly finished, so I ordered up materials for the rudder and stabilator, but it was many a long week after they had arrived before I was ready to work on them.

Week-end after week-end went by, each with its tally of a few cross stiffeners installed, or ply gussets glued in place. The fiddling stage arrived where parts had to be marked, masked off and painted before they could be glued in place. One has to wait for paint to dry and unless one has planned ahead for it one can lose most of a week-end over a couple of top skins.

I painted the inside white since if one wants to inspect anything inside it would be difficult to see much against non-reflective varnished surfaces. In the enclosed portion of the fuselage aft of the cockpit, my inspector would only allow me one coat of white paint over the colourless primer in order to keep the weight within bounds.

I have always disliked painting as being a necessary but unproductive chore and the painting of this relatively intricate structure nearly drove me to distraction. Trying to peer under cross-pieces or longerons to see that all the surfaces were covered got paint into my hair and all over my sweater. My little aeroplane may not merit many superlatives but it must certainly be the fluffiest.

A friend donated a castor just the right size for the tailwheel, so I went to our local forge and machine shop to get the tailwheel assembly made up on its spring steel leg. They were delighted to find themselves transported from the field of agricultural machinery into the aerospace industry and did a superb job at a giveaway price. I took it home rejoicing, tapped it through the slot in the sternpost and bolted it in place. Then I had to take it out again for painting and to fit the top and bottom skins at the after end, which are specially stiffened to take the rudder bushes.

The same little machine shop worked up the nylon rudder bushes for me and I fitted them in place using a wooden mandril turned to 2 in (51 mm) diameter, since the rudder tube had not arrived and I wanted to close in the fuselage.

I cut out all the parts for the control column to size and then Sellotaped

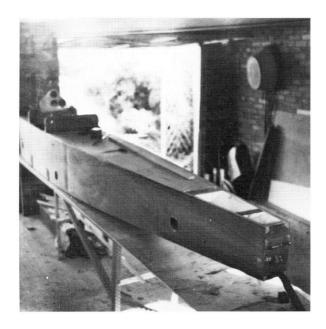

Top-skinning fuselage
on building table

them together for my inspector to take them to a certified welder of his acquaintance. I impatiently awaited their return so that I could install the stick and do a little simulated flying.

In the meantime I ordered a superb cushion from a neighbouring yacht builder. As a V.P.1's endurance is over $2\frac{1}{2}$ hours and the seat is an unyielding piece of $\frac{1}{2}$ inch (13 mm) plywood one could finish up like the little Lancashire lad who, on emerging from an air-raid shelter after an all-night blitz on Manchester, was heard to remark 'Ee by gum, Mum, my bum's numb'.

I had the cushion of 4 inch (100 mm) thick foam rubber tailored to the shape of the seat and fitted with press studs that clip underneath so that souvenir hunters would have difficulty in removing it and, more importantly, it could not slide forward and jam the stick.

No seat back is provided in the plans so I got an ultra-light one from a firm who make typist's chairs. This was necessary in order to bring my feet into comfortable contact with the rudder pedals. I must be the most comfortable of V.P.1 pilots.

One of the more unusual jobs turned out to be the making of the fibreglass fairing aft of the cockpit. I never expected to find that a couple of trowels would be part of an aeroplane builder's tool kit.

'Make up a plaster of Paris mould' say the instructions as though it is something one does every day. I searched in vain through all my text books for more detailed instructions and finally worked out for myself the following method which I think I would use again in default of any better suggestions.

The drawings give a plan view of the fairing and a fore and aft section through it. I laid out the plan view on a piece of scrap plywood and the section on a piece of one inch (25 mm plank). I laid a piece of half inch (13 mm) blockboard against the back of the aft bulkhead, where it projects above the after deck of the fuselage, marked it off and cut it out. I set this profile up on the plywood base and nailed it in position with one inch (25 mm) square blocks to steady it. Down the centre of the base I set up the longitudinal section profile and nailed the whole lot together.

I then got a pile of old newspapers, crumpled them up page by page, dipped each piece in water and squashed it into place on the base board until I had the rough shape of the fairing in wet paper.

I had bought ten pounds (4·5 kg) of moulding plaster which I thought would be plenty. This I mixed up with water and slapped on top of the paper shape, and of course it was nowhere near enough.

I had to get the car out late on a Saturday afternoon and tour all the chemist's shops within a radius of five miles buying up their stocks of plaster of Paris. I got another fifteen pounds (6·8 kg) in this way and it was still not enough. The following Monday I bought another ten pounds of moulding plaster and that just did the job.

So for this little fairing one needs about forty pounds (18 kg) of plaster. Moulding plaster is much better than plaster of Paris which shrinks abominably.

I started to do the rough moulding with my hands, but the plaster stuck my fingers together and got itself everywhere but on the mould. I soon found that it worked more easily using a wet trowel. I found too that a fairly sloppy mix is much easier and quicker to handle.

For the final shaping up I found that the only tools that were of any use were a Surform block plane, a Stanley smoothing plane and a one inch (25 mm) chisel. My sanding disc clogged up immediately and so did ordinary sand-paper. One essential tool is a wire brush for cleaning out the Surform plane after about every third stroke.

This sort of sculpture produces a pervasive dust and a considerable thirst so, to avoid domestic acrimony arising from chalky footprints on polished floors, it is as well to have a stock of beer actually at the site of the work.

Before starting on the fibreglass I went to a practical demonstration given by the firm who supplied the materials. This helped to give me a little much needed confidence. I have never liked the stuff, regarding it as an unnatural and unsympathetic material and its practitioners as dabblers in a necromantic black art.

The young demonstrator made the whole thing seem ridiculously simple, more so in fact than it turned out to be in practice.

One point that had worried me was a report in the American journal *Sport Aviation* to the effect that a number of cases had arisen of fibreglass fuel tanks flaking after some time in use. I mentioned this to the

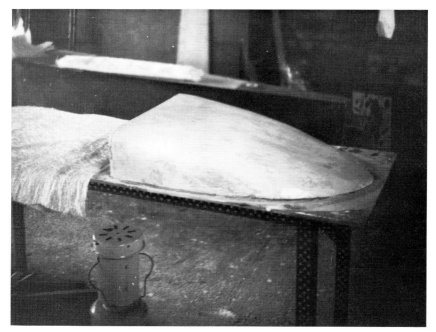

Plaster mould for aft fairing

demonstrator who said that this did happen in the case of tanks made with ordinary, general purpose resin. It is essential to use a chemical resistant resin for fuel tanks and this problem should not arise if the correct resin is employed.

As one might expect the chemical resistant resin is much more expensive than the general purpose one.

I came away loaded with yards of glass mat and Melinex sheeting as well as general purpose resin, chemical resistant resin, fire resistant wax resin, barrier cream, cleansing cream, bottles of catalyst, brush cleaner, brushes, a roller, glass tape, release agents and a stack of paper cups.

Came the great day and I laid everything out on the building table. The night before I had painted the mould with two coats of release agent No. 1, a sealant which dried very quickly and a coat of release agent No. 2 which did not show any signs of drying at all and was still wet the next morning.

Immediately on getting up in the morning I had driven the cars out of the garage, closed the doors and put the fan-heater on full blast to bring the temperature up to 60°F (16°C).

I coated my hands with barrier cream and studied the instruction sheet. Here came the first snag. The mix of catalyst to resin was given in ccs per pound. It took me a messy hour with my wife's cook-books to work out that this amounted to one teaspoonful of catalyst to one paper cup of resin. From then on all went well.

Glass fibre and resin on mould

I painted the mould with resin, slapped on a pre-cut sheet of glass mat, poured more resin on top and began stippling with a brush. The stiff sheet of mat melted onto the mould and I went to work with the roller.

A short pause to mix two more cups of resin. On with the next sheet of mat, more stippling and rolling, and the third, and final, sheet was on and curing all within forty minutes.

I took my beer break which somehow extended to an hour and a half. This was too long, so that trimming round the mould with a Stanley knife was very hard going and I had to finish off with a chisel.

The fairing lifted cleanly off the mould and I tried it onto the aeroplane. Amazingly it fitted perfectly. I left it to cure for a bit longer and after a spell of admiration and self-congratulation I went off to lunch.

Quite a while after lunch I replaced the fairing on the mould and drilled out the inspection hole on top using the tank cutter that I had used for the fuselage inspection holes. Then I washed the release agent off the inside of the fairing, sanded the mating surfaces, daubed resin on the top of the after bulkhead and onto the fuselage top deck where the fairing would sit, and put it gently into place. Probably quite unnecessarily I drilled a number of holes with my smallest drill and nailed the fairing to the bulkhead with brass brads before applying resin and glass tape round the joint between the base of the fairing and the fuselage sides and top deck. This last was a messy job and did not look too good when it was done, but it sanded down to a reasonable finish in the end.

I had hoped to save the mould for someone else but it cracked apart when I tried to take it off the building table. Incredibly the plaster and the paper it was formed on completely filled a standard rubbish bin and it was so heavy that the dustmen would not remove it so that I had to burn the paper and dispose of the plaster on the Council's tip.

Full of confidence after my relative success with the fairing I prepared to tackle the petrol tank which is moulded into the forward fuselage fairing.

I bought a sheet of soft aluminium to make the former for the forward fairing but, as I wanted to use it again to make patterns for the wing and stabilator ribs, I had to keep the sheet intact and could not trim it to shape. This was a mistake and I should have damned the expense. The weight of the sheet hanging below the fuselage on either side caused it to bulge slightly off the sides of the forward bulkhead leaving a rather unsightly gap.

The whole of this moulding had to be carried out in chemical resistant resin.

The major mistake that I made at this time was in being over-enthusiastic with the roller, so that I put ripples into the alloy former which, of course, appeared on the finished surface of the moulding.

With three layers of mat on the former, I finished off by laying a sheet of Melinex over the top and rolling it on, working from the centre outwards to exclude the air. The surface finish was lovely, but oh, those ripples.

The tank ends, bottom and baffles are all made out of flat sheet. The plans call for 'Alsynite' but, as this or its equivalent seemed hard to get, I made my own by laying a sheet of Melinex on the table, building up three layers of glass mat on it, placing a sheet of Melinex over all and rolling out the air, working from the centre outwards. Finally I placed a sheet of plate glass on top and left it to cure.

I had previously made paper patterns of the shapes I required so, after forty minutes curing, I removed the window glass, laid the patterns on top of the Melinex and cut round them with the Stanley knife. The result of this little effort was near perfection.

The tank sump was moulded round a six inch (150 mm) P.V.C. funnel. All the parts were then stuck together with glass tape and resin.

It is one of the sad facts of life that, by the time one has acquired the knowledge and the skill that one should have had before starting the job, the work is finished and remains for ever afterwards a monument to one's mistakes and ignorance.

Being impatient I made my fairings on male moulds. The purist will probably argue that I should have made fibreglass female moulds so that the gel coat would have finished up on the outside. I did consider this but it seemed to me that the primary mould would then have to be larger by the thickness of the fibreglass, and this would be difficult to make with any precision. Then again I felt that, in the case of the forward fairing which forms the petrol tank, it would be better to have the gel coat on the inside, in contact with the petrol. In any case the outside was going to be painted with polyurethane paint and there would have to be a certain amount of surface preparation for that.

Perhaps I am just making excuses for my own indolence and I must, in all fairness, admit that other builders have obtained finishes on their fibreglass work that put mine to shame, notably Tony Lang's Tango Lima which must be the most perfectly finished V.P.1 ever built.

Any good Muslim will tell you that to strive too hard for perfection is to challenge God Himself and so even the most beautiful of Persian carpets contains a deliberate mistake or lack of symmetry.

I comforted myself with this thought as I sanded out the ripples and other imperfections in my fibreglass petrol tank and aft fairing. Sanding, filling and rubbing down extended to over three week-ends until I decided that, imperfect though it still remained, the rubbing down had to stop.

Perfection is all right for those who have the time, but when one is nearing sixty one begins to be haunted by the spectre of the Demon Doctor ordering one to hang up one's goggles and I wanted to fly my little aeroplane after spending so much time and effort on it.

Before starting in to paint it seemed advisable to check the tank for water-tightness – or rather petrol tightness – and capacity. I set the tank

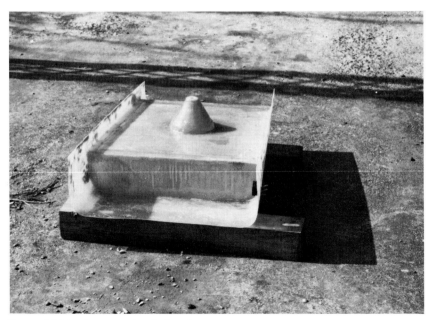

Forward fairing incorporating fuel tank

up on trestles, screwed the cock into the base of the sump and started to pour in measured quantities of water.

The water fairly poured out through the joints between the tank bottom and ends. These joints were made with a glass tape of rather open weave so I was not altogether surprised. I emptied the tank and left it to dry out for a week.

I then gave the joints a liberal application of resin and reinforced them with one ounce glass cloth before trying again.

There were still some minute leaks so I finished off with more resin and fine finishing cloth and finally poured resin into the tank and slowly rocked it from side to side with one end down at a time to allow the resin to penetrate the joint from the pressure side. That fixed it.

Finding the petrol cock was quite a saga in itself. After trying all the more likely sources without success, since modern motor cars no longer use them, it occurred to me that one should try the motor cycle suppliers.

I abstracted a list of addresses from the yellow pages and set out. After finding that the first three firms on my list had gone out of business I was beginning to get despondent when, down a side street, I spotted a display of bicycles and motor bikes on the pavement.

It was a little old fashioned shop with bits of bicycalia hanging everywhere inside and a little old man, who would never see seventy again, explaining in detail to a customer how, in his racing days, he had modified a Sturmey Archer to give him twenty four gears.

'Didn't do me no good though' he concluded sadly, 'I still had to pedal bloody hard'.

When I eventually managed to tell him what I wanted he cheered up and said 'About forty years ago a traveller sold me a whole lot of them. I never sold one; they must still be around somewhere.'

It did not take him long to find them and they were exactly what appears on the drawings – finger type strainer and all – and they were plated brass, not the rubbishy pot-metal things that are current today. They were in a variety of sizes so not being too sure of the size required I bought two of the largest for ten bob.

Before he would let me finally install the cock my inspector insisted that I should check that it would pass the maximum demand of the engine plus ten gallons per hour (45 litre/h). But what is the maximum demand of a 1600 cc Volkswagen engine with a prop on the front? No one could tell me but eventually I worked out, by extrapolation from the figures given in Bill Beatty's book *Flying the Evans V.P.'s*, that it would be 3·45 American gallons per hour, which I make 2·87 Imperial gallons. This meant a required flow of 12·87 gallons per hour (59 litre/h).

With stop-watch and measuring jug I determined that the two cocks would pass six and seven gallons per hour respectively at minimum head. Not good enough.

The bore of the larger cock was $\frac{1}{8}$ inch (3·2 mm) so I drilled it out to $\frac{3}{16}$

inch (4·8 mm) and tried again. This time I got a flow of 12·9 gallons per hour, so honour was satisfied, just.

The capacity of the tank came to six gallons and seven pints – just over eight American gallons (31 litres).

To back-track a little, before I put the bottom into the tank I had to fix the positions and install the bolts for the windscreen clips. To do this I had to have the windscreen. I was told about a windscreen repair shop in the town who also supplied perspex. It seemed a good starting point for enquiries so I went in and asked if they had such a material as 'Lexan', as specified in the plans.

Surprisingly they knew all about it and actually stocked the German equivalent 'Makrolon'. This is a polycarbonate, whatever that may mean, immensely strong and can be bent cold to any simple shape. They had a piece 18 inches (0·46 m) square and about a quarter of an inch (6 mm) thick, set in a wooden frame, which I was invited to try to smash with a four pound (2 kg) hammer. The hammer bounced right back and never even marked the Makrolon.

My piece of $\frac{1}{16}$ inch (1·6 mm) thick by 2 ft (0·6 m) square cost £4 plus 40p V.A.T. They were apologetic about the price but compared to other things aeronautical it was cheap.

I had made a cartridge paper pattern by trial and error. I laid this on the sheet of Makrolon and cut round it with the jig saw. A little sanding of the edges and the result looked really professional.

It seemed to me that there could be some interaction between the bottom edge of the Makrolon and the top of the petrol tank so, although it was not specified, I fitted a U shaped rubber strip to the bottom edge.

If you have not already done so you are reaching the stage where the fuselage has to come off the building table. I was impatient and got 007 down on the floor as soon as possible where it stood on its tail wheel with the front end supported on a tea chest, immobile and cluttering up the garage. Had I been sensible I would have had the undercarriage all ready to fit so that the fuselage could easily have been moved.

A friend, David Schofield, had offered to fabricate my undercarriage for me as he had alloy plate to spare and a home-made hydraulic press already set up. When I went to collect it I found that he also had a stock of stream-line steel tube for the flying struts, so two of my major supply problems were solved in the course of a pleasant days outing.

Fitting the undercarriage is probably the most anxious moment of the whole project since, if the bolt holes are at all displaced, one really has to go back to the beginning and start all over again. The holes *must* be truly vertical and exactly in the right position.

My method, and it worked, was to lay the fuselage upside down on trestles, mark the centre-line on the underside of the fuselage and then mark out the positions of the bolt holes, working from the centre-line and checking back from the outside skin.

Then, using the drill press, I drilled the holes full size. By the mercy of God they all came through in the right places.

I then inserted the bolts which were a tight fit in the holes, pushed them right through, smeared the ends with lamp-black and then withdrew them until they were below the surface of the fuselage bottom.

I then scribed the centreline on the top surface of the undercarriage, marked out the bolt hole positions from it, and lightly centre-punched them.

I then put the undercarriage very carefully in position, checking centre-line to centre-line, keeping it in place with a couple of sand-bags. Then I tapped the bolts into contact with it and, to my joy, found that the lamp-black spots coincided with the centre-punch marks. After that there were no more problems.

At Sywell that year I had been most intrigued by the undercarriage bracing on G-BAPP, the V.P.1 built by Flt. Lt. Norman Crow. His modification to the undercarriage bracing accorded with my own ideas and was almost exactly what I had sketched out for submission to my inspector.

Evans assumes that every builder has his own swage block so that the end fittings to the bracing wires can be swaged in place. Failing this you have to take the complete undercarriage assembly to the nearest rigger and trust him to get his dimensions dead right since there is no provision for adjustment.

I was unhappy about this and proposed to put a pair of rigging screws into the assembly which would entail eyebolts through the upper parts of the undercarriage legs. This was just what BAPP had, so I snapped happily away with the camera in order to provide acceptable supporting evidence to my inspector.

According to my calculations the greatest load one is likely to put into these bracing wires is about 1950 lb (885 kg). This calls for a breaking load in the wire of about 4000 lb (1800 kg) at a load factor of two and, turning to the manufacturer's tables, one finds that the only $\frac{3}{16}$ inch (4·8 mm) wire that will meet this requirement is 1×19 stainless steel – indeed there is one grade of $\frac{3}{16}$ inch (4·8 mm) wire with a breaking load of only 1920 lb (870 kg), so one could be in trouble if one picked the wrong grade and made a heavy landing.

It follows that all the other fittings should have a safe working load of at least 1 ton (1 tonne). I found that Gibbs of Warsash make stainless rigging screws for yachts with guaranteed safe working loads, so I bought a pair rated at a ton each. Mike was a little worried about their weight but as it would be slightly forward of the centre of gravity he let it pass.

David Schofield had told me of a firm call Zipkarts who make very good wheels to take $6·00 \times 6$ tyres but, in his experience, had proved to be indifferent correspondents. So on a high summers day of driving rain I motored up to Hoddeston, Herts, in search of wheels for my undercarriage. It was a dreary and tedious progress all across the Northern tentacles of London, but well worth the trouble. I got two wheels complete with brakes for less than £20.

I opted for roller bearings. With these bearings the wheels will not fit onto a Cessna axle, so I had to design my own axles to fit the $\frac{3}{4}$ inch (19 mm) diameter bore of the bearings.

If my assumptions on landing loads are correct, and I am assured by no less an authority than Evans the Aerodynamics that they are, the axles have to be machined out of medium (22 ton(ne) minimum) high tensile steel, to withstand the bending moment at the change of section from $\frac{3}{4}$ inch (19 mm) to $1\frac{1}{8}$ inch (29 mm) diameter.

A friendly Strut member lent me a scrap Cessna axle for checking purposes and to get ideas from. I was interested to discover that although this pattern was obsolete, having been overtaken by development design, it did not accord completely with the one shown on Evans' drawings, which must be an even earlier pattern. So it seems probable that other builders in the U.K. will be faced with producing their own modifications so far as the axles are concerned.

With 007 at last mounted on wheels I set about fitting brakes. I have always had a horror of the toe or heel brakes beloved of the Americans. It has never actually happened to me but I am always worried about

Undercarriage fitted

inadvertently applying brake on landing when all I want is a bit of rudder. The outcome could be hilarious for the spectators but unpleasantly surprising for me.

The nicest brakes I have ever used were the differential pneumatic brakes on the Hurricane and Spitfire, actuated by a hand lever on the spade grip of the stick. I could not aspire to anything so sophisticated on a V.P.1 but at least I could have differential, hand operated brakes.

Brakes are not required for taking off, flying or landing, only for taxying. For this it is nice to have a differential capability so that one can get into and out of tight corners, turn on a narrow strip or manoeuvre in close proximity to other aircraft on the ground.

I made up a pair of split levers which pulled on Bowden cables which are easily adjustable so that the levers work together.

Nothing easier you might think, except that they do not seem to make Bowden cables in England any more. One has to buy a made up length of cable from Italy and cut it down to length. They can be had from motorbike and scooter agents or repairers. One starts by cutting off the terminal on one end of the wire after first coating the area of the cut with solder to prevent the wire from unwinding itself. Then the wire is drawn out of the case and the case cut to length. The spare ferrule that one has bought has to be heated so that it will expand and slip over the case and its plastic cover. At one's first attempt the ferrule will distort in the blowlamp flame. At the second the edges curl over and then the damn thing melts and you have to start again with a fresh ferrule. Start with a good stock of spare ferrules.

Split brake levers –
parking brake Off

103

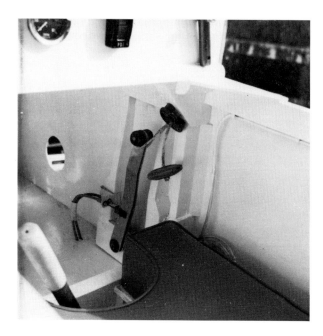

Parking brake On

After fitting the case to the aeroplane the cable is threaded from the lever, through the case to the brake actuating arm where the end can be drawn tight and clamped with a screw-down type of terminal. Then coat the cable with solder close up to the back of the terminal and cut off the stray end. Everything is then taped neatly in place. Give a few tentative pulls on the levers and make the final adjustments so that the levers are squared up together.

My parking brake cost just ten pence and weighs about an ounce. It consists of a loop of terylene cord which may be dropped over the knobs of the split levers, drawn tight by a toggle and locked in a jam-cleat. The jam-cleat cost the 10p. I made the toggle out of scrap and scrounged the terylene cord from my son's boat. And so, when I have finished with the parking brake, it is a simple matter to disconnect it entirely and stow it securely out of the way. The brakes can only then be applied by using quite a bit of force on the levers. This way I can know that the brakes are off and come into land with a quiet mind.

Rather to my dismay I found that in use these brakes were not as good as I had hoped and they slowly got worse over the first few months in active use until one day at Biggin Hill I taxied happily off the grass onto the gently sloping concrete approach to the runway only to find that my brakes would not hold me from running slowly forward. In front of me was Gerry Price in his elegant V.P.1 Esmeralda and, heave as I might on the brake levers, 007's flailing propeller crept nearer and nearer to his rudder. I was about to knock up the switches when a couple of heroes

104

grabbed my wing-tips and frustrated 007's murderous intentions.

Something had to be done about those brakes. I tried roughing up the linings with a rasp but the adamantine surfaces only blunted the tool, so I consulted my mechanical colleagues about it.

They concluded that go-karts go very fast on very small wheels that have very small brake drums and so, in order to absorb the heat generated by braking at 100 mph the linings have to be very hard indeed and require a big boot and a large hydraulic cylinder. Such linings are quite inappropriate for brakes operated by hand levers through Bowden cables at low taxying speeds. For our purposes we require the softest possible linings.

The local Ferodo agents removed and replaced them with soft linings which they rivetted in place, and now my brakes work so well that I can turn in the width of my strip, and they will even hold me against full throttle when running up on the ground. The message is clear. Anyone else who has go-kart wheels should get the hard linings changed for soft ones as soon as possible. It is not an expensive operation.

So much for the fuselage. Now you have something in which you can sit and hold the stick. You can feel the adrenalin beginning to run and I defy you to abandon the project now.

Chapter 5

Wings and things

With the fuselage off the table and, as it were, self-supporting, we can make a start on the flying and control surfaces – the wings and ailerons, stabilator and rudder.

The V.P.1 has a fully flying empennage and, never having been shipmates with one before, 'stabilator' was a new word in my vocabulary. Instead of the normal tail-plane and elevator there is a single horizontal surface, partly aerodynamically balanced, mass balanced against flutter and damped by an anti-servo tab. The rudder is also partly aerodynamically balanced and damped by an anti-servo tab; there is no fin.

This may sound very complex – it did to me, but in fact it simplifies construction. Being ultra-conservative I had reservations about its performance in the air but having flown it I have become a total convert. It flies very steadily and yet is very responsive in yaw and pitch. I have a feeling that the positioning of the rudder relative to the stabilator has much to do with the aircraft's reluctance to spin and its instant recovery from a deliberate spin.

I built the stabilator first but had the rudder tube been to hand I would have made a start with the rudder, if only because, when completed, it can be stored in position on the fuselage.

All the ribs for the wing, ailerons, stabilator and rudder are cut out from $\frac{1}{4}$ inch (6 mm) marine ply and the plans show how these can be got from the least amount of stock. You will save yourself quite a lot of time and storage space if you cut out all the rib blanks in one long session.

'Offset' plans are given for all the ribs. These are plans giving distances to the outside of the curved surface of the rib taken at given points along a base line, in the case of a wing rib, or a centre-line in the case of the stabilator and rudder which are symmetrical aerofoils.

Draw out the base or centreline, mark off the station points and draw through them lines perpendicular to the base or centre-line. On these perpendiculars mark off the offset distances and then draw a fair curve through the points so obtained.

I used a naval architect's splining batten and ducks for drawing the curves. My battens are made of ash, of a section that measures approximately $\frac{1}{16}$ inch (1·6 mm) by $\frac{1}{4}$ inch (6 mm) and they are 6 ft (1·8 m) long. Modern naval architects have them made of perspex but I much

106

prefer my wooden ones. The ducks are boat shaped pieces of $\frac{1}{4}$ inch (6 mm) mahogany about 6 inches (150 mm) long by $2\frac{1}{2}$ inches (63 mm) wide, loaded with lumps of lead, 2 inches by 4 inches by $1\frac{1}{2}$ inches thick (50 mm × 100 mm × 38 mm), screwed on top of them. With four ducks you can hold the batten in place with one edge passing through all the offset points so that you can run your pencil round the batten and draw a fair curve.

The batten will not cope with the small radius compound curve at the leading edge. For this you will need either French curves or pear curves. Naval architects use pear curves; ordinary architects use French curves. Both types are ridiculously expensive so it is better to borrow a set if you do not already have your own.

In the wings and stabilator the ribs are all essentially the same, merely being curtailed by the aileron on each wing and the trimming tab on the stabilator.

I cut a pattern out of soft aluminium sheet for a wing rib and one for a stabilator rib and used these for marking out the ply for sawing. The rudder ribs, being all different, I marked out directly on the ply sheet.

Having cut out all the ribs in blank form, I taped together in bundles and set aside the ones I did not require immediately.

The prospect of the rudder had caused me a lot of sleepless nights, quite unnecessarily as it turned out. The ribs have to be glued to blocks which are bolted to the 2 inch (50 mm) diameter alloy tube, which forms the axis, and the leading edge which is forward of the axis is rounded and tapered from top to bottom. I was worried about getting the blocks in exactly the right positions so that there would be no twist in the rudder and working the taper on that leading edge. Perhaps this made me unduly cautious.

I made and drilled the blocks, cut the slots in the leading edge spar to receive the noses of the ribs and cut slots in the trailing ends of the ribs to receive the trailing edge spar.

I then marked the tube for drilling, assembled the whole lot dry with the ribs lightly tacked to the blocks with brass brads not driven home so that they could be withdrawn later and then lamp-blacked the end of a bolt which I pushed through the bolt holes in the blocks to contact the tube.

The lamp-black spots coincided near enough with my drilling marks, so I went ahead and drilled the tube.

This done I reassembled the ribs and blocks to the tube, bolted the blocks in place, applied glue and hardener to the blocks and ribs, lined up the ribs by dry fitting the leading and trailing edge spars and then clamped the ribs to the blocks.

Thus I had the blocks in the right positions and the ribs all truly aligned. The only problem left was shaping the leading edge spar.

I cut out five female profiles gauges from soft aluminium sheet to conform to the theoretical nose sections of the ribs as shown on the offset plans. Using these in the right places and working away with the Karbo-Grit sanding wheel I reduced it to somewhere near its final shape and finished it off after it was glued in place.

The only other snag I encountered was when I came to assemble the rudder in the fuselage. I found that there was just no clearance to get the rudder horn in, though when I checked I found that everything had been built exactly to the specified dimensions. However, by inverting the horn fitting, and there is no reason why it should not be inverted, everything slipped easily into place. I think that one of the specified dimensions must have been changed in the course of development and the working drawings not brought up to date. This is not unusual in engineering practice in my experience. Indeed it is rare to find such a large set of drawings with so few minor errors.

The hollow box spar of the stabilator presented no real problems. All gluing was done with the assembly clamped firmly to the jig table over a sheet of Melinex to prevent any risk of sticking it permanently to the table-top. Before closing it up my inspector had a look inside and approved of what he saw.

I was worried about keeping everything straight in the final assembly on account of the double curvature of the aerofoil but in the event it turned out easy enough. I fitted the leading edges temporarily in place and then fitted and glued the trailing edges with the whole trailing edge clamped down to the table. This cocked the leading edge up in the air, but at least it was firmly anchored.

Assembly of Stabilator

108

I then lined up the leading edges using a string line between pins on the centrelines of the extreme ribs having checked that they were at equal heights above the table top. This seemed to work as there is no perceptible twist in the finished job.

I had been a little worried by other people's descriptions of fitting the leading edge ply with elaborate systems of rubber bands and wedges. Evans dismisses the operation without comment so I assumed that he must have nailed his down with brass brads.

Accordingly I glued and tacked the spar edge of the ply sheet to the filler on top of the spar and then, with a wooden straight edge, drew the ply down over the glued ribs to the leading edge where I glued and tacked it with brads. When I came to feather off the leading edge, the brass nail heads sanded away as easily as the ply.

The anti-servo trim tab really had me stumped. It is made of light alloy sheet folded into a hollow triangular section and is 43 inches (1·1 m) long. It seemed that one needed four hands and fingers 21 inches (0·5 m) long to hold everything in place for drilling and rivetting. So in the end I took all my bits and pieces to a local aircraft firm who laughed indulgently and agreed to do the bending and assembly for me.

Then after six months and numerous telephone calls to enquire about progress they finally regretted that they were unable to do it. This had me worried, since it was beyond my unaided capability, though it was obviously not impossible since I had seen at least three of the wretched things flying.

The next day I was telling a colleague of my latest set-back when he

Skeletal rudder and stabilator fitted to fuselage

remarked that we had an ex-aircraft sheet metal worker in our own organisation. At the first opportunity I hunted him down and sought his advice. He looked at the drawings and finally said 'Leave it with me and I will see what I can do'. The next day he rang up and said 'Your tab's ready'.

It was a beautiful bit of work and when I asked him how it was done all he would say was 'You mark it out, drill it and fold it. Then you take the dimensions for the tapered channels that support the horns from the work and drill and fold those. Then you will find that all the holes will come together for riveting.'

All I can say is that it would never happen for me in a hundred attempts and I still do not see how you get everything together without fingers twenty one inches long. Indeed a knowledgeable fellow that I talked to at Sywell told me he had made five tabs before he got one near enough right to install.

We have come to the conclusion that Bud Evans knows everything about metal work and has the resources of a huge factory at his back so that in this one case he fails to see the problems that confront the ignorant amateur. On carpentry, however, he is probably as much of an amateur as the rest of us so he has designed all the woodwork in his own aeroplane to make it as simple as possible for himself and, by extension, for us.

Which leads me to think that wooden aircraft for amateur construction should always be designed by professional engineers who normally practise on metal aircraft. The professional can very seldom see anything difficult in his own specialisation, forgetting that he has spent a lifetime learning it.

Towards the end of the last century Joshua Slocum, a retired sailing ship captain, got fed up with enforced idleness ashore, so he fitted out an old sloop and sailed off happily, single-handed, round the World by way of Cape Horn. To him there were no problems in seamanship or navigation; they were his job, and he was happiest doing it, exercising a well-learned skill.

On his return he wrote a marvellously entertaining account of his voyage with hilarious descriptions of how he discouraged piratical Indians in Tierra del Fuego with a box of drawing pins, of a goat that ate his charts and of his meeting with President Kruger of the Transvaal who was convinced the earth was flat – Slocum diplomatically agreed with him.

But that book, *Sailing Alone Around the World*, has drowned more amateur sailors than any other because Slocum made light of the real difficulties and dangers of the voyage and enlarged only on the many domestic crises which any landlubber could deal with just as well as old Joshua.

Therefore beware of the professional on his own subject. His problems are not yours. And what a sensible and modest man is Mr Evans to put himself on our level by building his own aeroplane in what must have been to him an unfamiliar material.

Building wings seemed to take for ever. From my diary I see that I started cutting out ribs in August 1974 and finally completed the wings in October 1975. If we deduct the five months waiting for the S514 steel that still leaves ten months of spare time and week-ends which seems far too long even for an unskilled, cag-handed amateur.

There is really nothing difficult about these wings. They are straight, of constant section with no taper or washout. I read in *Popular Flying* of all sorts of problems that other people had anticipated and of sometimes elaborate expedients that they had taken to avoid these imagined difficulties, all of which worried me considerably, but going on previous experience of the excellence of Evans' advice, I followed his instructions to the letter and found no serious snags.

The V.P.1 wings are as simple as it is possible to make them. Being of constant chord throughout the ribs are all essentially the same and, being carved out of flat ply, one only has to cut out the lightening holes.

Had the ribs been fabricated, as in the Currie Wot, they would have had to be built up in a jig from a lot of small parts with many gusseted joints. This is not difficult but it would have taken much longer. Had the wings been tapered it would have required several jigs and taken longer still.

The 'square' wing, though generally less aerodynamically efficient than the tapered wing has certain advantages for the low-powered and relatively slow aircraft, quite apart from the fact that it is easier to build.

The stall progresses outwards from the wing roots so that even at the point of stall one still has some aileron control. This can be a big help when making a precautionary landing in a short field or with a cross wind.

It is my belief that it is this wing that largely accounts for the V.P.1's remarkably docile behaviour at and near the stall.

I used one rib blank cut out exactly, with the centres of the lightening holes drilled through with a $\frac{1}{16}$ inch (1·6 mm) drill, as a pattern for marking out the remaining ribs. It is important to notice that, though they may look superficially alike, there are a number of small differences between certain ribs.

I failed to notice that the Number 9 ribs have two lightening holes omitted and in their place a couple of slots for the aileron pulleys.

Luckily I had enough $\frac{1}{4}$ inch (6 mm) ply to allow for cutting out two more number nines but I was left with two spare ribs. If this were the Garden of Eden 007 could have got himself a couple of female companions in a way that even Ian Fleming never thought of.

With all the ribs roughly cut out I planed the flat bottom of each to the pencil line, then clamped them together in batches of four on the jig table and sanded the top curve to match the master pattern.

Drilling the lightening holes was a tedious business. I had a cheap, spring steel type hole saw that did about two ribs before it died on me. I

Cutting out ribs

then bought a set of the bell type saws at enormous expense and half way through the job the drill motor burnt out.

I traded in my old single speed, $\frac{3}{8}$ inch (9·5 mm) chuck drill for a new two speed $\frac{1}{2}$ inch (13 mm) chuck machine and this saw me through to the end of the project.

With all the holes and slots cut out of the wing ribs, I got a pair of spruce spars, front and rear, out of the timber rack and tried them on the jig table. I cut them to length, gave them a lick or two with the plane to true them up and marked out centres for bush and bolt holes. I fitted and glued the centre cheek plates, tacked the ply wing-root end plates in position and then drilled the holes for bushes and bolts.

This done I threaded on the ribs, fitted the drag wire attachments and bushes – and realised that I was stuck until the S514 steel arrived for the wing root end plates. Stuck for five whole months.

I suppose I could have made a little further progress but I wanted to check the fitting of the wings to the fuselage before installing leading and trailing edges, torsion boxes, etc.

Everything comes to him who waits, even to aeroplane builders, and eventually the special steel arrived. Much more than I needed, but you cannot have less than a full sheet, so from penury I was transported to un-looked for and unwanted wealth. Unwanted because, with the excess, I had to pay much more than I had budgeted for. But at least I could get busy again cutting out wing root plates, flying strut ends and aileron horns.

Start of assembly of
starboard wing

I started on the flying strut ends so that they could go away for welding while I got on with the wings.

By experiment I found that an abrasive metal cutting disc used in a circular saw attachment for the electric drill would cut a slot in the flying strut ends the exact width required to take a 12 s.w.g. (0·104 inch, 2·64 mm) plate. What a stroke of luck! A further advantage of using the saw attachment is that one can use the fence to keep the slots running straight and parallel to the longitudinal axis of the strut.

These cutting discs rip through the work at a fair speed – one spends far longer marking out the slots than actually cutting them – but the discs wear down rather quickly and produce a great deal of grit dust. I needed two discs to complete the work so at £1·40 for 32 short slots they came quite expensive.

I cut the wing root plates out of the S514 sheet using the jig-saw attachment and I broke a lot of blades, but at least one can put a broken blade back in the collet and carry on cutting.

Mike had kindly offered to get the flying struts welded under his personal supervision so I fitted the end plates into their slots, taped them in position and thankfully handed them over. On Mike's advice I had not pre-drilled the end plates as it would be impossible to guarantee that the holes would line up after welding.

As soon as the struts were returned with the plates welded in place, Mike insisted that they be primed and painted externally and pulled through internally with lanoline. Then, as was his wont, he disappeared for some weeks to foreign parts.

I got the raw lanoline from a wholesale chemical supplier. There was something odd about the evil grin on the face of the chap who dug it out of the barrel with a thin wooden spatula and plastered it into a clean glass jar.

When I came to apply it I discovered why. Never have I got in such a mess. The foul stuff sticks to everything it touches, it will not come off and only spreads itself around when you try to wipe it off. Somewhere in the Far East, I reckoned, Mike must be having a good laugh at my expense. I could imagine him drinking sundowners with his aeronautical colleagues and the guffaws of knowing laughter as he tells them 'Back in England I left a fellow pulling through some flying struts with raw lanoline'.

When he returned I protested at the refined torture to which he had subjected me and he said 'Oh, didn't you know? You are supposed to warm it up in an old saucepan and then there is no problem'.

I could not wait to try a wing on the fuselage, even though the wing was only partly fabricated and only roughly squared up with binding wire. It went together without much trouble and I stood back to admire it. This was progress.

Half an hour later my wife came out to find me sitting in the cockpit grinning happily over the starboard side. 'Come off it, Ace' she said, 'even you can't fly on one wing'.

First trial fitting of starboard wing

'Come off it, Ace. Even you can't fly on one wing'

After the steel arrived I must have fitted the wings a dozen times, at each stage of construction, before they were structurally complete. Each time it became a little easier as I learnt the drill and found the essential tools and sequence of assembly.

At the first fitting I found that the bolts all went into place with only a little easing with a drift and only in a couple of places was it necessary to use a file, which I thought was not too bad considering that twelve bolts have to be passed through twelve bushes and twenty four plates, but Mike pursed his lips and had a good look before he would let it pass.

Having satisfied myself that the wings could be mated to the fuselage, they were returned to the jig table. At this stage I had to remove the compression struts because, in my earlier haste to assemble the wings, I had fogotten to paint the drag wire fittings. For springing the compression struts in and out I used a long screw jack that I had found lying around in my father's garage.

With the fittings properly painted and the compression struts back in place, I measured up for the drag wires which were made up to size with the rigging screws by my friendly rigger.

Now with the ribs lined up on their marks and the drag wires tightened up so that the whole wing was perfectly square, I started on the tedious business of gluing in corner blocks – hundreds of them.

I had not been able to get quarter round spruce so had to accept it square and plane it to shape. Fortunately, just at this stage, a young doctor moved into the house across the road bringing with him the finest collection of power wood-working tools it is possible to imagine. He had no sooner offered me the use of his spindle than I was there with my pile of spruce and in half an hour had saved myself two week's work.

The leading edges I planed roughly to shape on the bench and then cut out the slots to take the forward ends of the ribs and the intermediate nose ribs. I sprung them into place and glued and blocked them to the main ribs before fitting the nose ribs and finally sanded the leading edges to the correct contour using a female profile cut out of soft alloy sheet.

The trailing edges were easy enough to fit, clamped flat to the jig table over a sheet of Melinex.

With the aileron pulley boxes in place, I turned the wing over and glued on the bottom ply for the torsion box. Then I turned it right side up, fitted the stiffeners for the walkway and gave the whole of the inside of the wing a coat of varnish before gluing on the walkway ply.

I had built the ailerons during the period of waiting for the steel and these I now fitted in place on the wings and bolted them in the neutral

Bench assembly of port wing and aileron

position with a $\frac{1}{4}$ inch (6·35 mm) bolt through the leading balance weight hole and a hole through the end rib, with a $\frac{1}{4}$ inch (6 mm) ply spacer between the balance arm and the end rib.

Now I was ready for a fitting to measure up for the aileron control cables. On the next fine day I wheeled everything out into the garden, summoned my wife from the kitchen and we fitted the wings to the fuselage. Sheila had to keep dashing inside at awkward moments to check on the joint that was cooking in the oven.

Finally I released her and got out a coil of thin plastic coated garden wire, attached an end to an aileron horn and threaded it through the ribs until I arrived at the fuselage, only to find that I had forgotten to drill the holes in the fuselage sides to pass the cables through.

Sheila did not say very much, but she looked distinctly wintry when I dragged her out of the kitchen again to unrig everything in order to drill five holes in the fuselage sides – four for the cables and one for the pitot pressure tube.

After re-rigging, my three lengths of garden wire gave me the correct lengths for the aileron control cables, and these I took with the turnbuckles to the rigger for splicing up.

With the wings back on the jig table, I got Mike to look inside the torsion box before I fitted the top skin which I carried right over to the leading edge. At the same time I fitted the leading edge alloy to the outer ends of the wings.

This, in spite of reports to the contrary, is really no problem. I shaped the metal by letting a little hang over the edge of the jig table and beating it with a mallet. Then I moved it out a little more and repeated the dose again and again, until I had the approximate shape.

I punched a hole at each corner and tacked the leading edge alloy in place on the wing so that I could mark the location of each side of each rib in pencil on the underside of the alloy. Then I removed the metal from the wing, laid it upside down on the bench and punched the holes for the brads between the rib pencil lines. That way there was no problem and I never split a rib.

At this stage I could not fit the inner leading edge alloy as I had got neither the jury struts nor the extruded alloy angles by which they are attached to the main spars, but these arrived in due course and I had another wing fitting session to check the exact positioning of the angle fittings on the main spars, using a large set square. At the same time I fitted and checked the aileron control and balance cables. Mike attended this performance and declared himself generally satisfied except for the lead of one aileron cable which necessitated a new aileron horn.

The drawings are a little ambiguous regarding the stiffening of the underside of the end ribs, but some stiffening is obviously required to prevent distortion by the tautening of the fabric so, with Mike's approval, I glued in some $\frac{3}{4}$ inch (19 mm) square spruce which was satisfactory.

With the jury strut angle fittings painted and bolted in place and the inner leading edge alloy installed the wings were structurally complete and ready for covering.

With no further need for the jig table and winter coming on again, this seemed to be a good time to make and fit the transport gear so that the wings could be hung on the side of the aircraft, the jig table dismantled and 007 manoeuvred into its place so that we could get both cars into the garage again.

It only took a Saturday morning to make the transport gear and I had just finished fitting it when Michael Clarke, who was building an Isaacs Fury, arrived with his sister and two friends to collect a spare sheet of alloy I had promised him.

On the pretext of getting at the alloy, which was stacked against the wall behind the wings, I pressed the whole party into service to hang the wings on the side of the aeroplane. I think we were all surprised at how easily everything slipped into place though I, at least, should have got over my early amazement at the precision of Bud Evans's detail drawing and dimensioning.

And so, after two years and four months of leisurely, too leisurely, spare time work, 007's airframe was structurally complete though covering the wings and fitting the engine still remained to be done.

Port wing assembled to fuselage showing jury strut fittings lined up

Starboard wing showing aileron control leads, compression strut and drag bracing

Wings hung in 'towing configuration'

At the outset I was pretty incompetent in the use of tools and at the end I was not much better. I am also physically lazy.

That it got finished at all is a tribute to Bud Evans's brilliant and uncompromising design conception, beautifully clear drawings and descriptive text.

I do not even like building things. I took it on as a means to an end, because I love flying and I just cannot afford to hire other people's aeroplanes.

And so it seems clear that if I, of all people, can do it, anyone else can make him or herself a V.P.1 and so enjoy the sky.

Chapter 6

Fabric and dope

Married men should take a lot of careful thought before they embark upon the building of an aeroplane. As soon as there is something in the garage which is recognisably a fuselage one becomes, in one's wife's eyes, an expert on everything. No longer can you send for a plumber to change a washer on a tap. You can build an aeroplane, *ipso facto*, there is nothing you cannot do as well, if not better than anyone else. Though you speak with the tongues of men and of angels all your eloquence will not get you off the hook. Your wife will point to the Thing in the garage and, as far as she is concerned, *Re ipsis loquitur* – the Thing speaks for itself.

I should have known better. Twenty five years ago I built a boat and it took me ages to live it down, but since starting to build a V.P.1 I have had to mend leaking ball-cocks, hang a new door, install a loft ladder and, most galling of all, lose a fortnight of good doping weather painting the outside of the house.

Building aeroplanes is strictly for batchelors, or indeed spinsters, since in this age of women's liberation there is no good reason why a girl should not do it every bit as well as a man.

We reached a nadir of absurdity when my wife, after admiring my stitching along the trailing edge of one wing, thoughtfully suggested that I might consider making dresses for her. I pointed out that at my stage of the art I would have to staple the cloth to her fuselage before marking and cutting.

With the onset of winter I had stowed 007 in the garage with the skeletal wings hung in the 'towing configuration'.

I had manoeuvred it into the central position with its nose directly under the steel beam carrying the flat roof and as near to the supporting buttress as possible so that I could rig a tackle from the beam for installing the engine.

Somehow we managed to get two cars, two bicycles, our daughter's motor-bike and the motor mower into the garage as well as the aeroplane.

The winter is not a season conducive to working in a cold garage so I devoted the time to ordering the Ceconite for covering the wings and to getting some engine parts made up to the Peacock drawings.

Covering the aerofoils, doping and painting are the final stages in the construction of the airframe and certainly provide the most satisfaction and excitement as one sees the final shape of the aircraft appearing.

So far as the ordinary amateur is concerned there are only two types of fabric that can usefully be employed; mercerised and callendered Egyptian cotton or Dacron. There is a third material, Razorback glass cloth, but this is not easily obtainable in the U.K. and the methods of application and tautening are hardly a garden shed operation. It is also rather on the heavy side for use on a light aircraft.

There was a time when linen was widely, if not universally, employed but this has almost disappeared from the aircraft scene, probably on account of its cost and the fact that it is rather heavier than cotton.

So, effectively, we are left with the choice between cotton and Dacron. I used both and as a result of my experience I would, personally, go for Dacron every time. I built my rudder and stabilator long before the wings began to take shape and at that time Dacron was either not available in the U.K. or I failed to locate the source of supply.

Like most amateurs I was in a hurry to see the finished articles, so I bought cotton and covered my rudder and stabilator with it.

The Egyptian cotton fabric must be released to specification DTD 575. It is mercerised and callendered. 'Mercerised' means that the fabric has been dipped in a hot solution of diluted caustic soda which causes the material to shrink and develop greater strength and lustre. 'Callendered' means that it has been passed, wet, through a series of hot and cold rollers to reduce its thickness and provide a smooth finish.

Before starting to cover my rudder I read and re-read the article on Fabric Work in the *P.F.A. Handbook* and also managed to get hold of the C.A.A. papers on inspection procedures – BL 6-25 Fabric Covering and BL 6-26 Doping.

Thus fortified I unrolled my cloth on the dining room table, laid the rudder on top, folded the cloth over, marked it out with a good margin, took a deep breath and my wife's pinking shears and started to cut.

The shears just gathered the cloth into a line of wrinkles like the smocking on a small girl's party frock, but cut they would not. I took them out to the garage and tried to sharpen them with a saw file. This seemed to effect very little improvement but I managed in the end to get a rather ragged cut by playing around with the nut on the bolt that held the blades together. Feeling that I needed expert advice I appealed to my wife but all she said was 'Those damn things never did work'.

So I went to town and bought another pair that did and eventually the main cover was cut to size with the edges nicely pinked.

I doubled one edge under, stapled it to the side of the trailing edge, drew the bight of the cloth round the leading edge and stapled the other edge of the cloth to the other side of the trailing edge, also with the pinked edge turned under.

Then I started to sew the two open edges together across the trailing edge using the recommended overhand stitch, eight stitches to the inch (3 mm pitch), removing the staples as I went.

To my surprise it came together remarkably well, to a comfortably tight fit. Even my wife declared herself impressed.

Next I stapled the upper and lower extremes of the cloth to the edges of the top and bottom ribs, evening out the tension in the cloth, again with about an inch of pinked edge turned under. I cut pieces of fabric to fit the top and bottom ribs, stapled them in place and sewed the open edges together. The bottom piece had to have a hole cut out of it to pass the rudder post and I had stapled around this as close up to the rudder post as possible before starting to sew.

The final result did not look too bad, at least to my untutored eye, but Mike pointed out that I had forgotten the lock stitches at two inch (50 mm) intervals. He also asked for the ribs to be stitched through cotton tape, afterwards to be covered in the final stages of doping with linen tape, and also for the hole at the rudder post to be reinforced with a close fitting patch of fabric doped in place. Otherwise my first attempt at fabric work passed muster.

With the experience of the rudder behind me I set about covering the stabilator.

As the cloth comes in 54 inch (1·37 m) widths and the stabilator is 84 inches (2·13 m) wide the cloth had to be seamed and the seams have to run in the direction of the airflow. It would look unsightly with a single seam offset to one side, so I ripped one cloth down the middle so that I would have two seams symmetrically spaced about the centre-line and then trimmed the edges of the centre cloth so that the seams would come in the centre of a bay and not anywhere near a rib where they might interfere with the rib stitching.

These seams between cloths have to be doubled to form a 'balloon seam' and can be machined. My wife and daughters did this for me, ironing in the folds and pinning the seams together before putting them through the machine.

You should note that even the thread has to be released material, so make sure that your wife removes the delicate Silko and rewinds the bobbin with the proper stuff.

The cloth is sewn at the trailing edge using the simple overhand stitch, eight stitches to the inch (3 mm pitch) and a lock-stitch every two inches (50 mm). The edges of the cloth are turned under about $\frac{1}{2}$ inch (13 mm) and a gap of about $\frac{1}{4}$ inch (6 mm) left between the turned under edges.

Because the trailing edge spars are $\frac{1}{4}$ inch (6 mm) thick in the case of the V.P.1 I laid the turned under edges of the cloth up to the edge of the spar and stapled them in position, then removed the staples as I sewed.

At the roots and outer ends of the aerofoil I cut pieces of cloth to the shape of the ends, allowing extra for turning under, and stapled them to the vertical ply surfaces keeping the turned-under edges about $\frac{1}{4}$ inch

(6 mm) clear of the top and bottom surfaces. Then I sewed these together in the same way as at the trailing edge.

By the time the wings were ready for covering I had found the source of supply for 'Ceconite' Dacron at Shoreham, right next door to the P.F.A. office.

'Ceconite' Dacron is a polyester. It is cheaper than cotton and much cheaper than linen. It is heat shrunk so it requires less dope than cotton and ends up as a lighter covering. It is stronger and has a much longer life than any natural fibre material, does not mildew and is impervious to sunlight.

The only thing one has to watch is not to over-tauten and so damage the structure underneath.

When the Ceconite arrived I spent a chilly weekend in the garage laying the cloth out on the wings and cutting and marking it for seaming. I then talked my women folk into machining the seams for me.

I had actually manoeuvred a wing into the dining room when my father was stricken with flu and came to us to convalesce. The wing had to go back to the garage and I had to content myself with covering the ailerons.

My father, incidentally, claims to have been the first man in England, if not in the World, to have ascended as pilot in a helicopter. He was an apprentice at the A. J. Stevens works and the date was 1908. They had built this helicopter, with twin rotors driven by chains from a single engine, to the designs of an amateur enthusiast who insisted that it be test flown before he would take delivery. At this the works manager looked at the foreman, the foreman looked at the fitter who looked at my father who had no one to look at and so he had to get into the machine. The engine was started up, my Papa clutched in the rotors and opened up to full throttle. The contraption sailed magnificently across the yard and disintegrated against a brick wall. Father has had a deep mistrust of helicopters ever since.

At the same works he helped to build the engine for the dirigible 'Nulli Secundus' which was borrowed by Cody for use in the 'Cathedral' and is now in the R.A.F. museum at Hendon.

All the literature that I had accumulated on Ceconite and the people I had talked to about it led me to believe that one could simply stick the material to the frame with adhesive, thus saving miles of stitching, but when I put this to Mike, my inspector, he was not enthusiastic.

Mike, as behoves a good inspector, is markedly conservative, to the extent of believing that anything done by de Havilland's can be approved of as good practice, but these new-fangled American ideas are necessarily suspect. Eventually I wrung a great concession out of him. O.K., I could use adhesive – just as long as I sewed it as well.

I am reminded of a little verse, that appeared in Punch, concerning the issue to some battalions of our army of the F.N.280 semi-automatic rifle for evaluation in service. It was entitled 'The Conservative' and went:

A private soldier that I know
Was pulling through his 280
With copper-wire gauze and sand.
I remonstrated with him and
He dropped a curse and said to me
'I'll make this b....r 303'.

Dear Mike, he's not really as hidebound as all that and I have given up arguing with him as he invariably turns out to be right. He was doubly right in this instance because, when adhesive is used on a wing to avoid stitching, the fabric should be stuck to the leading edge ply, drawn under the wing, round the trailing edge and back over the top to the leading edge where it it stuck down with at least a 4 inch (100 mm) overlap. This calls for a ply covered, dee-box type of leading edge which the V.P.1 does not have, indeed two thirds of the leading edge is aluminium.

So I settled down to my sewing; eight stitches to the inch (3 mm pitch) and a lock-stitch every two inches (50 mm). There are more than seven thousand stitches in a V.P.'s wings.

However it is not as difficult as it seems in prospect. I found that I could sew up an aileron in two evenings and a wing in a weekend.

I had completed one wing and an aileron and was congratulating myself on discovering that Ceconite is easier to sew than cotton fabric when the March/April '76 copy of *Popular Flying* arrived containing Chris Morris's excellent article on 'Aircraft Covering Materials' in which he stated that Ceconite 'cannot be readily sewn'. I am glad that I did not see that before I

Cover being stapled to
wing ready for sewing

125

Sewing outboard panel
into wing

started; it could have been very demoralising. I think his statement probably derives from the fact that there is far less stretch in Ceconite than in cotton fabric; one must staple the edges to be sewn very much closer together – a gap of $\frac{1}{8}$ inch (3 mm) apart is quite wide enough, and it should be less or touch at the seams.

Incidentally I found that, in spite of what I had been told and I believe read somewhere, it is just as essential to wax nylon thread as it used to be with linen thread. After a couple of my threads had parted through chafing when I was sewing round the trailing edge spar, I turned the house upside down in a vain effort to find the lump of beeswax that had once been part of my sail repair kit. When I tried to buy some I found it impossible to obtain in any of the places where one might expect to find it.

I rang up my old sailmaker who lives near me and asked her to bring some home from her loft. 'Beeswax' she said, 'We haven't used any since we last made a sail for you.'

I have since discovered that this is not strictly true as sailmakers get their thread pre-waxed, and when I was having an old sail repaired the other day the cutter produced his own lump of wax from his trouser pocket.

In the end I got a piece from our neighbourly doctor and wonder whether he used it for sewing up his patients.

I was glad to see somewhere that Dacron is much less inflammable than cotton or linen as I once had a rather uncomfortable experience of this in a Hurricane.

The Hurricane IIcs that I flew had tin wings, rudder and elevator but the fuselage aft of the cockpit and the fin and tailplane were fabric covered. On this occasion I was pulling out from a rocket attack when the aircraft began to wobble all over the sky. When I got things sorted out I found that, though the aircraft was just controllable it was unbelievably sensitive in pitch and yaw.

I flew home very carefully and, after a somewhat spectacular arrival, I taxied in to dispersal. When my rigger climbed up on the wing to help me out, I tore him off a monumental strip for sending me out in an aircraft so badly out of trim.

He, good soul, stood there in silence until I finished and then said 'Would you mind standing up and looking back, Sir?' When I did so I saw that there was not a square inch of fabric remaining aft of the cockpit, just like a Bleriot. I suppose that an incendiary bullet must have passed through the fuselage and the whole lot evaporated in a puff of smoke.

I do not expect to be shot at any more but people, myself included, can be dreadfully careless with cigarette ends and it is easier to patch a little hole than to rebuild a whole wing.

There is quite a lot of written information about Ceconite and the heat shrinking process but it was only by talking to people who had used it that I was able to work out a sequence of operations for covering a wing. I can find no formal authority for it but for better or worse this is what I did and it seems to work.

Before starting to cover I painted the contact surfaces of the ribs and the leading and trailing edges with one coat of Adhesive 'A' thinned 50/50 and one coat at full strength. In way of the torsion box I painted over the ply on the lines of the ribs underneath and I also painted around fittings such as the jury strut anchorages and the aileron hinges and around holes for controls.

Once the cover had been sewn on and before attempting the shrinking process, I rubbed over the ribs, the leading and trailing edges and other pre-treated areas top and bottom with a rag well soaked in thinners to soften the adhesive underneath and draw it up through the fabric. I followed this up with two coats of Adhesive 'A' thinned 50/50, brushed on over the same lines. This divided the cover into panels ready for shrinking.

Shrinking, or tautening, of Ceconite is done before any dope is applied and is achieved by ironing the fabric with an ordinary domestic controllable electric iron. I found that the iron began to take effect with the setting on 'Silk' and this was fine for the unsupported areas. I had to move the setting up to 'Wool' for ironing over the ply covered torsion box and the alloy upper leading edge as these supporting areas seemed to act as a heat-sink and at the lower setting the iron had little or no effect.

One should start ironing at the points of maximum curvature and work into the flatter areas. This is said to minimise the bony appearance. Small wrinkles can be taken out by rubbing gently with the point of the iron. Even big wrinkles can be reduced to nothing with a little persistence. Chris Morris offers a good rule of thumb test; the correct tautness has been achieved when a penny just bounces.

The C.A.A. in BL/6-26 recommends three doping schemes; DTD 751 for low tautness, as in ultra-light aircraft; DTD 752 for medium tautness and, as one might expect, DTD 753 for high tautness. It is, however, always permissible to use the designer's specification provided it has been approved by the P.F.A., and in general it will be found to accord fairly closely with one or the other of the C.A.A. specifications.

Just remember that the more dope you use the greater the weight you are adding to the airframe.

Evans advises four coats of red oxide dope to fill the weave, two coats of silver and a finishing coat of 'auto enamel'. 'Auto enamel' being cellulose is compatible with the dope undercoats.

I needed red oxide tautening dope for my cotton fabric surfaces and since it has little or no tautening effect on Ceconite I used it for that as well.

Doping cotton is a most discouraging operation. Each coat seems to undo all the good work of the previous coats until it dries out and tautens up. The silver dope seems to take much longer to dry than the priming dope, about three days, during which time one wonders if it will ever come taut again or whether one will have to strip the lot and have another go.

Doping Ceconite is an entirely different matter. It is just as simple as painting a plastered wall.

Rudder covered and set up for spraying

Dope will stick cotton to the ribs and this is considered to be a bad thing for dope tautened cotton. This can be prevented by covering the ribs with clear plastic self-adhesive tape before applying the fabric. Ceconite, again, is different being tautened with a hot iron and is best attached to the ribs with adhesive so that the tautening can be carried out panel by panel as described above.

Some authorities, including the C.A.A. in its notes on doping (C.A.I.P., BL/6-26), recommend that plastic rings for inspection panels, drain-hole grommets etc. should be doped in place after the first coat of dope has been applied and that rib stitching should be carried out at this stage. Other authorities, including Evans, advise these operations after the second coat of priming dope. I followed Evans's advice.

I am still not clear why, if one uses Adhesive 'A' to stick the Ceconite fabric to the frame, one should also have to rib-stitch but most of the authorites, starting with Evans, insist upon it.

The purpose of rib stitching is to prevent the fabric being drawn away from the ribs by the reduction in pressure that results when air flows over the wing. This would distort the shape of the aerofoil, shift the centre of lift, so affecting fore and aft stability, and reduce the amount of lift, so initiating the stall. Not a nice thought.

I think I detected in Mike an air of relief when I did not argue about it but merely got out my cleopatric needle and got on with the job. This needle is ten inches (254 mm) long with a point at each end and a hole about two inches (50 mm) down from one end.

With the wing on trestles, the rib lines covered with self adhesive strip and the stitching positions measured and pencilled on, one shoves the short end of the needle down through the fabric close to a rib, until the eye appears underneath. One then threads the needle underneath the wing and draws it up, only to plunge it down the other side of the rib, long end first. At this point one unthreads the needle, ties a knot in the thread on the underside of the wing and repeats the process at the next stitching position.

When one gets to the middle of the rib one finds oneself crouching under the wing trying to thread the needle at arms.length in the dark. Of course one could always train a small boy to do the underwing work. As a grandfather of three I am all in favour of putting children to work but my wife says that this would be equivalent to sending the little darlings up chimneys or down the mines. I suspect that this solicitude is only to prevent their enthusiasms being diverted from assisting with the washing-up. A pity as they are just the right size for the job.

Doping is a job that I would gladly get someone else to do, but volunteers were few and far between. None turned up except the youngest grandson whom I would not trust with a magic colouring book, let alone a brushful of dope.

It seems very difficult to get a precise doping specification in regard to the coverage, so that one can work out exactly how much dope one needs to buy. The manuals are curiously non-specific and the merchants, or should they be called pushers, only seem interested in selling one as much as they can talk one into. Nowhere, so far as I could discover, is one told just how much area of fabric will be covered by, say, one litre of dope.

I stuck to Evans's specification of four coats of priming dope, two coats of silver and one coat of auto enamel. I actually used approximately 12 litres of priming dope, 6 litres of silver and 2 litres of auto enamel. I also used $1\frac{1}{2}$ litres of Adhesive 'A' and 8 litres of thinners. As the dope, adhesive and thinners are sold in 5 litre cans one is bound to finish up with quite a bit to spare.

The total area to be doped was 237 square feet (22 m²), from which it is easily seen that one litre of dope will cover approximately 80 square feet (7·4 m²) of fabric per coat.

I got talking to a chap who is a painter by trade and spent most of his war doping and camouflaging aeroplanes. We discussed the relative merits of brushing or spraying dope and paint. His advice was that if I intended to spray it was essential to get the proper equipment. He poured scorn upon the do-it-yourself type of spray gun that most of us could afford to buy and went on to say that amateurs seemed to think that the spray gun was a substitute for skill in obtaining a professional finish. In fact it requires as much skill and practice as the brush.

He advised me to stick to a brush throughout; a stiffish bristle brush for dope and a very soft brush for the enamel finish.

I had already tried spraying a finish on my rudder and stabilator and the results bore out his remarks. They looked distinctly mottled. I brushed a decent finish onto the stabilator but I was stuck with the rudder, as I had already sprayed on the decorative embellishments.

The problem of masking for the V.P.1 insignia, on a surface that curves irregularly in both directions, had me puzzled. I cut out a paper stencil but how could I make it adhere closely to the surface and yet peel off easily after the operation? A lady tracer in my office suggested egg white – and it works perfectly. Just don't leave it on too long.

The plastic rings for inspection and access holes were doped on after the second coat of priming dope, as were the soft alloy rings round the holes for the flying struts. I had to cut out the centres of the spring inspection cover plates to make the strut cover plates, and as the light alloy is very brittle, I broke one in the process.

I had to cut out the fabric in the centres of the inspection and strut holes in order to fit the struts and position the cover plates for marking and drilling holes for the self-tapping screws that hold them down. As I stood with my Stanley knife poised over the first one, I felt like a surgeon's apprentice on his first solo. Just suppose that it was in the wrong place, after getting so far towards completion. Fortunately it all worked out beautifully.

130

Dope is temperamental stuff and likes to be applied in an ambient temperature of 65°F–70°F (18°C–21°C) with humidity of less than 70%. Nothing dreadful will happen if the temperature is as low as 60°F (16°C) although the dope will take longer to dry. But one is not advised to work at any lower temperature.

The greatest enemy of dope is high humidity, especially when allied with low temperature. This causes blushing which leads to a reduction in the all important properties of water and air proofing.

Your inspector is likely to be hard to satisfy in respect of doping conditions – he may even require wet and dry bulb thermometer readings to be taken and recorded before starting – and you may even be driven to doing your doping in your centrally heated sitting room.

I was lucky. I had a warm and dry springtime for my doping but if you have to heat a room or a garage remember that raw dope is almost explosively inflammable so see that there are no exposed naked lights when you open the can.

In order to ensure a good finish you should rub the surface down with a pad damped with dope before each coat has dried on the fabric, in order to lay the fibres. Do this also over the tapes as they are applied.

The final finish can either be obtained with finishing dope, in which case you will have to rub down the silver undercoats with very fine 'wet and dry' paper especially in way of the tapes and other projections, or it can be auto enamel which effectively covers a multitude of minor sins with minimum effort.

I think that there is little doubt that finishing dope and a great deal of loving care produces the best finish but for my part I was glad that Evans specified auto enamel since I was in a hurry to get flying.

We have not, so far, mentioned the blessed word 'Madapolam'. This is a very light fabric to DTD 343a used only for covering and waterproofing plywood. It is doped onto the ply surface and both effectively weatherproofs the plywood and provides a good base for the final finish.

Before the days of polyurethane enamel paints this was the only way to weatherproof plywood and is probably still the best. However the modern two-pack polyurethane is cheaper, quicker, lighter and, properly applied to a clean surface over its own primer, just as effective.

Much has been said and written about the great strength and structural integrity of Madapolam covered plywood but I have had my doubts about this since I had a wing-tip knocked off a Mosquito over Athens and had to fly for two hours watching the wing getting shorter and shorter. To add to my troubles I had a rather stout and quite unflappable Geordie navigator who, when I briefed him on the drill for abandoning the aircraft should it become necessary, expressed doubts as to whether he would fit through the hatch with his chest-type parachute clipped on. Luckily we made it home without having to find out.

I painted my fuselage with two-pack polyurethane yacht enamel.

Internally my inspector limited me to one coat of white over one coat of colourless primer. On the outside he allowed me two coats of white.

After three seasons of fairly hard use, living in an open fronted hangar and flying off a rough strip that is, from time to time, well manured by cattle, the paint work shows no signs of deterioration. I am very happy with the result.

Chapter 7

The vital spark – V.W. engine conversion and installation

It is obviously better, if the airframe design provides for it, to use a purpose-built aero engine if you can get one or afford one. Compared to the Volkswagen (V.W.) engine it produces about twice the power for the same weight.

Unfortunately a second-hand 65 hp (48·5 kW) Continental A.65 in good condition, or even one fit for rebuilding, is inordinately expensive and the later 85 hp (63·4 kW) model is even further out of reach.

So most of us have to fall back on the well proved Volkswagen and consequently on designs which incorporate this engine.

Most of the early aircraft designed to use the V.W. engine employed the 1200 cc model which was the only one made at the time, but as there is very little, if any, difference in weight between the 1200 cc and the 1600 cc engines now available, one might as well use the largest capacity engine and have the benefit of the extra power for no weight penalty.

My own V.P.1 has the 1600 cc engine, climbs at 600 feet per minute (183 m/min) and cruises at 72 knots (83 mph, 134 km/h) true air speed (T.A.S.). I have flown another V.P.1 with the 1500 cc engine which climbed at 400 feet per minute (122 m/min) and cruised at 67 knots (77 mph, 124 km/h) T.A.S.

I think this is probably a fair comparison, though it is very difficult to be precise since so much depends upon the weight of the aircraft itself and upon the propeller that is fitted.

There are even larger engines and much research is at present in hand into the conversion and use of these engines; indeed plans have recently been published in the U.K. for the 1700 cc conversion. However these engines are appreciably heavier than the 1200 cc – 1600 cc range and, except in the case of an aircraft designed to carry the heavier engine such as the Evans V.P.2, one should seek expert advice from P.F.A. Engineering and one's inspector before acquiring one.

To the best of my knowledge the French were the first to come up with the idea of converting the Volkswagen engine to aerial use. The first details were published in *Les Cahiers du Sport de l'Air*.

I suspect that the breakthrough came when it was found that the crankshaft bearings could accept the thrust of a propeller so that no expensive or difficult modification was required in this respect.

The conversion and installation of the V.W. engine is relatively simple though perhaps not so ridiculously easy, when one comes down to details, as some authorities would have us believe.

There are a number of conversion schemes marketed in the U.K. and America, most of them very good, but beware; if you are converting an engine to be flown in the U.K. do not use American plans which provide only for single ignition.

The F.A.A. in America seem perfectly happy for ultra-light aircraft to fly around with one Vertex magneto replacing the distributor of the V.W. engine, whereas in the U.K. the C.A.A. will only allow single ignition in powered gliders. The rest of us must have dual ignition which entails drilling and counter-boring the cylinder heads for a second plug in each cylinder, and carrying and driving two magnetos.

Probably the most popular V.W. installation in the U.K. is the Peacock conversion and, in the U.S.A., the Ackerman. Of necessity they are very different. I used the Peacock conversion though I have to confess that I did very little of the work myself.

The original engine that I acquired through a happy encounter at a Strut meeting came out of a gyrocopter that inadvertently took off without its pilot. The engine was about all that was left. It had a single Scintilla magneto in place of the distributor and drove a pusher propeller from the gear-box end of the crankshaft which, on the Peacock conversion, drives the magnetos. Being bottom mounted in the gyrocopter the lugs had been turned off the bell housing so that a new crank-case was required if it was to be installed in the normal recommended manner.

Being a second-hand engine it had to be stripped, all moving parts, including the crankshaft, crack tested and all clearances measured and recorded before re-building in a new crank-case.

The conversion consists essentially of:

(a) Fitting a propeller hub in place of the dynamo and fan drive pulley.
(b) Trepanning the flywheel and fitting to it a sprocket to drive the two magnetos.
(c) Mounting the two magnetos, fitted with sprockets, on a plate which positions them below the engine and in line with the top, driving sprocket.
(d) Drilling and tapping the heads to take a second plug in each cylinder.
(e) By-passing the oil-cooler.

There is rather more to it than that, of course, but you will get the idea and the details can be had from whichever set of conversion plans and instructions you decide to buy.

Perhaps the greatest merit of the Volkswagen engine, from the amateur's point of view, is that it requires no welded engine mount. It is simply bolted directly to the firewall through spacers that give clearance for the magneto chain drive. This is a beautifully simple, cheap and strong arrangement.

The problem that most plagues the purist is the fact that the 1600 cc engine, for example, gives peak performance of 53 hp (39·6 kW) at about 4000 rpm. Different propellers will give different results but about the most that can be attained with a fine pitch propeller is 3400 rpm in the climb at which the engine is developing 50 hp (37·3 kW). An even finer pitch propeller, while allowing the engine to run faster and develop more power, would itself be less efficient and give less propulsive thrust to the aircraft.

My own relatively coarse propeller climbs at 3100 rpm giving out about 46 hp (34·3 kW) and I cruise at 2700 rpm and 41 hp (30·6 kW).

One can always get at that extra horsepower by gearing the engine, for a weight penalty of 25 to 30 lbs (11 to 14 kg) and there are several sets of plans for this on the market. Of course one will lose some power in the gearing, since no system can be 100% mechanically efficient, and one can expect the fuel consumption to go up; you can't get 'owt for nowt'. Most of us opt for the simple solution of the direct drive.

The biggest and trickiest job in the whole conversion is the drilling and counter-boring of the cylinder heads to take the second plug. This is an operation that calls for a great deal of expertise and care but fortunately there are experts who will do this for you and they can be found in the advertisement columns of *Popular Flying*.

The propeller hub and retaining ring can also be had from specialists. Other items such as the oil bypass, the engine mounting spacers, bolts and studs can be made up by any local machine shop and the magneto plate and flanges you can cut out from alloy plate with jig-saw, drill and file. It is important for one's own ego to do some of the work oneself.

It is popularly believed that engineers know all about engines. In fact, for most engineers nothing could be further from the truth. For most of my working life I have been involved in the design and construction of large, immobile objects such as bridges, buildings and quay walls, and the location of railway tracks, generally in the remoter parts of the world.

In my apprentice days I spent some time in ship's engine rooms and fell in love with those great steam driven monsters whose connecting rods marched in time with the willowy dance of the valve rods swaying on the cams. Those I could understand. You could see and feel the power as the huge cranks tramped round at a hundred and twenty revolutions a minute. Manoeuvering called for a team of men, one to each throttle valve, one to each reversing lever and one, generally me, on the engine-room telegraph, keeping the movements log.

Somehow I have never managed to come to terms with the internal combustion engine with its unimaginably high rate of revolution and its busy little parts beavering away at tiny clearances, all hidden away in a black iron box. It is wonderful of course, almost magical and a triumph of man's ingenuity, but it lacks the sympathy of steam. Shades of Hiram Maxim and his steam driven aeroplane.

I had taken my ex-gyrocopter engine home and dumped it on the dead end of the jig table where for months it lay and glowered at me, daring me to touch it.

I bought a set of metric spanners but then my courage gave out and so long as there was work to be done on the airframe I could ignore it. Eventually I ran out of excuses.

I made a start by removing all the accessories which I dumped into a cardboard box under the bench. Stripped down to the bare block it looked more menacing than ever.

I made a half-hearted attempt to shift the retaining nut on the propeller hub and, when this proved unsuccessful, I decided to leave it until the next week-end.

A few nights later I was talking on the telephone to my friend Richard about propellers when he mentioned that a mutual friend and P.F.A. member, Alan Newnham, was an absolute whizz with Volkswagen engines, having done a most successful conversion on his own power plant. I wondered whether he would be willing to give me a hand, if only with advice. Richard thought he would and a few nights later, after a glass or two of ale, we three went out to look at 007 in the garage.

Most of my friends know plenty about boats but precious little about aeroplanes, so I do not mind showing off my handiwork to them. Submitting it to expert scrutiny, however, was a very different matter and I confess I took them out there with my heart in my boots. However they were more than kind; perfect guests in fact, and I hoped they were not just being polite.

Then they turned on the engine. They pulled it around and peered in all its dark recesses. They turned out the box of bits and pieces that I had stripped off it and all the time I stood in the background and hoped they would not condemn my bargain outright after it had terrorised me for so many months.

Eventually Alan stood back and said that he thought that he might be able to find a good crank-case for it and a flywheel for trepanning, provided everything inside was in fair shape, and he could see no reason why it should not be.

Finally they packed everything up and carted it out to Alan's car, when I realised with delight that at last the brute was going to get the treatment which it had for so long defied me to attempt.

The next morning I went carefully through Donald Peacock's excellent conversion plans and very detailed instructions to abstract and list all the accessories and components that I might have to buy in.

Round Dural bar I had, sufficient to make the spacers that hold the engine off the firewall. A phone call to a friend produced a promise of the $\frac{1}{4}$ inch (6 mm) thick dural plate to carry the magnetos. Then I rang the recommended supplier for the carburettor and hit the first snag when he told me that the Zenith twin float Type 32 KLP 10 is no longer available. This meant setting in train another hunt for an acceptable alternative. The way of the aeroplane builder is beset with these time-consuming and frustrating researches. Hard rubber pads for the engine mounts promised another trail of detection since A.J.S. motor bikes are no longer made. I supposed that it would all come together eventually; but when?

A few nights later Alan rang up to say that he had got the engine apart and, subject to crack-testing, it all looked good. At the first opportunity I ran over to Alan's place where he showed me my monster all in bits and finally tamed. It looked so innocuous that I wondered what on earth I had been worried about, but that is always the way in the presence of experts – watch the fluent ease of a great trapeze artist doing a triple bunt, and then try it yourself, if you dare.

Alan handed me my heads to be sent away to have the second plug-holes drilled. The following Wednesday I had to deliver two grandsons to London Airport to fly out to spend their holidays with their parents in the Western Pacific. So I put my cylinder heads in the back of the car and went on from the airport to deliver them to the great Roy Watling-Greenwood who, in a wonderfully equipped little workshop in a small village some miles north of Lewes, bores second plug-holes in Volkswagen heads and also produces those beautiful propellers that grace so many home-built aircraft.

For the inexperienced let me say at once that if you want to visit Roy don't start from London Airport. With a short stop for lunch it took me four hours to do the journey through the narrow built-up lanes and winding streets of South London's suburbia – and it rained all the way.

While at Roy's place I asked if he knew of a source of supply for S.R.4 magnetoes, whereupon he produced a pair, which disposed of another supply problem.

From then on I fed Alan parts of the Peacock V.W. conversion as they came to hand until one evening, at a P.F.A. Strut meeting, Alan asked how 007 was coming along and I said I was just about ready for the engine.

Alan looked thoughtful and then said that because of pressure of work and P.F.A. activities he had not got very far with my engine, but would I like to trade mine for his as he would not be needing an engine for at least a year?

I fairly jumped at this very generous offer and a few nights later I collected the engine, bore it home and parked it on the end of my wife's garden bench close up to 007's firewall.

The next week-end I borrowed a handybilly tackle with a brake on the top block from a sailing friend, slung the engine from the steel roof beam and carefully inched it into position.

One thing that had caused me a lot of anxiety was whether or not the pre-drilled holes in the firewall would line up with the bolt holes on the

Engine being offered
up to firewall

engine. They fitted perfectly – but the top bolts were half an inch too short! I had deducted half an inch from the dimensions given on the Peacock drawings because they were for a $1\frac{1}{4}$ inch (32 mm) thick firewall, whereas mine was only $\frac{3}{4}$ inch (19 mm) thick. I found there was a thickening of the flange on my 1600 cc engine that did not appear on the drawings of the 1200 cc engine of the original conversion. So I needed the longer bolts after all, though the bottom ones were a perfect fit.

Waiting for the new top bolts to come delayed installation for a week and Alan talked me into taking a day off to go flying with him. It was a delightful break from the steady slog of work on 007.

We went first to Goodwood where I got in an hour's flying with ex-night fighter Doug Adams of Vectair to make my licence legal again. On to Shoreham, where we found everything closed because it was the Easter public holiday. However we lunched well there and afterwards went to the hangar and looked at Gerry Price's V.P.1, Esmeralda from which I learnt an awful lot. Then back to Goodwood for another half hour of solo each and finally home refreshed in the cool of the evening. A lovely day to remember.

The new top bolts arrived and were fitted so that I could release the block and tackle and get on with the hook-up of controls.

For most of a year, ever since John Derrick had given me the throttle unit, I had been looking for someone to make up the push-pull controls but without much success.

138

Engine installed – port side

I had managed to get a piano wire choke control for a car that just happened to be exactly the right length, but the throttle and hot-air controls would have to be specially made to fit and, in any case, the throttle would need a much heavier gauge of wire.

Now that the need was urgent I started a systematic search and eventually, quite by chance, I unearthed the only remote control specialist in the county, less than a mile from my office.

In no time at all he had made up my throttle and hot-air controls and also the copper tube with nuts and olives that connects my oil pressure gauge to the engine.

I had previously fitted a nylon tube with compression end fittings to the oil pressure gauge but Mike rejected it on the grounds that an engine fire would melt the tube and it would thereafter feed the fire with hot oil. Not a pretty thought.

The throttle had presented me with a problem. The actuating mechanism on the V.W. carburettor consisted of a small quadrant of about one inch radius with a little arm and ball to take the socket end of a rod. I measured the chord of the movement of the little arm as $\frac{3}{4}$ inch (19 mm) and calculated the length of lever required to give a little less than the full travel of the throttle control in the cockpit. The problem was how to arrange a bell-crank system to operate on the little arm and its ball joint.

For a whole fortnight I worried over it until one evening, when I was gazing at it despondently, I suddenly began to wonder what was on the other end of the little shaft on which the quadrant worked. I looked and found a nut and a 10 s.w.g. spacer. When they were removed there was a squared end all ready to receive a lever. A quarter of an hour later the job was done.

Mike was not very happy about the lack of support for the carburettor, which was only held on by two bolts through a flange welded to the inlet manifold which, in turn, was free to rotate in the rubber connections at each end.

It was a problem to find a suitable support point on the crank-case. I got over it by making a 10 s.w.g. (0·128 inch, 3·25 mm) stool of Z section. One leg of this was bolted to one of the oil filler studs and the other leg supported the hot-air box. It was secured to the bottom of the hot-air box with a $\frac{3}{16}$ inch (4·8 mm) bolt.

The $\frac{3}{16}$ inch (4·8 mm) bolt would not be accessible once the whole lot was assembled, so the stool had first to be bolted on to the hot-air box, the hot-air box fitted to the carburettor, then the whole lot rotated down until the other leg of the stool was half way down on the oil filler stud. At this point one could install the fuel pump and bolt it down, before the carburettor plus hot-air box and stool could be rotated to its final position and the last nut on the oil filler slipped on and tightened up.

Later on, urged on by Alan and Richard, I fitted another support at the other end of the carburettor just to make sure.

Evans recommends the use of an electronic marine type tachometer. This is clearly because of the impossibility of getting a reasonably straight run from engine to instrument.

There are, I discovered, two types of electronic tachometer. One works by induced current in thin wires wrapped round the plug leads. At first sight this seems the easier solution but, with dual ignition, one must at some point bring together the two leads firing the plugs on the same cylinder in order to wrap the thin wire round both leads. This would call for an inordinate length of H.T. leads since the ones for the top plugs are naturally run over the top of the engine and the others feed in from the bottom. I suppose it could be done but I opted for the other type which works off the earth switch side of the magnetoes.

This requires a change-over switch and quite a tangle of wiring, but it is all in the short space between the instrument and the mag switches. I made it easy for myself by drawing a simple wiring diagram and colour coding the wiring (see fig. 7.1).

After my experience of the electronic tachometer and having seen the troubles that many of my friends have had with the direct drive type, I would never consider using anything else. It is so much easier to install and mine has given no trouble whatever in service. The 6 volt dry cell battery lasted for two years in the first instance and would probably have gone on much longer had I not changed it. It is also cheaper.

I feel that the magneto switches should be outside the cockpit where the

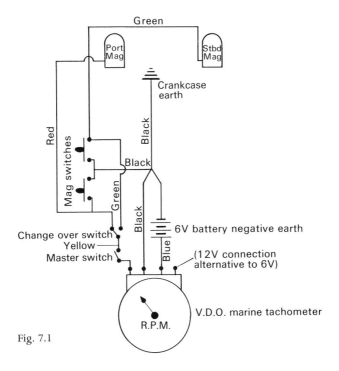

Fig. 7.1

chap swinging the prop can see them, as was always the case on the aeroplanes in which I grew up.

After all these years I have just discovered why the switches apparently worked back to front. On the call of 'Switches Off' one checked that the switches were down and replied 'Switches Off'. At 'Contact' one turned them up. This is because when the switches are down the earth circuit is made and the mags are earthed. When the switches are up the circuit is broken and the mags can spark. The switches work in the correct sense; the orders are ambiguous. This must have been obvious to an intelligent engine fitter but to this dim-witted pilot it seemed just another quaint survival from the rotary engine and piano-wire days.

Incidentally I don't suppose that there are many around today who recall the old R.F.C. toast 'Suck In'. Not that I am old enough to have been in the R.F.C. – I got it from a Jesuit Monsignor who had flown in McCudden's squadron – but I think it is worth preserving. It is only the P.F.A., E.A.A. and R.S.A. pilots who call 'Suck In' these days as a part of their starting drill.

So to all those worthies who gather month by month at the P.F.A. Strut meetings, to whom I am so much indebted, I raise my glass and say 'Suck In'.

It is possible to fit an impulse unit to the port magneto to make starting by prop swinging easier, but I did not do this, even though I had acquired some of the parts, as I was told that the impulse units for Lucas S.R.4 magnetoes were apt to fly to pieces in the air. I also met a chap who had sprained his wrist swinging an installation equipped with an impulse mag. According to him the wretched things were designed specifically to dismember prop-swingers.

Recent correspondence in *Popular Flying* has revealed that these units are designed for direct shaft drive through a fibre coupling to allow for slight misalignment of the shaft and they cannot accept the side loads imposed by a chain driven sprocket – so my first informant was correct, and I am glad I did not fit one.

The carburettor has to be a side-draught type equipped with a hot-box against carburettor icing. My carburettor is the one that came with the engine, the Solex 32 PHN 1, with the automatic choke changed to hand operation. There are also good reports of the Solex B 30 AHG model.

Whatever you fit you will have to play around with the jets during the ground running phase in order to get the optimum mixture.

These carburettors are not, of course, suitable for inverted flight and if you want to indulge in aerobatics you will have to start by obtaining a suitable carburettor. You cannot in any case fly a V.W. engine inverted for more than the few seconds it takes to go over the top of a loop for example because it has a wet sump and would soon be starved of oil and seize up. There you would be; 'upside down and nothing on the clock'.

From the beginning I regarded my hot air system as a bit of a joke and doubted whether it was really necessary or, indeed, whether it would work under real icing conditions at all. I exercised it more as a matter of habit.

However, once when flying a friend's V.P.1 fitted with the same hot air box I got very definite icing at 3000 feet (900 m) and much to my relief the hot-air control cured it in about ten seconds – it could only have been about ten seconds but it seemed like half an hour with very rough Devon country underneath me and the engine sounding as though it was choking to death. It really works.

I have the V.W. fuel pump that came with the engine and it has proved very satisfactory in service. Its only disadvantage lies in the fact that it cannot be hand-primed. This can be overcome by using a Peugeot pump (SEV 46 C or D according to engine model) and details of this will be found in the proprietary conversion instructions.

One incidental advantage of the Peugeot pump is that it has a lower profile than the V.W. pump. I have had to mould an unsightly bump into my cowling to cover the V.W. model.

The propeller, or airscrew as it is more properly called since only a pusher configuration can truly claim a propeller, is a fairly large indivisible cost and I seriously considered making my own. It did not strike me as an impossible task for an amateur since it only consists of gluing up a number of laminations and shaping the resulting lump of timber.

I had great difficulty in finding any literature on the subject but eventually I found some information in Hoffman's *Engineering for the Amateur Aircraft Builder* published by the E.A.A. I had actually gone so far as to make up the jig and profiles from Hoffman's charts when another lucky encounter at a P.F.A. Strut meeting put me in touch with an importation of Canadian airscrews for 1600 cc V.W. installations and I grabbed one at about half the going price in the U.K.

Since that time Eric Clutton has published his *Propeller Making for the Amateur* to make a useful reduction in the cost of getting airborne.

Before it can be flown the engine must be run-in and the fuel flow checked. The engine can be run in a test rig or in the aircraft itself. This is necessary in order to bed-in all the new parts, to ensure that there are no blockages in oil or fuel passages and to adjust the carburettor and the magneto timing to give optimum performance.

Detailed instructions for this test running will be found in the *P.F.A. Handbook* or in the instructions which come with the engine conversion plans.

My own engine was ground run for $6\frac{1}{2}$ hours before it finally took to the air. At that stage I was getting impatient to fly and wasted no time at all. Alan had run it for 5 hours 15 minutes before passing it on to me so as soon as it was installed I got right on with the fuel flow test.

Mike had told me to arrange a gravity feed directly to the carburettor and lead a pipe from the fuel pump into a bucket, then, at the critical moment with the engine at full bore, to transfer the pipe into a measuring vessel for one minute and afterwards read the quantity obtained.

Temporary fuel supply for fuel flow test

Fuel flow test set-up

My Volkswagen handbook gave the maximum pump delivery as 400 cc per minute, so it seemed to me that a litre measure would be adequate. I asked my wife if she had one and, proud of the fact that she was as metricated as anyone else, she produced a transparent plastic jug with graduations up to one litre.

Alan lent me a gallon tin with a tap soldered into the bottom and a length of plastic pipe. I put half a gallon in it, sat it on top of 007's tank and lashed it in place.

007 was positioned on the concrete at the entrance to the garage with the tail lashed to the bumper of my car, chocks under the wheels and the brakes locked on.

I carefully swept the garage floor to ensure that there could be nothing that could fly into my lovely new propeller and damage it. Then I went into the starting routine:

Magneto switches Off
Master switch On (to energise the tachometer)
Mixture Rich
Four priming strokes on the throttle
Turn engine over two revolutions (Four blades pulled through)
'Contact'.

Considering that the engine had not run for eighteen months I was pleasantly surprised when it started on the third blade with a hearty crackle.

144

To my dismay there was no sign of life from the rev counter. I ran the engine by ear for a few minutes but this was obviously no use for precise evaluations. The engine sounded marvellously healthy. I could detect no mag drop at all by ear and, at the end of the run, I tried the hot-air control. This did produce a detectable drop in revs so maybe it worked.

I shut down and removed the little six volt accumulator which was supposed to energise the tachometer. It was flat. It seemed that I had misread the indications on my trickle charger, had charged it at 12 volts instead of 6 volts and had ruined it.

Down to the village to get a couple of 3 volt dry cells which I connected up in series to give 6 volts and then we had another try. On the first run the tail had tended to lift when any great amount of power was applied, so I lashed the tail skid down to a couple of old car batteries.

This time everything went perfectly. A little running at idling revs (1100 rpm) then up to 1800 rpm for a mag check – no more than a flicker of the needle on the dial – and then up to full power. The maximum static speed seemed to be 2850 rpm.

I dropped it down to 2500 rpm for the fuel flow test as my wife, who was in charge of the end of the tube and the litre measure, could not work in the slipstream at full power.

Once the one minute sample had been obtained I throttled back to ask her what the measure showed. A thoroughly disgruntled woman, her face, hair and frock flecked with black grease off the mag drive chain, peered over the side of the cockpit and announced 'Seven eighths of a litre'.

Imperially British to the last, the firm who made her litre measure had scorned ccs or millilitres and had calibrated it in *eighths* of a litre. A little conversion sum gave the flow at 875 cc per minute, rather more than the 400 cc per minute given in the handbook, probably because it was not working against any back pressure.

My open exhausts produced a hearty bellow at full throttle; as Alan put it 'She doesn't half bark'. That sort of noise may be music to the ear of the constructor but a lot of people are genuinely offended by it.

There is no need for us to be aggressively masculine in this matter, indeed the less noise we make the fewer the objections that are likely to be raised against our innocent sport.

I had read in *Sport Aviation* a tip for tranquilising the Volkswagen exhaust. It was suggested that if the end of the open exhaust pipe were to be squeezed in the vice until it was oval with a smaller dimension of half its original diameter and then a row of $\frac{1}{4}$ inch (6 mm) holes drilled in the side of the pipe, it would result in a marked reduction of the exhaust noise.

I thought it was worth trying, especially as it cost nothing – and it really worked.

My 007 is by no means a 'whispering angel', as the gentlemen of the press insisted on christening the Beaufighter, but it is a lot quieter than it was and I can detect no loss of power.

Chapter 8

The big rig

Now that all the major components have been fabricated up to final finish, we have reached the stage of assembling the complete aircraft, weighing for centre of gravity determination and applying for registration ready for flight testing and certification. The excitement mounts; the tension and, so far as his family and friends are concerned, the constructor are becoming unbearable.

If the aircraft is one that can be folded – such as a Fred – or one that is easily rigged and de-rigged – such as a V.P. – the Big Rig is best done in the garden at home where you have all your tools, stocks of nuts and bolts, locking wire etc. readily to hand, as well as plenty of assistance in the way of wife, family, friends and neighbours who can be pressed into service as and when required.

As this will be the first complete assembly under the eye of your inspector you are going to learn a great deal from it that will be useful on future occasions so carry a clip-board with plenty of foolscap on it for making notes about the order of assembly of particular items, special tools required and spares to replace items dropped and lost in the grass such as safety pins, split pins, clevis pins, nuts etc. If you can drop and lose them once you will surely do it again.

Since it will all have to come apart again for transport to the airfield use plain assembly nuts rather than lock nuts.

If the aircraft is one that cannot be folded or easily de-rigged it will probably have to be taken in bits to the airfield where you intend to make your first flight and assembled there; but as it is likely to be some time before you receive the Permit to Fly it would be as well to arrange hangarage, at least until the aircraft is ready to fly.

The order of assembly is the first problem to be solved. In my own case this was the first time the wings had been fitted to the fuselage since they had been covered and it took me most of the morning to discover that the flying struts had to be fitted to the wings before the wings could be offered up to the fuselage.

Biplanes have their own peculiar rigging problems and generally call for special trestles, bridge props and a band of assistants. As I recall the two bay biplanes were easier to rig than the single bay types as the wings could be 'boxed up' standing on their leading edges on the ground and were, temporarily, self supporting on the fuselage once the root bolts had been passed. Unfortunately, so far as I know, all the ultra-light biplanes are single bay jobs. Years ago, before the war, I knew a chap who had an Avro 504 N which he used to rig with a pair of tuning forks, one for the flying wires and one for the landing wires. I do not suppose that anyone does that any more.

It was a sunny Saturday morning when I rolled my 007 out from the garage. With the wings hung along the sides on the transport gear it looked like a butterfly emerging from the chrysalis. We carefully bridged the flower border and rolled 007 onto the front lawn where it sat surrounded by rose beds.

The wings came off the transport gear and were laid on trestles on either side. Then we started trying to put the jig-saw puzzle together.

Impatient as I was the pace of work was, necessarily, slow as passers-by kept coming in to ask questions and be shown round; every child in the neighbourhood had to be lifted in and out of the cockpit.

Fortunately we were having a cold lunch so that I was able to command the full attention of my wife and daughter. It was lunch time before we had the wings in position.

I found that an essential tool for lining up the strut and root bolts is what, in the shipyards in the days of riveted plates, we used to call a drift – a length of $\frac{5}{16}$ inch (8 mm) round mild steel bar ground down to $\frac{1}{4}$ inch (6 mm) diameter at one end. With this and a mallet the bolts go home with the minimum of effort and bad language.

Fitting the stabilator is a fiddling but not a difficult job. The really tricky part is fitting the shims to take out all the side-play in the eye-bolt hinges. I must confess that I did not do this until the final rig before flying and then it was done for me by the professional ground staff at the airfield. I noticed that they used a special pair of pliers with long, pointed noses bent at right angles. They looked like dentist's tools and perhaps they were as I have never been able to get a pair for myself.

Connecting up the control cables to the stick is a muscle-binding, neck-cricking job. There is so little room to work through the $3\frac{1}{2}$ inch (89 mm) diameter inspection hole, especially if you have fingers like pork sausages. Lying on one's back under the fuselage, trying to get fork-ends to meet holes in the cross plates at the bottom of the stick and pass a clevis bolt through the three holes is a great advance on the most refined of Chinese tortures. I simplified the problem by tying a bit of string round the swage above the fork-end and leading it out through the hole in the opposite side of the fuselage to a point under the wing where my wife or daughter could pull on it. That helped.

Now is the time to check the mass-balancing of the ailerons and the stabilator, with the aircraft levelled in the flying position. This mass balancing was a nagging worry to me, right up to the time I first flew my aeroplane. I had made the balance weights exactly to the dimensions

147

shown on the drawings, but when I came to check the actual balance of the stabilator I found that quite a lot more lead would be required to achieve a perfect balance. I was reluctant to add any extra weight, especially at a lever arm of some 128 inches (3·25 m) behind the centre of gravity, so I let it go, feeling that I could always add more weight later if it was necessary.

At the time of the trial rig the friction in the cable and pulley system and the weight of the cables themselves must have been enough to compensate for this under-balance. It has never given me the slightest trouble in flight. So it would seem that it does not have to be a perfect, knife-edge balance, so long as everything will stay in the neutral position without having to be held there with the stick.

The next job is to check the movement of the rudder, ailerons and elevator or stabilator to see that they accord with those shown on the drawings. On the V.P.1 these movements are really very small; 15° each way on the ailerons, $13\frac{1}{2}°$ each way on the stabilator and 15° each way on the rudder.

All these movements seemed minute to me but my inspector did not seem unduly worried and they have proved to be perfectly adequate in flight. Indeed I suspect that this limited movement accounts for the V.P.'s reluctance to spin, since an inadvertent spin is generally the result of over-controlling.

Incidentally, before you fly your aircraft you must have an independent check on the controls. It has actually happened, and once quite recently, that an unfortunate pilot has taken-off with one of his controls crossed. The outcome of this sort of oversight is generally fatal.

Now, with everything in place, we approach the centre of gravity (c. of g.) determination. This generally seems to worry the less mathematically minded among us but there is really no need for anxiety on this score. It is very simple logic.

Back in 250 B.C. or thereabouts, Archimedes enunciated the theory of the lever when he said 'Give me where to stand and I will lift the earth'. This is the principle of 'moments' on which the whole of modern engineering design depends. It is the Law and Archimedes is its prophet, so next time you drive over a bridge or fly away in a jumbo jet, or even take off in your home-built aeroplane, give thanks to that randy, boozy old Greek.

What he was saying, in effect, was that for equilibrium a force, or a weight, acting through a distance or a lever-arm, must be balanced by the product of another force and another lever arm. To put numbers to it, a weight of, say, 500 lb acting through a distance of 20 in produces a moment of 500 lb times 20 in = 10 000 lb in and, for equilibrium, this must be balanced by a similar moment of 10 000 lb in.

If your other weight is 250 lb it must act through a lever-arm of 40 in to produce the same, balancing, moment of 10 000 lb in.

Let us see how this works out in practice.

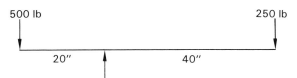

500 lb   250 lb

20"   40"

The first thing to do is to calibrate your bathroom scales. I had long suspected that my bathroom scales were badly in error and so I tried to borrow some more accurate ones. The result of my researches was to establish the fact that all bathroom scales are congenital liars so I set out to calibrate my own.

With three half-hundredweight (56 lb, 25·4 kg) weights I found that it had a straight line error as one would expect since it is spring controlled, the proportionate error being constant throughout the range. My wife was delighted to discover that she weighs eight pounds (4 kg) less than the scales indicate and abandoned her diet forthwith.

Using two wooden blocks, each the same thickness as the scales so that I could swap them around with the scales without affecting the levelling of the aircraft, I set 007 up level, in the flying attitude, and introduced the scales under each wheel in turn. Precise reading of the scales was made difficult by the fact that the slightest breeze set the pointer swinging.

Two sets of readings of the weights on each wheel are required. The first set are taken with the aircraft empty, without pilot or fuel. This set of readings gives us the empty weight of the aircraft and can also be used for calculating the maximum forward position of the c. of g. The second set of readings, with the pilot and if necessary passenger and baggage or ballast in lieu, are for the determination of the maximum aft position of the c. of g. If the fuel tank is forward of the c. of g. then it must be empty; if aft it should be full.

In the case of the V.P.1 the fuel tank is forward of the c. of g. so this set of readings is referred to as 'the gross less fuel'. This gross less fuel weighing for the maximum aft position of the c. of g., with myself in the cockpit, was beyond the capacity of the scales. It was necessary to construct a bridge consisting of a plank supported on blocks at one end and the scale platform at the other, the wheel being on the middle of the span. The reading was then doubled to give the weight on the wheel. The accuracy of this reading was easily checked knowing my own weight and the increment on the tail wheel.

My results were very satisfactory. Although the total weight exceeded that of the prototype, nearly all the excess was accounted for by modifications interposed by the designer and by U.K. regulations such as the torsion boxes on the wings, the jury struts, dual ignition, steerable tailwheel etc.

The positions of the c. of g. accorded very closely with those on the prototype and were comfortably forward of the furthest permissible aft position. The work sheet looked like this:

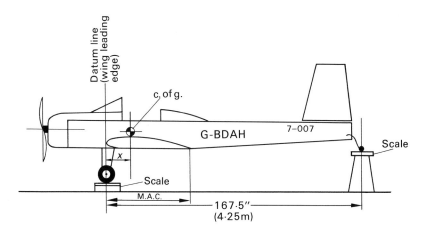

	G-BDAH 7-007 Weight lb (kg)		**Prototype** Weight lb (kg)	
Empty				
Port Wheel	247·5	(112)	205	(93)
Starboard Wheel	247·5	(112)	205	(93)
Tail Wheel	42	(19)	35	(16)
	537	(243)	445	(202)
Mk 1 Mods			37	(17)
			482	(219)
Gross less Fuel				
Port Wheel	319·5	(145)	280	(127)
Starboard Wheel	319·5	(145)	280	(127)
Tail Wheel	61	(28)	55	(25)
	700	(318)	615	(279)
Mk 1 Mods			37	(17)
Fuel	47	(21)	47	(21)
All Up Weight	747	(339)	699	(317)

CENTRE OF GRAVITY

Empty

$$x = \frac{42 \times 167·5}{537} = 13·1 \text{ in } (0·33 \text{ m}), \ 26\% \text{ M.A.C.}$$

Gross less Fuel

$$x = \frac{61 \times 167·5}{700} = 14·6 \text{ in } (0·37 \text{ m}), \ 29\% \text{ M.A.C.}$$

M.A.C. stands for Mean Aerodynamic Chord and in the case of a 'square' wing it is the same as the chord. On the V.P.1 it is 50 in (1·27 m).

The equivalent figures for the prototype were 12·8 in (0·32 m) and 14·5 in (0·37 m), and the maximum permissible aft position is given as 15·5 in (0·39 m). The prototype was air tested in the States at 750 lb (340 kg) all up weight. This included aerobatics and spinning.

Still confused? The problem is to find the unknown distance x from the datum line – a known position on the airframe – to the centre of gravity. The datum line on the V.P.1 is on the vertical plane through the centres of the wheels which, in the flying attitude, touches the leading edge of the wing.

It is clear that all the weight forward of the centre of gravity acts through the centres of the main wheels and all the weight aft acts through the tail wheel. If it were not so the aeroplane would tip up on its nose.

Hence we can say that the weight on the two main wheels times the distance x must equal the weight on the tail wheel times the distance between the main wheels and the tail wheel less the distance x.

Now since the weight to distance relationships are simple in this equation, uncomplicated by squares and other functions beloved of mathemagicians, it is clear that the distance x must be in the same proportion to the distance between the main and tail wheels as the weight on the tail wheel bears to the total weight of the aircraft. Thus, taking the case of the c. of g. of the empty aircraft, we can say that

$$\frac{x}{167\cdot5} = \frac{42}{537}$$

which simplifies to $x = \dfrac{42 \times 167\cdot5}{537}$ or 13·1 inches (nearly).

You can check this result by multiplying the weight on the main wheels by x to get $495 \times 13\cdot1 = 6484\cdot5$ lb in which should be equal to the weight on the tail wheel times the distance between the main and tail wheels less x, or $42 \times (167\cdot5 - 13\cdot1) = 42 \times 154\cdot4 = 6484\cdot8$ which is near enough and straightforward Archimedes.

You may ask why is all this necessary? Why should the boffins in the C.A. or the F.A.A. want to know where the c. of g. lies?

Without going into the complexities of the Lift/Weight and Thrust/Drag couples, it is sufficient to say that they know, from the designer's plans and calculations deposited with them, the characteristics of your wing and exactly how the centre of lift moves slightly fore and aft according to the speed of the airflow over it and the angle of attack. They know from this the limits within which the centre of gravity may be positioned relative to the centre of lift so that the aircraft will always pitch down, and so remain under control, should the power be cut off or the wing be stalled.

A tail-heavy aircraft can be dangerous to fly and would not receive a permit. Now you will appreciate your inspector's concern to keep the weight down, especially aft.

If your work-sheet should reveal a tail-heavy condition it can be corrected by fixing ballast weights to the firewall. This will involve you in further Archimedian calculations but, more seriously, it will reduce your manoeuvering limits, so it is as well not to finish up with a tail-heavy aeroplane.

Before the aircraft can be flown it has to be registered with its national authority. I did this at quite an early stage, not appreciating how much work still lay ahead or how quickly and easily registration could be effected.

It had occurred to me that towards the end of the project I could be mighty busy and would not want to be held up by clerical work that could have been foreseen and done at leisure, so I wrote to the C.A.A. for the forms.

They came by return so I filled them in, attached my cheque for £5 and sent them back. Within the week I had my registration, G-BDAH; Golf Bravo Delta Alpha Hotel.

Now anything so bureaucratic as a registration is bound to be covered by statute in so far as size and type of lettering is concerned so I searched through all the books and papers that I had acquired but nowhere could I find the slightest reference to it.

In the end I rang up the C.A.A. who very long-sufferingly found and read out the regulation over the telephone. For the benefit of anyone else who may find himself in the same quandary here is the gist of 'Part B, Schedule 1'.

> Letters shall be Roman capitals and there shall be a hyphen between the G and the subsequent letters. The letters shall be painted on the underside of the left hand wing, equidistant between the leading and the trailing edges with the tops of the letters towards the leading edge.
>
> The letters shall also be painted on both sides of either the fuselage aft of the cockpit, or of the tail.
>
> Lettering on the wing shall be not less than 50 cm (19·685 ins) high, and on the fuselage not less than 30 cm (11·811 ins) high, or on the tail not less than 15 cm (5·906 ins) high.

There was a bit more to it than that of course but for the chap doing the work the above should be sufficient.

The inch dimensions should obviously be 20, 12 and 6 inches respectively but the metric dimensions enable one to make them just that little bit smaller and that can only be good. There are so many nice little aeroplanes disfigured by ungainly and ill-proportioned lettering.

But even though I kept the fuselage letters to the very least dimensions they still look disproportionately large. One wonders whether the C.A.A., who seem a pretty reasonable crowd, could not be persuaded in the interests of aestheticism to allow ultra-light aircraft to proportion the letters to the space available. Interestingly the F.A.A. in America have just authorised a reduction in the size of registration numbers on aircraft under their control.

Incidentally the cost of registration has now gone up from £5 to £12 for aircraft under 6000 lb (2703 kg) all up weight and the C.A.A. now charge a fee of £100 if you require a special combination of letters such as your own initials. It seems an excessive fine for a little harmless vanity, unless, of course, you equate vanity with pride which puts it among the seven deadly sins.

Now that you are getting near to flying you should fit yourself into the cockpit and make yourself as comfortable as you can.

I had a beautiful fitted cushion made by a local yacht yard that could be clipped in place so that it could not slip forward and jam the stick. I also fitted a seat -back to ensure that my feet would rest comfortably on the rudder pedals. If your legs are any shorter than mine you may have to fit blocks to the rudder pedals to ensure that you get the full movement.

If you have not already fitted it, now is the time to install your shoulder harness.

I have never understood how those ridiculous lap-straps came to be allowed in single-engined aircraft. I certainly would not like to face the prospect of a forced landing without the comfort of full shoulder restraint.

The F.A.A. in America recommends that each strap should be able to accept a load of 800 lb (363 kg) and this should adequately protect a person weighing 170 lb (77 kg) against a 9g acceleration, or should it be deceleration.

I made up my own harness out of 2 inch (50 mm) wide nylon webbing, said to be good for a 1600 lb (726 kg) static load. I punched in $\frac{1}{2}$ inch (13 mm) diameter brass eyelets at 4 inch (100 mm) centres and pinned them together with a $\frac{3}{8}$ inch (9·53 mm) coach bolt cut down to $1\frac{1}{4}$ inch (32 mm) length, the cut end ground round and an $\frac{1}{8}$ in (3·2 mm) hole drilled through it to take a spring steel safety pin. Just like the old Sutton Harness. I have heard it said that the Sutton Harness saved more lives than the parachute and I can well believe it.

It may be said that this type of harness does not allow enough freedom of movement, but our cockpits are so small that very little movement is required. With a cockpit that only comes up to one's waist it is very comforting to be firmly and solidly strapped in.

I have the bolt attached by a string through a $\frac{1}{8}$ in (3·2 mm) hole through the domed head to the top eyelet in the upper right hand strap.

I put the bolt, with the domed head against my chest, through the second hole in the upper right hand strap, which happens to be the highest comfortable position for me. I then attach the bottom left hand strap followed by the bottom right hand strap, both as tight as possible,

Basic Sutton Harness

and finally the upper left hand strap. The spring steel pin, attached by a string to the top eyelet of this upper left hand strap, is pushed through the hole in the end of the bolt to make all secure.

This used to be the official drill for securing Sutton harness in the R.A.F.

Harness locking pin and safety pin

154

Incidentally this, in the cause of weight saving, is the lightest possible harness. Most of my friends use a proprietary type with a locking box that weighs all of 4 lb (1·8 kg).

During the engine run you will have checked that the engine instruments, the tachometer and the oil pressure and temperature gauges, are working. The altimeter should be connected up to the pitot static line and you should have seen this working with the daily changes of barometric pressure.

The air speed indicator should be checked to make quite sure that the pressure and static sides are correctly connected, then get someone to blow *gently* into the pitot head and see that you get a reading on the instrument – a reading in the right sense.

If you have a venturi driven gyro instrument, such as a turn and slip indicator, the venturi should ideally be positioned within the arc of the propeller at two thirds of the distance from the centre of the hub to the tip. This is not easy to attain in a very small aeroplane. Mine should be 17·7 in (0·45 m) out from the centreline and is in fact only 13·3 in (0·34 m), or just half the distance out from hub to tip, but it seems to work quite well, perhaps because the starboard aft exhaust pipe blasts straight into it.

If the aircraft is in the garden it will probably not be convenient to swing the compass at this stage but, if you have not already done it, now is the time to make and fit a holder for your deviation card. I made mine out of scrap Makrolon polycarbonate sheet, the sections glued together with Araldite. Just to remind yourself that it has to be done, put a blank card in the holder.

You are legally required to have fixed in the cockpit a metal plate carrying the registration letters of the aircraft together with your name and address. A friend volunteered to make mine and a beautiful job it was, in brass $\frac{1}{8}$ in (3 mm) thick. It need not be as heavy as that.

Two other things you should carry are a fire-extinguisher and a first aid kit. Any car accessory shop will have a selection of fire extinguishers, so get the smallest and lightest one they have and fix it in the cockpit where it can easily be reached from outside. You will not, in any case, be able to use it in the air. If your aeroplane is on fire in the air you will have to turn off the petrol, open the throttle wide and side-slip like crazy to keep the flames away from the petrol tank and cockpit until you are on the ground. Then hop out taking the extinguisher with you.

I could find nothing laid down as to what the first aid kit should consist of, so I got a charming young lady member of St John's Ambulance Brigade to give me a list of what she considered essential and it comprises:

1 Triangular Bandage, 50 in × 36 in (1·27 m × 0·90 m)
5 Sterile Gauze Pads
1 Bandage, 2 in × 20 ft (50 mm × 6 m)

1 Tin of assorted First Aid Plasters
1 Large Safety Pin
1 Small pair Scissors

I put it all in a plastic food bag and attached it by a string to the underside of the spring inspection panel in the top of the aft fairing. I then painted a little red cross on top of the panel. I only hope that young lady is around if ever the first aid kit is needed for I doubt that I would know what to do with it.

Try to arrange a simple and secure stowage for your maps so that they are easily withdrawn and replaced. There are few things more unsettling than trying, in mid-air, to recover a map that has got itself under the seat – especially if you are getting lost and need it badly. We have all done it at some time or another.

I had noticed that all the other V.P.1s that had flown in the U.K. before mine had a trimming tab on the port aileron. I therefore made and fitted one bent to approximately the same angle as the others. This was a mistake as, in the event, it was not only unnecessary but gave me a heavy list to port on my first flight. It had to be removed.

Nonetheless, if I were again about to make a first flight, I would have an aileron trim tab made up and ready for fitting should it prove necessary. It is probable that some trim will be required if only to overcome the propeller torque and one could waste a whole day's flying if one had to go home and make one.

By now you should have the last of the construction stages signed out by your inspector in the little green constructor's log book.

The next move is to request from the P.F.A. a form of application for the issue of a Special Category Certificate of Airworthiness (Form 71/1/2).

When this is received you should complete it, have it countersigned by your inspector and return it to the P.F.A. office together with:

The Constructor's Log Book
The V.W. Engine Conversion Report if applicable
A Log of the Engine Running up to date
The Fuel Flow Test Record
The Work Sheet showing the weighing and c. of g. computations

These should all have been signed by your inspector who must by now be suffering from writer's cramp.

If all this paper work is in order you will receive by return a 'Permit to Fly' under 'A' Conditions and a Flight Test Schedule. The Schedule must be flown and the form completed and returned to the P.F.A. office before the Certificate of Airworthiness can be issued.

Curiously in all the papers I received there was no mention of what 'A' Conditions actually are. They are obviously defined in some statute, so knowing that ignorance of the law is no defence, I was about to ring up the

C.A.A. again when I remembered an article in *Popular Flying* that had something to say about it. Half an hour with my back numbers produced an article by John Pothecary in which he quotes from Air Navigation Order 1970. These 'A' Conditions are as follows:

1. The aircraft shall be either an aircraft in respect of which a certificate of airworthiness or validation has previously been in force under the provisions of the Order (ANO 1970) or an aircraft identical in design with an aircraft in respect of which such a certificate is or has been in force.
2. The aircraft shall fly only for the purpose of enabling it to:
    (a) qualify for the issue or renewal of a certificate of airworthiness or of the validation thereof or the approval of a modification of the aircraft, after an application has been made for such issue, renewal, validation or approval, as the case may be: or
    (b) proceed to or from a place at which any inspection, test or weighing of the aircraft is to take place for a purpose referred to in sub-paragraph (a).
3. The aircraft and its engines shall be certified as fit for flight by the holder of a licence as an aircraft maintenance engineer entitled in accordance with the provisions of Schedule 4 to this order so to certify, or by a person approved by the Board for the purpose of issuing certificates under this condition.
4. The aircraft shall carry the minimum flight crew specified in any certificate of airworthiness or validation which has previously been in force under this Order in respect of the aircraft, or is or has previously been in force in respect of any other aircraft of identical design.
5. The aircraft shall not carry any passengers or cargo except passengers performing duties in the aircraft in connection with the flight.
6. The aircraft shall not fly over any congested area of a city, town or settlement except to the extent that it is necessary to do so in order to take off from or land at a Government aerodrome in accordance with normal aviation practice.
7. Without prejudice to the provisions of Article 17(2) of this Order, the aircraft shall carry such flight crew as may be necessary to ensure the safety of the aircraft.

So much for 'A' Conditions. So far as our aircraft are concerned we may fly them to the place of test, we may fly them on test and we may fly them home again. We may fly only over open country and we may not carry passengers. It all seems pretty reasonable to me and I doubt that anyone would quarrel with any of it.

Mention of passengers reminds me that if yours is a two seater aircraft you will have to carry ballast in place of the passenger. Such ballast must be properly secured in position, a sand-bag held only by a lap strap will not do. Details of ballasting should be found in the building instructions for the aircraft, but if in doubt consult with your inspector and/or P.F.A. Engineering.

One final bit of paper-work before you fly concerns the insurance. The least that you may carry is third party liability for which the minimum is presently £100 000.

Insurance is one of the amateur builder's biggest operating costs, so it is advisable to go to one of the brokers specialising in aviation insurance.

To the amateur builder his aircraft is probably the most precious of his possessions and when he comes to insure it he is thinking not just of the market value of the machine but of the hundreds of hours of work that has gone into it. And so he is unlikely to stop at third party insurance but to want comprehensive cover as well. This is very expensive. A good broker will steer him into a 'home builder's clause' which can make his premium look rather more sensible.

The home builder's clause will read something like this:

'It is understood and agreed that in the event of any claims becoming payable under Section 1 hereof in respect of any repair to the aircraft or the replacement of any components, parts or accessories;

1. the liability of the Insurers shall be limited to the cost of any material, components, parts or accessories not made by the Insured himself when building the aircraft which are required for repairing the aircraft and the cost of transporting the aircraft from the scene of the accident to the Insured's workshop.

2. the Insured will be responsible for and will pay all costs and expenses in respect of the labour incurred in the repairing of the aircraft and the installing of components, parts and accessories.'

You are undertaking to repair the aircraft in the event of an accident in exactly the same way as you built it and I doubt if you would want to do anything else.

Chapter 9

First flight

It is said that there are old pilots and bold pilots, but no old, bold pilots. My sixtieth birthday occurred some six months before I flew 007 on her maiden flight and I had then been flying for some forty years so, in terms of the adage, that must make me a cringing coward.

However, after three years of work all directed towards this very moment, it was only in the few minutes taken to put on my overalls prior to the momentous swing start that I found myself wishing that I had stuck to stamp-collecting.

Then the engine caught and fired and we were in business and very busy.

I climbed into the cockpit, strapped in and tested the controls for full and free movement. Everything seemed to be free and moving in the right sense so I put the choke control to normal, opened up to 1800 rpm and tested the mags. All seemed well so I released the brakes and taxied out.

At the run-up point I went through the old drill:

T   Trim – fixed and nothing I could do about it now
M   Mixture – normal
P   Pitch – fixed
F   Fuel – Tank full and cock On
F   Flaps – none
G   Giros – only one and that would have to wait until we got some airspeed

There must be something I could do, so I re-set the altimeter microscopically to zero.

The brakes would not hold her against full power so I checked the mags at 2200 rpm and taxied onto the runway. I let her run straight for a little and then opened up to full bore.

She unstuck very quickly at an indicated 50 knots (58 mph, 93 km/h) and immediately there was a noticeable vibration.

'Oh, my God' I thought, 'Flutter'. So I landed straight ahead, turned off the runway and taxied back to the apron.

On the long drag back I thought it could not possibly be flutter because I had not felt it on the stick and anyway it could hardly happen at fifty knots. Could the engine bolts have worked loose?

159

I consulted with the experts who had gathered to watch me and eventually one of them, the youngest and brightest of us all, said 'It's got to be wheels. Try a touch of brake after take-off next time.'

So I taxied out and had another go.

This time the same vibration occurred but a touch of brake stopped it immediately and I climbed out at 60 knots (69 mph, 111 km/h) indicated.

She seemed to have far too much trim on the port aileron; I had copied the tab from the other V.P.1s that I had seen. Mike, my inspector, had been opposed to this from the start but I thought I knew better and now, as always, I was proved wrong. Bud Evans, the designer, had also queried it saying that very few of the many V.P.1s that he had seen required any aileron trim at all.

Apart from this minor defect which I had built into her myself, she flew impeccably. I took her up to 800 feet (240 m) and flew a gentle circuit at an indicated 65 knots (75 mph, 120 km/h) which seemed to require only 2500 rpm. I made a glide approach at 60 knots (69 mph, 111 km/h) indicated and put her down reasonably gently rather a long way up the runway. In view of the advice to keep a first flight to ten minutes only, I decided that this would have to do for the day.

The panel of experts had scrutinised my take-off with care and reported that there was visible fore and aft vibration of the undercarriage immediately after take-off, but it had damped out quickly, presumably when I had applied brake.

Next morning I reported all this to my engineering friends who promptly picked her up by one wing tip when it was seen that, as soon as the ground load was removed, the undercarriage leg moved inwards under the weight of the wheel and axle and the bracing wires went slack.

But I am getting ahead of myself in my eagerness to report that 007 is a veritable flying machine and not just groundworthy.

To backtrack a few weeks, I had filled in the application form for a Permit to Fly as soon as it arrived from the P.F.A. office, got Mike's final signatures and sent it off together with the constructor's record book and photostat copies of the weighing sheet and the fuel flow test record sheet.

At the same time I wrote to Air Chief Marshall Sir Thomas Prickett, who ran Goodwood, to ask if he would admit my non-radio aeroplane for test flying. So far as I can see there is no prohibition against doing one's test flying from a private strip, but never having done it before I felt that I would like to be as nearly into wind as possible with plenty of runway on which to land straight ahead if necessary or desirable.

Almost by return I received a Permit to Fly together with a 'Good Luck' message from John Walker of P.F.A. Engineering and a charming letter from Sir Thomas saying that I was welcome to use Goodwood out of hours.

I arranged some leave and rang A.T.C. at Goodwood to let them know I was coming. The next day, helped by a neighbour, I loaded 007 onto a friend's trailer.

We were having a beer before taking to the road when the local press arrived. God knows how they had got to hear of it and I am afraid that I was rather short with them in my hurry to be off. But they got a good picture of 007 folded up on the trailer with my neighbour, Basil, standing grinning beside her. He later got a rocket from his wife for horning in on the act – but he is much more photogenic than I am.

My wife, Sheila, came with me to help with the rigging and especially to recruit assistants for the heavy and difficult bits like offering up wings to the fuselage.

We rigged 007 on the grass under the shade of the trees. Sheila recruited two excellent assistants, one of them a very friendly German. I almost curled up with embarrassment when I heard Sheila blithely telling him that I had operated in Hurricanes, Spitfires and Mosquitos, and prayed he would not wonder how many of his countrymen I had accounted for.

However he did not seem to hold it against me and we soon had the rigging completed.

Mike had asked his friend, the Chief Ground Engineer, to do the final checks on rigging and controls. Bob Edwards called on us and suggested that we move 007 to the Maintenance Hangar so that he could give her the once over. In the event it was a twice and thrice over before Bob was satisfied.

Accordingly I started her up and, for the very first time, taxied her under her own power the few hundred yards to the hangar. I found her wonderfully easy to handle on the ground, far more so than the Piper Cub.

Bob found quite a lot in my rigging of which to disapprove and suggested that I leave her for the night and come back in the morning when he would show me what he required doing before he could sign her off.

His principal objection was to the rather sloppy fit of the $\frac{3}{8}$ inch (9·53 mm) diameter bolt in the eyebolts of the stabilator. This we packed out with washers and shims until all the slop had been taken out. He also found amusement in my unprofessional methods of doing up locking wire.

One way and another it was 4.30 p.m. before we were all signed up and I could taxi her over to the fuel point to take on 4 gallons (18 litres) of Avgas; which is where we came in.

I flew her again the next evening for thirty minutes to get the real feel of her. Without the trimming tab her aileron trim was near perfect – just a hint of starboard wing down. I found the hardest thing of all was to get the straight and level attitude correct. In this she reminded me very much of the Hurricane with its sloping nose which was not obvious to anyone but the pilot. Indeed, though it may sound ridiculous, her handling in the air had very much the feel of the Hurricane; even the glide approach to land brought back memories.

Perhaps it was because of this that I came in much too fast and went round again without touching down. The next approach was much better, a steady 60 knots (69 mph, 111 km/h) indicated all the way down to a quite reasonable landing even though, being flapless, she floated for an awful long way.

I lost the next two evenings flying as the engine got temperamental and would not start. Eventually we traced the trouble to over-priming. All part of the business of learning the tricks.

Before the next flight I replaced the trim tab but this time bent ever so slightly downwards. Now she flew straight and level with hands and feet off.

I took her up to 3500 feet (1070 m) to check the stall which occurred at 41 knots (47 mph, 76 km/h) indicated with a very gentle downward break and hint of roll to starboard. It was the gentlest stall I have ever encountered. She just nodded down with apparently plenty of aileron control. I got a more definite break by pulling the nose higher at the start, but the end result was the same.

I dislike spinning but at the same time I am not happy about flying an aircraft that I have not spun. It seemed to me that this was as good a time as any to try the spin so I pulled the nose up high, cut the throttle and, as she nodded into the stall I banged on right rudder. She wheeled over in a lovely stall turn and as the nose plunged down the speed built up and she went into what could only have been a spiral dive.

It was anything but comfortable and the sensation was not unlike a spin, but the airspeed was fluctuating between 40 knots (46 mph, 74 km/h) and 60 knots (69 mph, 111 km/h), and a speed of 20 knots (23 mph, 37 km/h) above the stall is no spin in my book.

On the second turn I thought she showed signs of inverting. Not fancying this at all, I brought her out. Recovery was immediate on centralising the rudder.

I tried again, to port, with a similar result and decided that I had frightened myself enough for one day. If I could not make her spin properly maybe she would not spin inadvertently, so I need worry myself about it no further.

I think this reluctance to spin probably derives from the very small amount of movement allowed to the rudder and stabilator. This effectively limits the amount of over-controlling by the pilot, which is the prime cause of inadvertent loss of control.

Add to this the great inherent stability of the aircraft and we have a very safe and docile little aeroplane. She will never win prizes for aerobatics but she will certainly look after her pilot.

So back to the circuit to practise a few landings. The trick, I discovered, was to keep the approach speed down to 55 knots (63 mph, 102 km/h) indicated, otherwise she would float for ever. On one approach at 60 knots (69 mph, 111 km/h) plus I rounded out just above the runway numbers and touched down at the mid runway turn-off point.

The next night was the occasion of the two hour endurance test. On the way up I checked the rate of climb from 500 feet (150 m) to 1500 feet (460 m) at an indicated 55 knots (63 mph, 102 km/h). I timed it to be 550 feet per minute (168 m/min), and with correction for a ground temperature of 77°F (25°C) this works out at 590 feet per minute (180 m/min) – not at all bad.

I levelled off at 2500 feet (760 m) and patrolled backwards and forwards from Ford to Shoreham. At 2750 rpm she was flying hands and feet off at an indicated 66 knots (76 mph, 122 km/h). A time check on four runs gave a true airspeed of 72 knots (83 mph, 133 km/h). Again not bad at all for an apparently aerodynamically dirty little aeroplane.

I was getting rather chilly sitting in a draught at 2500 feet (760 m) and I was getting bored with this bit of Sussex so I dropped down to 1500 feet (460 m) and went on a tour of Chichester Harbour, the bit of Hampshire where I was raised.

At 2500 rpm I seemed to be getting a steady cruise at 55 knots (63 mph, 102 km/h) indicated, but it was getting late and cold and 007 was getting low on fuel. I had to get back to the circuit.

We were approaching the minimum five hours after which the full test schedule could be flown. There were a number of minor adjustments to be made and the compass to be swung, so I got to the field early next day.

Bob Edwards had asked me whether I had balanced the wheels and I had confessed that I did not know I had to. He explained that there should be a mark on the tyre which should be lined up with a mark on the tube which would be somewhere near the valve.

I went and looked at the tyres and, sure enough, there was a red mark on each tyre but in each case it was nearly opposite the valve. Here was the cause of the vibration after take-off.

That afternoon I flew her for 45 minutes before I started the test schedule. I had to get in another four landings to complete the fifteen required. The first was pretty ropey but the rest came off reasonably well – and that vibration had disappeared.

I climbed away from the last touch-and-go into the timed climb through 500 feet (150 m) to 1500 feet (460 m). On up to 3000 feet (914 m) for the stalls, the sideslips and the maximum speed dive. All the way through she handled like the perfect lady that she is, and at last down to the whistling glide and a perfect landing.

I taxied in, switched off, picketed her, put on the covers and went home to fill in the test schedule form and get it in the post.

Regrettably I had to earn a living so it was a whole week before I was able to fly her again.

It was a blustery evening with a fair cross-wind component on the runway in use. I tried to get a calibration on the 2500 rpm cruise and got some very odd results, patrolling between Goodwood and Thorney Island.

It could have been the inconstancy of the wind or, on the other hand, a characteristic that the P.F.A. President, Air Commodore Chris Paul, noticed when flying Richard Husband's V.P.1. If after labouring along at an indicated airspeed of 55 knots (63 mph, 102 km/h) one just lowered the nose a little and allowed the speed to build to 60 knots (69 mph, 111 km/h) she would hold this higher speed when returned to straight and level.

With everything against me, a gusting cross wind, turbulence on the approach and a heck of a wind gradient I pulled off the best landing I have ever performed in this or any other aeroplane. I sat there for quite a few seconds waiting for the bump that never came. Very odd. For once I must have been giving proper attention to the business in hand instead of woolgathering as is my wont.

The following Friday the C. of A. arrived and I was free to fly cross-country to Jim Espin's strip at Popham where she was to be stationed, at least temporarily, but for various reasons it was the Sunday before I could make the trip.

The long hot summer had broken and the visibility was pretty marginal, indeed it was raining softly when I took off but the tower gave me cloud base at 6000 feet (1800 m) so I could see no reason why I should not go.

I climbed to my safety height and set course over Goodwood racecourse. Almost immediately the ground disappeared in heavy rain and I was on instruments with my very limited panel. To add to my discomfort it was excessively turbulent.

I told myself that this was the orographic effect on the seaward slope of the South Downs and it would clear before I reached Petersfield.

We are enjoined to fly only in V.M.C. (visual meteorological conditions), but in view of my assessment of the situation I preferred to carry straight on rather than attempt a 180° turn on my magnetic compass in heavy turbulence which could well disorient me.

Five minutes later I was reminding myself that I had not opened a book on meteorology for thirty years or more and maybe I had forgotten something, when trees and a winding road appeared below. There were a lot of cars on the road and where, I asked myself, would all those cars be going if it was not Petersfield.

The rain died out, the visibility improved a little and there, ahead, was the glint of the Petersfield lake dead on track.

Twenty two minutes after setting course I was over the snakes and ladders of the end of the M3 and there was Jim's strip, just where it should have been.

Never having landed there before I flew a couple of wide circuits making a careful inspection and then I came down for a low pass to reconnoitre the approach and the overshoot. Jim and the Stone brothers were out by the signals square waving madly as I went past ten feet (3 m) up. For a moment I wondered whether I was flying against the T. I pulled off a nice approach and landing and could have stopped in a third of the length of the strip, which was nice to know.

The Popham reception committee gave me a great welcome. As it was starting to rain again, they helped me to park 007 under the wing of a resident J3 Cub and put a temporary cover over the cockpit before we adjourned to the hangar for a cup of tea while we waited for Sheila to arrive from Goodwood with the covers and pickets.

It took her an hour and a half to make the journey by road that I had done in 22 minutes by air and I was imagining every kind of catastrophe that could have happened to her by the time she turned up.

And so, after three years of pleasurable work, 007 had made it into the air, and just what sort of an aeroplane she is is best shown by her performance figures:

	Indicated Air Speed (I.A.S.)			True Air Speed (T.A.S.)		
	knots	mph	km/h	knots	mph	km/h
Stall	41	47	76	43	50	80
Take-off	50	58	93	52	60	96
Climb	55	63	102	58	67	107
Cruise	66	76	122	73	84	135
Glide	55	63	102	58	67	107
Approach	50	58	93	52	60	96
V_{ne}	93	107	172	104	120	193

Rate of Climb	590 ft/min (180 m/min)
Fuel consumption	2·4 Imp. gallons/hour (10·9 litre/h)
Endurance	2·9 hours
Range in still air with	200 statute miles
30 mins reserve	(322 km)

Flying her is a quite delightful experience. She has the feel of a much larger, more powerful aircraft and yet she seems an extension of oneself in the way she responds without effort to one's every wish. And yet she is the simplest, most basic of all aeroplanes.

I suppose there is a paradox here, that her simplicity lies in the sophistication of her design.

So much for my own first flight in my V.P.1 and subsequent flight testing for the C. of A. Now let us take a more reflective and analytical view of the whole procedure.

For some weeks or months before the event you should have been studying the pilot's notes and any other flight reports you can get hold of such as those published in *Popular Flying*, *Sport Aviation* or *Les Cahiers du R.S.A.*

The pilot's notes will contain tables of speeds for the stall, with and without power, climb, cruise, glide and landing as well as the V_{ne} – the velocity never to be exceeded. These will be given as true air speeds and probably in miles per hour. If your air-speed indicator is calibrated in knots, as mine is, you will have to convert this data to suit your instrument.

There may also be a graph of true air speeds plotted against indicated air speeds for the prototype and possibly a table of cruise air speeds and power settings.

The air-speed indicator is bound to suffer from both instrument error and position error. These are unlikely to be the same as those on the aircraft for which the pilot's notes were compiled. It is also possible that you have neither the same engine nor the same propeller as the prototype so that your power settings and performance may very well differ from the original.

You can assume your stalling speed to be near enough that given for the prototype and you are stuck with the V_{ne}. All the other speeds, true and indicated, you will have to determine for yourself.

So before you can do much analytical air testing you will have to calibrate your air-speed indicator. On your first flight you will note the indicated air speed at which the aircraft unsticks, which is likely to be about 10 mph above the indicated stalling speed – at least on P.F.A. type aeroplanes.

Later on you have to check the indicated air speed at the stall, find the best climb and gliding speeds and determine the true air speed at several different indicated cruising speeds by making a number of runs as nearly as possible up and downwind over a predetermined base line between two prominent land marks about ten miles apart.

You should then have enough information on which to make a rough calibration graph of T.A.S. against I.A.S. from which to determine approximately, by extrapolation your indicated V_{ne}.

The graph which I finally obtained did not resemble the one in the pilot's notes at all. When I faired the line it came out near enough straight which was odd because an air compression graph, which is what we are plotting, should in theory be a parabola.

However, after nearly half a century of flying I have learnt not to be unduly surprised by my instruments so long as they are consistent in what they tell me. One can always blame the Reynolds Number as hardly anybody understands that.

Be that as it may, before we can start flying we must first find a place to fly from. As I have said before, I can find nothing laid down that says that one cannot make one's first flight from a private strip, but it is important, if one wants to check on whether an aircraft has a tendency to swing when the power is poured on, to make one's first fast taxi runs and take-off into wind. One also needs enough length to land straight ahead if necessary. This calls for a minimum run of 2600 ft (800 m).

166

Even if your private strip is long enough you may have to wait for days until the wind is in the right direction and if your leave is limited this can be frustrating.

It is therefore as well to come to an arrangement with your nearest licensed airfield which has a choice of three or more runways, preferably grass.

You will probably have to fly outside normal operating hours as I did, so mid-summer with plenty of daylight is the best time of year for it.

Before starting any test runs one *must* have an independent check on the flying control connections and have this signed for. Any such statutory check should be signed out as, in the event of an accident, the validity of one's insurance could otherwise be called into question. In my experience insurance companies will look for any loophole through which to wriggle out of their commitments. I suppose one cannot blame them; they are in business to make money out of us.

One should also carry out a thorough check on fuel filters, magneto points, tappets, security of engine control connections etc. Also, if you have not already done it, now is the time to change the oil after the running in period and flush the oil system through. It does not take long, an hour at the most, and the last thing one wants is to have an engine fail or even falter on one's first flight.

The next item is a full external check including, most importantly, tyre pressures. A big difference in tyre inflation could produce a swing on take-off that is not normal to the aircraft. Check that the pitot cover is off and the pitot head is undamaged and clear, and see that all control locks are removed.

Now you can get in, do up your harness, check the stick and rudder for full and free movement and, even though you may think it will not be required, see that you have a map – you never know, you might find yourself flying.

No doubt you have given some thought as to what you are going to wear on this occasion, even if it is only a pair of goggles and a flat cap back to front. I would suggest that by far the best clothing, at least for test flying, is a suit of 'surplus' R.A.F. overalls. They are designed to give you a smooth outline so that you will not get the stick up your trouser leg or snag the throttle with your sleeve. They also have useful built-in knee boards and lots of accessible pockets for spare pencils, chewing gum to relieve the dry mouth, folded maps in case you lose the circuit etc.

Unless one is testing a prototype there should be no need for a parachute. The services wear them all the time because they expect that one day they will have their aeroplanes shot off them. This is not likely to happen to civilian aircraft in peacetime, though I met a chap once who told me how, one winter afternoon when homing to his strip in bad weather, he found himself following a pheasant down a line of guns who put more pellets into his Luton than they ever put into the pheasant. I wonder if they would have entered him in the game book if they had shot him down.

After starting carry out the normal engine checks. See that the oil pressure is steady; the oil temperature will probably not be registering yet but keep glancing at it throughout the flight – and throughout all flights for that matter.

Check the mags at full throttle; the mag drop should not exceed $2\frac{1}{2}\%$ or 75 rpm at 3000 rpm. Check for a drop in revs when the hot-air control is exercised. If all is well, wave the chocks away and taxi out.

Check the brakes while taxying and at the same time check that your compass and turn-and-slip indicator respond to these turns. Thoroughly explore the ground handling, with and without brakes, at low taxying speeds. It should be possible to handle the aircraft on the ground, in still air conditions, without brakes at all just by the use of rudder and occasional bursts of engine.

If there is much of a cross wind the aircraft may show a tendency to weathercock into wind unless one uses the brakes to keep straight. This will be more pronounced with high-wing and biplane types than with low wing aircraft. But even if there is a fair amount of wind one can still get a good idea of the ground handling by taxying up-wind and swinging the nose from side to side.

By the time you get to the holding point for the runway you should have a fair idea of the aircraft's controllability on the ground.

The drill of 'vital actions' is apt to be somewhat restricted on an ultra-light with fixed trim, fixed-pitch airscrew and no flaps. It comes down to: Mixture – normal; Fuel – on and sufficient for the flight; Altimeter – set to QFE (or QNH on cross-country flights) and a mag test.

Wait for a green light from the tower if you are being controlled or, if not, take a good look round the circuit, a deep breath and turn onto the runway.

Let her run straight for a short distance and then open up firmly and smoothly to full power.

With a tail-wheel aircraft move the stick forward with the throttle to lift the tail as soon as possible. Only when the tail is up can you tell whether or not she has an appreciable tendency to swing.

In my experience a tendency to swing on take off is associated with large diameter propellers developing a lot of torque. The little tooth-pick airscrew on the usual Volkswagen installation could hardly be expected to produce a noticeable swing.

I think a lot of imaginary swings are caused by ruts and other irregularities in the ground, especially if the tail-wheel is not lifted quickly enough. I do not think my reactions are any faster than anyone else's but I have regularly failed to detect 'vicious' swings in aircraft which other people have reported as being prone to this vice. Indeed the only aircraft which impressed itself on my memory as being liable to swing on take-off was the Mosquito, which had two great big Merlins both turning in the same direction. As I recall one had to lead with the port throttle right up to the gate before starting to open the starboard one.

Except perhaps on prototypes, which I have never flown, I see little value in protracted fast taxi runs without leaving the ground. With a well proven design you will discover all you need to know about an aircraft's behaviour in this mode within two seconds of the tail coming up.

As the aircraft gathers speed it will need less and less forward pressure on the stick to keep the tail up and then, all of a sudden, your treasure will be flying. Be ready to note the speed at which this occurs and, if possible, the rpm. Don't worry too much about the latter as you can record it on any subsequent flight.

If you have any doubts about anything (an unusual vibration, noticeable heaviness on one wing, or excessive nose or tail-heaviness) land straight ahead, taxi back to the tarmac and have a good think about it before making any adjustments and having another go.

If all seems well climb out at about 10 mph (16 km/h) above the unstick speed. Climb steadily to 400 feet (120 m) before turning crosswind and continue the full throttle climb to at least 800 feet (240 m) before turning downwind.

Once the turn to the downwind leg is completed, level off and see how the speed builds up. You will probably get another 20 to 30 mph (32 to 48 km/h) above the climbing speed at full throttle, straight and level. Only then ease back the throttle to about three-quarters open and note the speed to which the aircraft settles down.

By now you will probably be too far downwind to start a normal approach to land, so fly crosswind to the dead side of the circuit and go all the way round again, feeling the trim in all three planes – rolling, pitching and yawing.

There should be no hurry to get down. Take all the time you want to get the feel of the aircraft and make notes of alterations required to the trim. Adjust the throttle to a smooth and comfortable straight and level flight. Note rpm, oil pressure and temperature.

Only when you are good and ready position yourself for the approach. I personally like to make glide approaches, having been brought up to this from an early age, but V.W. engines seem to prefer a trickle of power.

Use your first climbing speed for the glide approach. It will probably prove to be rather faster than the best gliding speed and may produce a somewhat protracted float in ground effect, so that you will have to sit there and wait for her to settle down, using a lot of runway.

If you have not previously flown an ultra-light you will probably find the controls, especially in the pitching plane, unusually sensitive. This may cause you to 'balloon' in the final stages of your first flare-out, so, if you are the least bit unsure about making a good landing, pour on the power and go round again. It is all useful experience on the new type.

Once you have landed from your first flight put the aeroplane to bed and go away to study your notes and reflect on what you have learnt. And you should have learnt a great deal.

You should have recorded the unstick speed and rpm. The climbing speed you have used will probably be higher than the best climbing speed for the type and so, of course, will the rpm, so these particular readings are not yet of much significance. You will also have recorded the maximum straight and level full power indicated speed and rpm, and the cruising indicated speed and rpm. Both of these will be of great use in your deliberations and on future flights.

You do not yet have enough information to do an accurate calibration of your air-speed indicator but with a bit of intelligent guessing we can get some idea of how it is performing.

If we make a trial assumption of the unstick speed as being 10 mph (16 km/h) above the indicated stalling speed, which will be near enough for most P.F.A. type aircraft, and assume that the true airspeed at the stall and maximum straight and level are the same as on the prototype, then we have approximate indicated and true airspeeds for both ends of the speed range. If we then plot these on a graph and draw a straight line between the points so obtained we will have a rough approximation for the airspeed corrections and can make a good estimate of the best climb and glide speeds. These figures will be useful for the next flight and can be up-dated as more information comes in during the subsequent test flying.

Let us assume, for illustrative purposes, that the indicated unstick speed was 60 mph and guess from this that the indicated stalling speed would be 50 mph. Suppose, too that the maximum straight and level indication was 85 mph. If the true airspeeds for the prototype were given as stall 45 mph and maximum straight and level 90 mph our graph would look something like this:

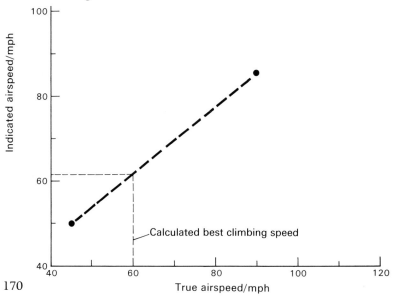

Now Norman Macmillan, writing about aeroplanes not dissimilar to ours in *The Art of Flying* published back in 1928, gives the best climbing speed as the stalling speed plus a third of the speed range. Our imaginary aircraft has a true stalling speed of 45 mph and a true maximum straight and level speed of 90 mph so our speed range is 45 mph. Our best true climbing speed will therefore be 45 plus 45/3 which equals 60 mph T.A.S. From our graph we see that our air-speed indicator should show 61·5 mph.

If we apply the same rule to the indicated air speeds we arrive at a climbing indication of 61·6 mph.

If we go on to assume that the line should be parabolic rather than straight, as we have drawn it, we could guess that a T.A.S. of 60 mph would give an I.A.S. of about 59 mph so let us stand on 60 mph as our climbing speed until we can definitely establish it in climbing tests.

The other essential information you will have gleaned is the state of trim. You can estimate what adjustments may have to be made before you fly again.

A very thorough inspection of the airframe is advisable after the first flight. Up to the first take-off the airframe has been loaded, generally statically, only in the landing mode. Now, for the first time, it has been subjected to dynamic loading in the flying mode – the opposite sense to when it is on the ground. Flying struts that were in tension on the ground have now been subjected to compression – or vice versa in the case of a high wing type. Similarly the loading on the main spars and all other parts of the aircraft has been reversed. Anything that can possibly work loose will have been thoroughly shaken and will show up now.

Go round with a spanner, make any adjustments to the trim that may be required and carry out the normal daily inspection before flight.

The next flight should be a gentle excursion to check the trim. Only when this is satisfactory should you carry on to check the stalling speed and flight characteristics at the stall.

Climb up above 4000 feet (1200 m), check your harness and engine instruments, take a good look round and underneath (the normal HASEL check) and then, with flaps up if you have flaps, throttle back and glide, gradually reducing speed until the aircraft stalls. Record any stall warning such as a buffet and the speed at which it occurs, the speed at the stall and the aircraft's behaviour such as a wing drop.

My V.P.1 would not show a stall like this and just mushed gently downwards with the stick hard back. I could only get a definite break by pulling the nose well above the horizon.

If the aircraft shows any signs of an incipient spin off the stall, which is not exactly rare, be ready to catch it with opposite rudder and the stick eased forward.

I deliberately spun my V.P.1 and only discovered afterwards that this manoeuvre is prohibited because the type has not yet been cleared for spinning in the U.K.

Spinning is not part of the Flight Test Schedule so I suppose that it did not occur to anyone in authority to tell me not to do it. I only knew that the aircraft had been spun in the U.S.A. and put through positive 'g' aerobatics (loops, barrel rolls and stall turns) and I had gone so far as to mention this on the application form for a Special Category C. of A. So, if you want to perform any unusual manoeuvres in your home-built aeroplane, first check with your national authority that they are permitted. Personally I would have been quite relieved to have been told I must not do it.

However, as a service trained pilot, I did not regard spinning as a particularly unusual manoeuvre since it is a regularly practiced exercise at all stages of service training.

I never liked spinning. It is an uncomfortable experience and I once had a nasty fright when spinning a Harvard Mark 1, an AT-6 to our American cousins.

I put it into a spin at 6000 feet (1800 m) and took normal recovery action after a couple of turns – and nothing happened. She went right on spinning. With full opposite rudder I tried rocking the stick and bursts of engine, all to no avail. Passing through 2000 feet (600 m) I decided it was time to go, released my straps and was half way out over the side when she straightened herself out of her own accord. I got back in and eased her out of the dive at little more than tree top height. So the way to get a Harvard Mk. 1 out of a spin is to lean right out over the side.

As a result of this experience I have an almost morbid interest in how any aircraft that I may have to fly will recover from a spin. I am truly sorry if, inadvertently, I broke the rules on this occasion, but I am much happier in my own mind knowing that a V.P.1 is very reluctant to spin – just as reluctant as I am – and will snap out of it with the minimum of corrective action.

Perhaps I should add that without the assurance of the favourable report in Bill Beatty's *Flying the Evans V.P.s* on the type's spinning characteristics I would never have attempted a spin without wearing a parachute. I am not a bold pilot.

Having established the stalling speed we can make some runs to calibrate the air-speed indicator (A.S.I.) at various throttle settings.

Pick out two easily recognised points about 10 miles (16 km) apart on your map and, as nearly as possible, up and down-wind. For one set of readings I used the road roundabout just south of Shoreham Airport and the intersection of the runways of Ford airfield and made two runs in each direction at a normal cruising setting of 2750 rpm.

I had problems getting a consistent calibration at 2500 rpm as mentioned before. I even once recorded a better ground speed upwind than on the previous downwind run and this played havoc with my averages.

By now we should have an accurate record of the indicated stalling speed and a knowledge of the cruising regime so we can up-date our airspeed calibration graph with accurate figures for the stall and cruising speeds. We can also check our best climbing speed, predicted by Macmillan's formula, by making a number of trial climbs at full throttle and varying speeds.

These trial climbs are made against the stop-watch by taking the time to climb from 500 feet (152 m) to 1500 feet (457 m). The results you obtain will have to be corrected for temperature for purpose of comparison.

John Pothecary's simple rule is to add 4 feet per minute (1·2 m/min) for every 1°C above 15°C ground temperature and deduct 4 feet per minute (1·2 m/min) for every 1°C below 15°C ground temperature. Suppose we take two minutes to climb from 500 feet (152 m) to 1500 feet (457 m), this would be a climb rate of 500 feet per minute (152 m/min). If the ground temperature were 20°C, then the corrected rate of climb would be 520 feet per minute (158 m/min). But if the ground temperature were only 5°C for the same recorded rate of climb of 500 feet per minute (152 m/min), the corrected rate would be 460 feet per minute (140 m/min).

If you do all your trial climbs under the same conditions you need not correct the results in order to find your best climbing speed, but if they are done on different days then they must be corrected for temperature in order to get a true comparison. In any case it is as well to know exactly what your best rate of climb amounts to.

Before we can fly the full test schedule we must complete 5 hours flying which may include the mandatory flight of at least two hours duration. We must also make 15 satisfactory landings.

The immortal Pilot Officer Prune used to claim that a good landing was one you could walk away from. Be that as it may we all know that the start of a good landing is a well set up approach. It is very difficult to make a good landing off a bad approach. Tim White in *England Have My Bones* tells how he once pulled off a 'greaser' from an appalling approach and heard his instructor mutter through the Gosports 'That one was born in the vestry'.

I found that my best approach speed was the same as my best climbing speed. This is often the case, so I would start investigating the approach and landing by setting up this speed at the start of the glide and holding it right down to the flare out.

One of our worst problems is coping with turbulence and wind shear on the approach. Our little aircraft are far more affected by these phenomena than are the heavier 'Spam cans' on which most young pilots are trained and this sensitivity comes as quite a surprise to most home-builders on their early flights. I recall once approaching to land at Hurn in near gale conditions when suddenly, at 200 feet (60 m) on finals, my airspeed almost disappeared and I had to give full throttle to restore my approach speed. At the same time the turbulence rolled me sharply through 50°. It is not often as bad as that but we do, always, have to be rather more alert when approaching to land than do pilots of more conventional machines.

So a good approach is one on which we manage to hold our glide straight and our speed steady in spite of all that wind shear and turbulence can do to us.

We need to investigate normal powered and glide approaches and, particularly if we are going to be based on a private strip, the powerd precautionary slow approach and short landing.

As we gain more of the confidence which comes with experience of the type we can investigate the behaviour of the aircraft in cross-winds, both taking off and landing. High wing and biplane types are inclined to be more capricious under these conditions than low-wing aircraft. My little low-wing V.P.1 is relatively easy to handle in a cross wind. I once returned to my narrow, rough and sloping strip after a week-end away to find a full gale blowing at $70°$ to the runway. It took me four attempts to get down, but once I had gauged the drift correctly she sat down quite delicately from a prolonged side-slip and handled as easily on the ground as if there was hardly any wind at all.

Our little aeroplanes are probably just as robust as the club and school machines in which we learnt to fly, but after all that work they are much more precious, so it is probably unnecessary for me to advise you to have no false pride about going round again if you have the slightest doubt about making a good landing.

When visiting a strange strip I never attempt to land without first making a low pass off a trial approach in order to reconnoitre for obstacles such as farm power lines on the approach, the state of the strip and the wind effect, and for any obstacles on the overshoot. Only then do I make an approach with the firm intention of landing. Perhaps I am unduly cautious, but the thought of another three years work appalls me.

Before we start on the two hour endurance flight we must, if we have not already done it, swing the compass. We should also ensure that the tank is filled right up since this will be our first chance to check on the fuel consumption at cruising revs. We must also remember our maps.

A two hour flight to nowhere in particular is a good opportunity to do A.S.I. calibrations and this should keep you amused for at least an hour. It will also impress upon you the importance of a comfortable, thick, cushion and, if it is at all chilly, the need for good windproof clothing.

By far the best sort of clothing for open cockpit flying is the old R.A.F. Sidcot suit, designed by Sidney Cotton of photographic reconnaissance fame, but they seem hard to get in this day and age. Surplus Store R.A.F. overalls are fine as overalls but they contribute little in the way of warmth.

Silk next the skin is always a good start. The R.A.F. used to provide its pilots with beautiful silk gloves to wear inside the fleece lined leather gauntlets and every fighter pilot had his square of parachute silk to wear as a scarf. This was not, as the Bomber Barons and some others supposed, a dash of glamour-boy mystique such as leaving the top tunic button undone (Pilot Officer Prune was reported to have said 'I don't have a top button. It was shot off.') but served a very real purpose in saving the neck from chafe through rubber-necking for Germans on one's tail and it kept one's neck beautifully warm.

When I went back to open cockpit flying I dug out my old leather helmet and there, inside, were my old silk gloves and parachute silk scarf.

We do not fly high so that our feet should not get cold, especially if we wear pure woollen socks as we should since, in the event of a fire, melting acrylic socks can give one a very nasty second degree burn. And so it is only the hands and upper part of the body that need special attention.

I wear an overall and silk scarf and, in cold weather, a Morgan 'Channel' sailing jacket and silk gloves. I find that I keep very comfortably warm.

With five hours flying and fifteen landings behind us we can proceed to fly the 'Flight Test Schedule'.

The aircraft must first be loaded to maximum all-up weight and the c. of g. recorded. This means another weighing session with the tail jacked up in the flying attitude.

You have to certify that you have the Permit to Fly in your pocket together with a valid third party insurance certificate and that the aircraft has shoulder harness installed.

The ground checks consist of:

(a) Flying and trimming controls for backlash, friction and correct functioning.
(b) Instruments for correct functioning. Set altimeter to 1013 mb and record outside air temperature. (The International Standard Atmosphere at sea level has a pressure of 1013·25 mb (14·70 psi, 101·33 KPa) and a temperature of 15°C.)
(c) All controls, including engine controls, for correct functioning.
(d) Run engine up to full throttle and record outside air temperature, rpm at run-up, magneto drop, oil pressure and oil temperature.

During taxying the undercarriage must be checked for ease of ground manoeuvering and freedom from binding. Brakes (if fitted) should be checked for satisfactory functioning.

The take-off is to be made with full power and flaps (if fitted) at take-off position. As soon as possible after unstick record the unstick speed, the engine rpm, the oil pressure, the oil temperature and any unusual handling or functioning characteristics on the take-off.

For the purpose of checking the rate of climb, the time taken from 500 feet (152 m) to 1500 feet (457 m) should be recorded. Before commencing each climb the airspeed should be allowed to settle to the appropriate climbing speed. Power should then be increased gradually to maximum climbing power (full throttle for normally aspirated engines) and the aircraft eased into the climb, endeavouring to maintain climbing speed. Care must be taken to ensure that the aircraft has settled in the climb and the airspeed should be kept within plus or minus 3 mph (5 km/h). The climb should not be carried out near cloud or turbulent air and a steady heading should be maintained.

For the stalling check the aircraft should be trimmed to a speed approximately 40% above stalling speed, which I took to represent the gliding attitude, and the aircraft should be stalled by pulling the control column gently back so as to reduce the speed at a rate not exceeding 1 mph per second (1·6 km/h/s) until the aircraft stalls. Record the stalling speed with power off and flaps up, the natural buffet speed, the behaviour at the stall and the degree and order of nose or wing drop and any abnormal characteristics during stall or recovery.

Lateral and directional stability are checked at normal approach speed, power off with full flap if fitted. Medium rudder sideslips are to be carried out to port and starboard. The aileron and rudder controls are then to be released in turn and the ability for the down wing to rise and the nose to swing into the turn are to be checked respectively. The test is then to be repeated with the engine at full power.

The maximum speed test is to be made in smooth air conditions. The aircraft is to be dived at one-third throttle to its maximum permissible speed, V_{ne}. Check any unusual behaviour of the aircraft and whether control forces appear normal and whether or not there is a degree of self-centering to small movements.

For a simulated baulked landing set the aircraft in the approach configuration and note the behaviour in a simulated overshoot. Record the engine rpm, the oil pressure, trim changes and throttle response.

When you have done all this you can fill in the form, send it away and wait for the Certificate of Airworthiness to come back.

If one lacks time on ultra-lights and especially if one has experience only of tricycle undercarriages but has built a tail-wheel type, one would be wise to get a pilot, experienced in ultra-lights to do one's test flying for one.

Unfortunately, as Flecker noted in *The Golden Road*, 'It was ever thus. Men are unwise and curiously planned.' Few people who have spent years building an aeroplane are going to forego the esoteric thrill of flying their own creation for the first time. I'll be damned if I would.

So, if you have built a tail-wheel type – and most ultra-lights are of tail-wheel configuration – try to get in some tail-wheel time on something as small as possible, like a Piper Cub or a Condor.

When you come to fly your own aircraft the first thing you will notice is the sensitivity of the controls, especially in the pitching plane, and it may take you two or three circuits without landing to get used to this.

Just do not rush things. Take it easy and relax and you will suddenly find that you are enjoying flying more than you have ever done before.

Chapter 10

Free to fly

Long before reaching the flying stage we should have thought seriously about how we proposed to operate our aircraft, about a place to hangar it and from which to fly it.

It is always advisable to keep any aircraft under cover; this is particularly important with wood and fabric aeroplanes. Picketing out in the open for a night or two in summer is all very well, but any longer in the wind and the rain does not do an airframe much good.

So our first thought must be for hangarage. This can be a problem even at the best of licensed airfields. Perhaps I should have said especially at the best of licensed airfields, because the best are run by the nicest and most efficient people and everybody wants to fly from them so that their hangars are bursting at the seams in spite of the high cost of hangarage at any such formal establishment.

If you wish to fly regularly from a licensed airfield they will probably insist that you have radio. This represents an additional load on the aircraft and may well cost half as much as the aeroplane itself.

No one would be so foolish as to deny the real value of radio aids, but they are only aids and by no means essential to the art of flight. Indeed I would go so far as to suggest that they are of far greater assistance to the aerodrome operator than they are to the pilot, although there are today many pilots who rely on radio aids almost to the exclusion of a good look-out, map-reading and normal good airmanship. This is to be deplored.

I never for one moment intended to install radio in my V.P.1. Apart from the weight and the cost, neither of which could I afford, part of the fun of our sort of flying comes from relying on our own map-reading and airmanship to get ourselves safely from A to B.

So, having no radio, we may have no option but to fly from a private strip.

Practically all owners of private strips are farmers – I know of none who is not. They nearly all operate under the 28 day rule which says that if the strip is not active for more than 28 days in the year no planning permission is necessary.

Farmers have to be good neighbours and so, by extension, do their guests. This includes trying to avoid annoying the owners of adjacent properties by flying low over their roof-tops. On the strip that I fly from we try not to fly at week-ends and make all our circuits over forest land to the north of the strip.

Strip owners are therefore understandably coy about who they will admit to their hangars and are unlikely to accept a stranger without the strongest recommendation from someone they can trust as to his good sense and good airmanship.

There are plenty of strips dotted around the country. The problem is to get established on one.

Most farm strips are rough and narrow and some are none too long. Being free of crops, apart from hay, they tend to be used as tractor roads or even as headlands on which the ploughs are turned. So large soft balloon tyres are a great help in negotiating them.

Most farmers seem to prefer the rugged Cessna 172 with its barn door flaps for their personal air transport and drive it like a tractor. However if a 172 can get in and out of the strip it will do for most ultra-lights, though aircraft with small and relatively hard wheels may have problems with ruts and the long grass which is prevalent at haying time.

Until I had actually flown my aeroplane I found it very hard to get wind of any strips at all. I have a feeling that nobody takes the home-builder seriously until he is actually airborne. Only then will people start dropping hints to the effect that if one gives old Tom a ring he may be able to fit you in.

Down on the Farm. V.P.1 and Falconar F11, *Ken Burtt*

It is quite astonishing to see the number of wind-socks that are displayed on lonely farms and the number of sheds away out in the country with, projecting from them, raked rudders that cannot quite be concealed. The farmers, God bless them, must be the hard core of private flying, at least in Britain.

Probably the best way to find a strip is to try the P.F.A. grapevine. This will always, in time, produce something though it may not be just where you want it, convenient to your home and outside controlled airspace. If this does not produce the results you want you should decide on the area from which you would like to fly and then make enquiries over a drink or two in the local pubs.

Having found a strip and agreed terms for hangarage with the owner it is as well to reconnoitre it on foot before flying in. Ask about any local restrictions in the way of areas to be avoided, power lines on the approach and whether or not stock will be grazed on the strip. Sheep are quite compatible with aeroplanes but cattle are not; they seem to like the taste of dope and can soon reduce an aeroplane to a tattered skeleton.

If the strip runs through two or more fields the gaps in the hedges may sometimes be closed with an electric wire fence if cattle are to be grazed in one of the fields.

A friend of mine once returned to his strip after a week away and, failing to see the electric wire across the gap, hooked it with his tail wheel and arrested himself. This sudden arrival dropped him rather hard from about four feet up and spread his undercarriage. I wish I had seen it, it must have been hilarious. He was lucky not to have caught the wire with his main wheels – that could have been fatal and quite un-funny.

So, whenever you fly away from the strip for a day or two, always make a low pass and have a good look before landing back.

Another minor hazard is bird strikes. Many farmers raise pheasants and partridges for shooting and the young birds seem to prefer the open strip to the cover of the crops on either side. They will generally scuttle out of the way when you are taking off at full throttle. But they often do not seem to notice an aircraft landing until it is right on top of them when they will fly straight up into the propeller or the leading edge of the wing and one lands in a cloud of feathers.

One chap I know records his bird strikes with pictograms of little supine birds along the side of his cockpit just as some fighter pilots recorded their victories with swastikas.

Bird strikes of this nature do not seem to damage the aircraft at all, the speed being only some 40 mph (64 km/h) at impact; at least I have never suffered damage from this cause in spite of hitting several birds both with the propeller and the leading edge of the wing.

Once you are settled on your strip, devote some days just to flying around noting the principal land marks and the bearing of the strip from each of them. It may be easy enough to find the strip in good weather but it can become very elusive when thick haze builds up or when you are forced down low by cloud and rain.

So get to know your own area from the air for about ten miles (16 km) around. One day you may be short of fuel after a long trip and unable to afford the time for a square search looking for your landing ground.

Map reading navigation is of prime importance to the ultra-light pilot even if he has a radio since all the radio aids there are will not help you to find a friend's private strip three counties away if you cannot locate yourself accurately on the map.

As one who learnt to fly before the days of radio and electronic aids I have always preferred to map-read my way around the country and even when I have the aids available I only turn them on when it is absolutely essential to go onto instruments.

I suffer from an inbred mistrust of black boxes or anything electrical engendered by a lifetime of working with electrical engineers. They can spend months or years designing, checking and erecting huge installations, but when the moment comes to pull the switch and set everything in motion the looks of amazement that invariably appear upon their faces when the thing works I find deeply disturbing.

I suppose that most young pilots today are brought up on V.O.R., D.M.E., Radio Compasses and all the other new-fangled gadgetry. This must be why, at two recent rallies, young men have looked at my very modest array of instruments in my non-radio home-built and have asked how on earth I found my way there. It would seem therefore that a few words on how it is done would not come amiss.

The three basic instruments of pilot navigation are the compass, the airspeed indicator and the watch.

Start by swinging your compass. This is not difficult; indeed it cannot be or the R.A.F. would not have required pilots to do it. It was not a popular chore and was traditionally performed by the sprog – the latest joined pilot. Once upon a time, by dint of pulling every string I could lay my hands upon, I succeeded in wangling a posting to what was acknowledged to be the best photo reconnaissance squadron in the R.A.F. What I had not bargained for was the fact that, because it was so very professional and an incredibly happy outfit, we did not lose pilots or aircraft on operations and when pilots were nearing the end of a tour they invariably applied for another one. This left me swinging an average of two compasses a day for the best part of two months. By the end of that time I could swing a Spitfire in ten minutes flat.

There are three coefficients that affect the compass and must be corrected for.

Coefficient A arises from misalignment of the compass in the aircraft. If, at the end of the swing, you find a constant error of the same sign on all headings this is coefficient A. It is removed by loosening the fixing screws, turning the compass the required amount and re-tightening the screws.

Coefficients B and C are slightly more abstruse and are caused by fixed magnetic material in the aircraft – the engine, the roll-over bar etc.

Coefficient B covers deviations on east and west headings and coefficient C deals with those on north and south headings.

The old standard corrector boxes had the hole for the corrector key in the fore and aft plane for coefficient B and in the athwartships plane for coefficient C. We remembered them by B for British fore and aft and C for Chinese athwartships. My present compass, an E2A, has both holes fore and aft and labelled B and C. Some Air Ministry boffin must have discovered that the rumour about the Chinese was quite without foundation. Possibly a case of 'personal reconnaisance is never wasted' as we are told in the Field Service Pocket Book.

As you are unlikely to have access to a concrete compass base with the cardinal points painted upon it you will have to make do with a landing compass. I have no idea why it is called this; the Navy calls it a hand-bearing compass. An Army prismatic marching compass will do just as well.

First empty your pockets of all magnetic material, keys, penknife etc and, if you have a steel buckle on your belt, remove the belt and keep your trousers up with your tie.

Wheel the aircraft out to a level site, well away from hangars or other steel built buildings, and point it north. Check this with the landing compass by standing about thirty feet (10 m) behind it and sighting down the centre-line of the aircraft. Note the aircraft compass reading. Now turn the aircraft to point east by the landing compass and again note the aircraft compass reading. Do remember to leave the landing compass well away whenever you go to check the reading of the aircraft compass or you will get some funny results.

Now turn the aircraft onto south and this is where you start work. Note the aircraft compass reading.

Now let us assume that when the aircraft was heading north the compass read 006° and now that it is heading south it reads 184°. You have recorded deviations of +6° and +4° so that the algebraic difference between south and north is +2°. Divide this by 2 and you have found that coefficient C equals 1°. Put your corrector key in the hole marked 'C' and gently twist it until the compass reads 183°.

Now turn the aircraft onto west. Let us suppose that when it was heading east it read 098° and on west it reads 260° so that you have recorded deviations of +8° and −10°. The algebraic difference of these is +18° (Come, come, surely you have not forgotten the business of 'change the sign of the bottom line and add'). Divide this by 2 and you have found coefficient B equal to 9°, so insert the key in the hole marked 'B' and gently turn it until the compass reads 269°.

Now you have done all the brain work and it did not hurt at all. Did it? Now all that remains to be done is to do a check swing, calculate and take out coefficient A if you must, and prepare the deviation card. Put the aircraft on each of the cardinal and quadrantal headings, noting the compass reading and deviation on each. Your work sheet should look like this:

Course (M)	Compass	Deviation	Coefficient A	Residual Deviation
360	005	+5	−1	+4
045	047	+2	−1	+1
090	089	−1	−1	−2
135	136	+1	−1	0
180	183	+3	−1	+2
225	225	0	−1	−1
270	269	−1	−1	−2
315	318	+3	−1	+2
	Total = +12			

$$\text{Coefficient A} = \frac{12}{8} = 1\tfrac{1}{2}, \ = 1° \text{ say}$$

I know of at least four ways of presenting a deviation card. Only remember that you have very little room to spare on your instrument panel where it will have to go and make it as small as possible. My own measures 2 in × $1\frac{1}{2}$ in (50 mm × 38 mm) and fits into a perspex holder. For this swing it would read:

For	Steer
N	004
045	046
090	088
135	135
180	182
225	224
270	268
315	317

Write it out neatly and clearly in Indian ink on a piece of stiff card and keep a copy in your 'nav. bag' for use when making out your flight plan.

The above swing would be a pretty satisfactory one and the deviations could almost be ignored except on north. My own compass has deviations of up to 10° due to being fixed to the underside of the roll-over bar and my deviation card is of the utmost importance to me.

One swing will probably last for a whole season, but do check your compass from time to time by flying your aircraft on known bearings between points that you have marked on your map just to see that the compass reads what you think it should.

Remember too that electrical storms or even flying near large cumulus clouds can upset an aircraft's permanent magnetism to an alarming extent so that a check swing is advisable after any such phenomena. I remember a glorious spring day in the eastern Mediterranean flying between ranks of towering cumuli and watching my compass needle swinging to point to each cloud in turn as I passed it by. After a quarter of an hour of this my compass was useless and I had to carry on by guessing the precession on my gyro direction indicator and re-setting it every twenty minutes or so until I got home. That particular aircraft had to be swung every day for a fortnight until it settled down again.

Almost as important as the compass is the air-speed indicator (A.S.I.). Nearly all A.S.I.s suffer from position errors and one cannot accept them at their face value. Mine reads 66 knots for a true air speed of 72 knots. So calibrate your A.S.I.

Pick a couple of easily identifiable features about 10 miles (16 km) apart on the map and approximately up and downwind. Choose a reasonably quiet day and make at least four runs between them, two each way, timing each run. It is important to maintain a steady height and air speed with the engine set at cruising speed. Average the times and so obtain your true air speed at cruising revs.

It pays to have the best watch you can possibly afford, with a full sweep second hand and a large, clean and easily read face. You will not need the date as you are not likely to fly into tomorrow. I strap mine over my overall cuff with the watch on the inside of my wrist. Thus I do not have to wave my arm around in order to read it in my very confined cockpit.

We are now ready to start navigating. Most of it must be done on the ground before ever we take off.

There are two scales of map in general use, the 1:250 000 and the 1:500 000. I carry and mark up both maps but prefer to use the 1:250 000 as it has much more detail. This is a purely personal preference and I have a good friend who travels widely in a Currie Wot and uses only the 1:500 000 for the very reason that it has less detail to confuse him. There is a lot to be said for this argument, but I still prefer the 1:250 000 scale.

I use a plastic scale rule with statute and nautical miles to both these scales, and a Douglas protractor. For our sort of flying a Dalton computer is not necessary.

Because of Terminal Control Areas, Military Air Traffic Zones, Danger Areas etc. you will seldom be able to fly directly to your destination, so study your maps and pick out easily identifiable turning points. I find that airfields, even long disused ones, are among the best landmarks. Large towns are easily recognised but as one should try to avoid overflying them it is not easy to get a precise time check from a recognisable spot within them, such as a railway shunting yard.

On my last trip to Sywell I turned on Booker and Wing. I could have gone directly from Booker to Sywell but, by deviating slightly to Wing, I got an intermediate time check and it set me up for another check where my track crossed the M1 at a distinctive point.

Draw your track lines on the map and a use a good thick coloured pencil which can be easily read in the air. Calculate how far you will fly in five minutes at cruising speed in still air. In my case it is six nautical miles (7 statute miles, 11 km). Mark off your track lines in five minute intervals restarting at each turning point.

Now, from your starting point and from each turning point draw lines at five degrees and ten degrees on either side of your track. These are your drift lines. They should be drawn lighter than the track lines and preferably in a different colour so that there is no risk of confusion.

Like most of us I fly from a farm strip which has no telephone and is forty minutes drive from my home. This means that a forecast wind is hopelessly out of date by the time I get airborne.

The slower you fly the more the wind affects you. This is our biggest problem since very few of us fly at all quickly. I have never placed a great deal of trust in the forecast wind, even when I could get one, and have always preferred to find the wind effect for myself in the air.

The psalmist knew a thing or two when he sang of the inconstancy of the wind that 'bloweth where it listeth'. I am not suggesting that you should fly a 'three drift wind' or anything complex like that, just estimate your drift from your drift lines and correct for it. And so when making out our flight plan on the ground we take no account of the wind.

You will need a knee pad, preferably with a block of printed forms on it. The 'Airtour' or 'A.S.A.' knee pad and flight log will do very well, but you can quite easily make up your own.

Having drawn your track lines look along them and pick out any obstructions near your track, such as high ground or radio masts, whose heights are given on the map. Make a guess at the barometric pressure difference between your base and the highest ground or obstruction that you have located, using the latest synoptic chart – failing anything better the weather chart in the morning paper on which isobars are drawn and quantified in millibars will do – and allow thirty feet per millibar. If you are not sure which way to apply it, add it to the height of the highest ground or obstruction. Add five hundred feet to the result and this is your safety height. Write this at the top of your form.

Note also the height of your base and of your destination airfield above sea level and, when setting your altimeter before take-off set it to the height of your base above sea level and you will have a good enough approximation to the QNH. This will help you to avoid flying into airways instead of under them – and do not forget to note in your log the maximum heights at which you may fly under airways.

Study your map carefully and pick out all unmistakable landmarks. Sizeable towns, of course, but not villages as they are often too indeterminate from the air. Motorways are fine but A roads are often indistinguishable from B or C roads. Rivers, canals, lakes and gravel pits show up well if they are big enough to be marked on the 1:250 000 scale map. Railways, provided they are still there and rail-over-road or rail-over-river bridges are fairly easily discerned. Airfields are the best landmarks of all from the air.

With all this you should have enough information to write up your log. As an example of my own working, I offer a copy of the log of my last trip to Sywell (see next page).

On take-off try to restrain yourself from wheeling onto course while still climbing out from base. We all do it but it is sloppy flying and we start with an in-built error of a couple of miles. Climb to your stage or safety height, set course right over the middle of your base and *note the time* in your log.

Fly a steady course at cruising revs and constant height. After five minutes estimate your drift from your actual position relative to the five minute position marked on your track line, using the drift lines as a guide. Let us say it is six degrees to port of your desired position. Alter course twelve degrees to starboard and this should put you back on track at the next five minute position. You will then alter course six degrees to port and continue on your original compass course plus six degrees. You have not found the wind, only the effect of the wind on your course, but unless you are flying to maximum endurance the actual wind strength and direction will only be of academic interest.

Our cockpits are too small and draughty for us to do more than read the maps, note the times in the log and do the simplest of mental arithmetic.

It is of prime importance to get a drift five minutes after each turning point and correct for it. So long as you do this you should stay more or less on track for the rest of the leg.

Do not worry if your landmarks fail to come up on time, it just means that you have a head-wind component, but do note the times at which you pass each mark and compare them with the still air times that you have calculated on the ground. And remember to read from the map to the ground; never try to read from the ground to the map – that way lies panic.

There is no room in our cockpits to open out a map. Hence one has to fold it so that it is only necessary to turn the map over. The problem arises when one runs off one map onto another. I get over it by stuffing both maps back to back into a clear plastic envelope. Once, trying to handle two maps at once while returning from Biggin Hill via Shoreham, one of them blew out of the cockpit and is probably stuck in a hedge five miles north of Petersfield.

Remember that the compass is subject to turning and acceleration errors

Specimen Log.
Base to Sywell. 2 July 1977

1. Vital Notes

Highest Ground	857′
Allow for barometric variation (2 mb)	60′
Safety margin	500′
	————
Safety Height	1417′

Maximum height under Airways (M4 to Princes Risborough) 2500′
Elevation of Sywell   429′
Elevation of Base   440′

2. Flight Plan

Stage	T.A.S. (knots)	Height (feet)	True Track	Magnetic Track	Compass	Distance (Nautical miles)	Time (minutes)
Base/Popham	72	1500	043°	050°	060°	12½	10
Popham/Booker		2000	032°	039°	048°	29	24
Booker/Wing		2000	007°	014°	018°	17½	14
Wing/Sywell		2500	356°	003°	004°	24	20
					Totals	83	68

3. Log.

Timing	Observations	Watch Time*	Elapsed Time*
	Airborne and climbing	10.40	
0	Base set course Popham	10·52	0
5	Worthy Down	10·57	5
10/0	Popham s/c Booker	11·03	11/0
5	Basingstoke to Starboard	11·08	5
9	Road Bridge over Railway	11·13	10
14	Reading – River	11·19	16
19	Henley to Port	11·25	22
24/0	Booker s/c Wing	11·30	27/0
6	Princes Risborough to Port	11·36	6
9	Aylesbury to Pt – Halton Stbd	11·40	10
14/0	Wing s/c Sywell	11·45	15/0
5	Bletchley	11·50	5
9	Lake – Newport Pagnell to Stbd	12·00	10
12	M1	12·03	13
15	Forest	12·07	17
20	Sywell	12·13	23
	Landed	12·24	

* These two columns filled-in in the air

so, when making a turn, pick a distant point which you estimate to be approximately on your new course, make the turn onto it and wait for the compass to settle down before making minor corrections to the proper course. Never chase the compass or you will finish up going in circles.

Our sort of flying is apt to be a spur-of-the-moment activity. It's a nice day and, with an hour or so to spare, we run out to the strip just to see that the treasure is all right. Arrived there we might as well run the engine to circulate the oil a bit. Before we realise what is happening we are airborne and ten minutes later we are lost. You may well laugh indulgently and say it could never happen to you. Maybe, but it has happened to me. So I spend the odd half hours in my study during the winter evenings, plotting my way around the country and making out specimen logs. And I carry a card in my credit card holder of still air courses and timings for every conceivable turning point within ten minutes flying of my base.

I could ramble on indefinitely, for example about the use of motorways, rivers and railways as position lines, but these are dodges that you can work out for yourself.

I would not suggest that anyone should slavishly follow my method; I only say it works for me. In my experience people generally get the best results from forms and systems that they have dreamt up for themselves. At least they have thought about it and understand what they are doing.

If you want to go into the subject in greater detail, and I hope this has whetted your appetite to do so, the best book ever written on air navigation is A.P.1234 – the R.A.F.'s old manual. Get the oldest copy you can find in the second-hand bookshops. My copy is dated 1941, but the earlier editions included an excellent section on meteorology.

Just remember that we have neither the time nor the space in our cockpits to do any paper work that could have been done on the ground. I still get lost if I neglect any part of the drill. It happened quite recently only ten miles from home and I felt remarkably foolish.

Probably the greatest anxiety of the home-builder/pilot, isolated in a draughty hangar out on his private strip, centres around the day to day maintenance of his little aeroplane. Inspection and maintenance of the airframe is probably no great problem since it is all the work of his own hands, but the engine is a horse of a rather different colour – rusty black?

Aircraft engines come complete with very detailed maintenance manuals laying down inspection schedules, oil changes etc. Even if the engine is second hand the manual can usually be obtained without much difficulty. Unfortunately no such comprehensive guide is available to the owner of a converted V.W. engine.

It would be untrue to say that the information on what to expect when your newly converted V.W. engine first crackles into life is not available, but you do have to hunt for it and there do not appear to be any formal pilot's handling notes, which surprises me in view of the motor's wide use and popularity.

Some of what you need to know is contained in Don Peacock's notes to his excellent conversion plans. On page 19 you will find that the oil pressure should be between 30 and 40 lbs per square inch (207–276 kPa) and on page 14 one is told that the oil temperature should stabilise at between 60° and 90°C.

So far so good, but what happens if these figures are exceeded or not achieved? At what point does one start gnawing the knuckles and looking for a good forced landing field?

With a low-technology piece of machinery such as the Volkswagen one can expect individual engines to produce a fair spectrum of differing indications. Performance figures will obviously be affected by the diameter and pitch of the airscrew and by the all-up weight and form of the aircraft. So any figures from one particular aeroplane must be viewed in the light of the installation as a whole and only regarded as indicative in a general way of what to expect from any other V.W. conversion.

The motor on the front of my V.P.1 is of 1600 cc capacity attached to a Steinhilber airscrew of 53 inch diameter × 34 inch pitch (1·35 m × 0·86 m). This is relatively coarse and a finer pitch could be expected to give more revolutions. Contrariwise a larger diameter would tend to slow things down a bit, so 'you fits your prop and takes your choice'.

Before I started up my new engine I got together all the technical information I could acquire, including two different workshop manuals, on the principle that you cannot have too much of a good thing. The trouble was that not all my sources were in total agreement so that there were still large areas of doubt in my mind when I took the first swing.

On the subject of oil pressure Manual A said 'Oil pressure (hot with S.A.E. 20 Oil) 7lbs per square inch [48 kPa] idling; 28 lbs per square inch [193 kPa] at 2500 rpm'. Manual B said 'Oil pressure 42 lb/sq in [290 kPa] / Aluminium 28 lb/sq in [193 kPa] for S.A.E. 30 at 70°C at 2500 rpm', whatever all that may mean. It also said that the idiot light would come on in the car at 6 lb/sq in (41 kPa) and the relief valve would operate at 42 lb/sq in (290 kPa).

On the question of oil temperature only Peacock had anything sensible to say and that was to the effect that it should be between 60°C and 90°C.

Knowing very little about the technicalities of lubricants I turned to Kempe's – the engineer's bible – from which I found that motor oils are classified for viscosity at temperatures of 140°F (60°C) and 210°F (98·9°C) so presumably one is not likely to be in trouble so long as the oil temperature stays between these figures.

In the event my engine turns at 2850 rpm when on the chocks, 2900 rpm when climbing at full throttle and 3100 rpm at full throttle straight and level. I normally cruise at 2750 rpm for a consumption of 2·4 imp. gallons per hour (10·9 litre/h) at an airspeed of 72 knots (83 mph, 133 km/h) T.A.S. She seems very smooth and happy cruising at 2500 rpm at a T.A.S. of 64 knots (74 mph, 119 km/h), but I have yet to check her consumption at this setting.

On starting from cold the oil pressure rises to 40 lb/sq in (276 kPa) and the temperature slowly climbs to between 70°C and 75°C where it normally remains.

In the early days the oil temperature would go up to between 90°C and 95°C. This seemed a bit on the high side to me so I added some Wynn's to the sump which brought it down to between 70°C and 75°C. Perhaps this was quite unnecessary but it looks better to my untutored eye with the needle to left of centre. If I handle the engine at all roughly by, for example, sustaining a climb at full power, the temperature will still climb up to 90°C plus, but five minutes cruising at 2500 rpm will bring it down again to between 70°C and 75°C.

Once the engine has warmed up the pressure drops to between 30 and 35 lb per square inch (207 kPa–241 kPa) where it has so far remained.

The problem of what fuel to use had me very worried. My manual says only that the compression ratio is 7·7 to 1 which is not very high by today's standards. The C.A.A. urges us to use nothing but Avgas 100L and this is all that one can generally get on a licensed airfield, but I was not altogether happy about this having regard to the fact that mine is an aerialised motor car engine and not a true aero engine.

I consulted one of my mechanical engineering colleagues who confirmed my fears that, in a relatively low-compression engine, Avgas, a leaded fuel, would tend to burn out the exhaust valves, corrode the pistons and cylinder heads and erode the spark-plug points. He advised me to put 2 star motor fuel in the tank, which is what he believed the engine to be designed for.

Still vacillating I discussed it with an ex-R.A.F. test pilot friend who now runs a garage. He advised me to use 2 star petrol in the summer and 3 star in the winter for easier starting. He also suggested that I should carry a can of Redex to add to the fuel if I ever had to accept 100L. I am not quite sure what this is supposed to do and I have not, in fact, done it assuming that dilution with the remaining motor fuel in the tank would be sufficient to keep temperatures within bounds.

I compromise by using 3 star and always filter the fuel through a chamoix leather as we did in the R.A.F. I always fill the tank right up after flying as this minimises the risk of condensation in the tank.

Before flying I always check the low level filter and water trap. So far I have never found a trace of either water or dirt in it.

I personally regard this low level filter and water trap as being of prime importance, in spite of the fact that it has never yet had to operate. I have seen one or two aircraft on which it does not feature, presumably partly because there does not appear to be a mandatory requirement for it and partly on account of the cost.

I originally proposed to install the same sort of filter and trap as is used on the Cessna 150 with which I was familiar, but I was brought up short when I enquired the price which was then about £50. It just happened that I had the very simple filter and trap that is fitted to the fuel tank of a Stuart Turner marine installation. I had acquired it some years before when I was overhauling the fuel system on my boat and found, in the event, that the old one was still serviceable. I have no idea what it cost but would be surprised if it ran to more than two or three pounds at today's prices and it seems to do the job just as well as the rather pricey Cessna pattern.

It was only $\frac{1}{8}$ inch (3·2 mm) bore but it was no trouble to drill it out to $\frac{3}{16}$ inch (4·8 mm) to match the rest of my system. It is obviously not so convenient as the Cessna pattern on which one only has to press a little lever to let the petrol run out at the bottom. With the Stuart Turner pattern one has to remove the brass bowl, look inside it and replace it, but this hardly takes longer than pressing a lever. Anyway it has passed the scrutiny of two professional inspectors and has performed perfectly in service, and so it should since it has nothing to go wrong.

Another commonly neglected source of trouble is the tappets. I never looked at mine at all until 100 rpm mysteriously went missing. When I tried to start the engine I detected a hiss from my number 3 exhaust valve and, on opening up the rocker box cover, I found that the gap had closed right up. My handbook gives the correct gap as 0·006 inch (0·15 mm) and none of the tappets conformed to that.

Of course it was a new engine and the valves could be expected to bed themselves in, so that the tappet gaps would be bound to close up a little and 0·15 mm is really very little. Anyway I now include tappets in my pre-flight inspection.

One sure deterrent to easy starting is the least bit of oil or dirt on the magneto points. Where on earth it comes from I cannot imagine, but if there is a speck of dirt drifting around it can be guaranteed to find its way onto my points.

Ideally, I suppose, one should include checking the contact breaker gaps and cleaning the points in one's daily inspection, but I would think that once after every ten hours flying should be sufficient. There is nothing difficult about it but it takes time. If one checks everything on every occasion it leaves precious little time for flying.

Fouled plugs can make starting difficult, so I carry a spare set along with my tools and other impedimenta in the back of my car. In my service days I could always get plugs cleaned by taking them to the M.T. Section who invariably had a sand-blasting machine, but I have yet to discover a local garage in England which has this useful facility. I have therefore acquired a plug cleaning tool which consists of a closed tube full of fine steel needles. You remove the plastic stopper from one end, screw the plug into its place and shake hard for a minute or two. It is inexpensive and works quite well.

My manual advises an oil change after 3000 road miles (4800 km). At my cruising speed of 72 knots (83 mph, 133 km/h) this works out at 36 hours.

Having regard to the difference in operating conditions I have set myself an oil change period of 25 hours.

When the first oil change was coming up I consulted my mechanical colleagues who recommended the following procedure:

(a) Drain out the old oil.
(b) Remove the filter and wash well in petrol.
(c) Replace the filter and plug and fill the sump with flushing oil.
(d) Run the engine for five minutes.
(e) Drain out the flushing oil and remove and wash the filter.
(f) Replace the filter and plug, not forgetting a new gasket, and fill up with new oil.

In all innocence I went to my local garage and asked for a gallon of flushing oil. They had none and I rather suspect that they did not know what I was talking about. I tried several other garages with the same result, so back I went to my mechanical friends who advised me to get a gallon of the cheapest oil I could buy and use that instead. I never knew there was so much difference in the prices of oils.

Now, having done everything that we should have done in the way of pre-flight checks and maintenance, we check petrol on, a few priming strokes, suck in, Contact – and nothing happens.

I have swung that prop for two hours on end without achieving anything more than a few surly kicks back. Other times it will go on the third or fourth blade.

I thought I had solved the starting problem by using some stuff called 'Easy Start' – raw ether in an aerosol can. An eight second burst into the air intake and she would start every time. I was delighted when, at the Wessex Strut's rally at Henstridge, I found that a lot of other chaps were using it. This seemed to be the answer to all our starting problems.

But, at Biggin Hill, I got talking to Bill Wilks who told me that it was fine for diesel engines but with flat-four petrol engines it could be guaranteed to crack the piston rings. I might have guessed that it could not be as easy as all that.

I toyed with the idea of fitting an impulse unit to the port magneto but was advised against this for the reasons given before.

Eventually I aired my problem in the columns of *Popular Flying* and no less an authority than the General Manager of Rollason Aircraft Engines Ltd replied;

'It would appear that most of your starting problems stem from the fact that you are treating what is an ordinary car engine as if it were a Merlin engine installed in a Spitfire.

'The sooner people realise that this engine should be treated exactly the same as a car engine the better, then more of their time will be spent flying than starting.

1. Turn on fuel, prime fuel pump if left more than 24 hours.
2. Close throttle, pull out choke.
3. Switch on both magnetos.
4. Proceed to swing as though expecting it to start on every swing.

'When engine starts gradually push in choke until engine runs smoothly.

'This operation can be speeded up by putting a trickle of throttle on after engine starts.

'These starting procedures apply mostly to the Ardem engine fitted with the Zenith 32 KLP10 carburettor, but can be adapted for any conversions that have choke control. The main thing to avoid is priming the engine by pumping fuel in with excessive use of the throttle.

'Stopping the engine: Allow engine to idle for a few moments, then throttle right back and switch off ignition – turn off fuel.'

Well, there you have it, straight from the oracle and it does work.
To summarise, then, my daily inspection routine is as follows:

(a) Spray all round with WD-40.
(b) Remove cowlings.
(c) Check fuel filter and water trap.
(d) Check oil level.
(e) Check tappets at 0·006 inch (0·15 mm).
(f) Check all control terminals for security and exercise controls.
(g) Grease magneto chain if necessary.
(h) Every 10 hours clean and check magneto points and plugs [magneto gap 0·014 inch (0·36 mm), plug gap 0·015 inch (0·38 mm)].
(i) Every 25 hours change oil.

I should emphasise that the foregoing is just a description of what I do and I have no formal authority for any of it. However I have laid it before the Olympians of P.F.A. Engineering and so far no thunderbolts have been flung in my direction.

Last of all remains the problem of what to do with our aeroplane now that we have got the freedom of the skies.

No doubt for the first year or two the happy pilot will be content just to fly, pottering around his local area and jaunting off to rallies all over the country to stand beaming by his little treasure, modestly confessing to all enquirers that he built it himself and trying not to look too pleased about it. He may even use it for serious personal transport, though unless it is fully airways equipped he will have to accept that he will frequently be weather-bound. There used to be a saying that 'If you have time to spare go by air'. I have a nasty feeling that it is still true, even of commercial flying. Returning from Malta recently we were delayed 14 hours by fog at Heathrow.

A lot of pilots take to aerial photography and this is something that I can claim to know a little about since the R.A.F. devoted a great deal of time and trouble to teaching me to take photographs from the air.

Most people take oblique photographs using an ordinary hand-held 35 mm camera or a pocket instamatic type and are disappointed to find that the detail obtained is too distant and vague to be of interest.

The more determined ones find they get better results using a long-focus lens. A telephoto lens is really too much of a handful in a tiny open cockpit, but a long-focus lens used at 600 feet (200 m) or so can produce very pleasant and interesting pictures.

I had thought idly for some time about fitting a vertical camera into my 007 and converting her into a photo-reconnaissance unit (P.R.U.) aircraft. It had never really been a serious intention, but one's mind grapples onto these silly little problems and worries out a solution until things begin to come together and, all at once, it is done.

The theory is easy enough. Take an ordinary 35 mm camera with, say, a 45 mm focal length lens, then, by similar triangles, it is clear that by flying at a height of 738 feet (225 m) above the target one will produce a photograph to a scale of 1/5000. Enlarge this by 4 and you have a scale of 1/250 which is quite acceptable.

Each exposure will cover 175 metres and one will need a run of at least four photographs, each overlapping the previous one by 60%, so that one can use a stereoscope to bring up the contours and detail. Each exposure must therefore advance 40% of 175 metres or 70 metres (230 feet). My airspeed is about 70 knots or 127 feet per second, so that I would need a two second time interval between exposures to give the correct overlap.

The apparently insoluble problem was how to wind on the film between exposures. A number of my colleagues at work are keen photographers, so I put the problem to them. It seemed that most of the more expensive camera outfits can provide a bulky and very expensive motor drive for their products at an all-in cost of about £400. This was out of the question. However there used to be a German camera called a 'Robot' which incorporated a clockwork film transport. This opened up a possible line of enquiry.

It happened, then, that I found myself one day in London's Bond Street with time on my hands, so I went into a well-known camera shop to pursue the matter.

A charming and knowledgeable gentleman told me that Robots had not been made for a number of years and, in any case, only the last model, the 'Robot Royal', would be of any use to me as the previous models used special cassettes which could be difficult or impossible to obtain. Robots, he said, were becoming collector's items and only rarely came on the market. I decided to forget it.

However it was only a week later that I was walking past a camera shop in my home town and there, in the window, was a Robot Royal. I went in, arranged a trade-in on my own Japanese 35 mm camera and I was back in my old trade as a P.R.U. pilot.

I made up a polystyrene mounting on a piece of $\frac{1}{4}$ inch (6 mm) ply, glued it into the bottom of 007's fuselage just aft of the aft bulkhead, cut the hole for the lens and 007 had become a veritable spy in the sky.

I had hoped to use a long cable release coming up through the stick to a button on top, but this would have required a greater length of cable than is commercially available, so I had to settle for a bulb release. This leads to a position near my left (throttle) hand – a bit like the rocket release on the Hurricane.

So, with everything installed, I set off on my first photographic sortie for thirty-three years. I was interested to find that with 4 lb (1·8 kg) of camera 26 in (0·66 m) behind the normal c. of g. she trimmed, in cruising flight, to a very slight climb. I cured it by reducing the revs to 2600 which conveniently brought my cruising speed to a little under 70 knots (81 mph, 130 km/h).

The target was my friendly farmer's farm house. I took a wide sweep round, ran up at right angles to the proposed photographic line, steep-turned on and made four exposures, counting the time interval 'One and Two and Press'.

I turned off reckoning I had done a pretty good job. Everything seemed to be where it should have been in relation to my line of flight.

Alas, when the film was developed, I had missed the target by 100 feet (30 m). It seemed I would need an awful lot of practice before my hand regained its cunning.

Of course with a 35 mm camera at 740 feet (225 m) one has far less latitude for error than we had in the Mark XI Spitfires with twin f 36 inch (0·91 m) cameras at 40 000 feet (12 000 m) and that was difficult enough.

I recall that on one of my early operational sorties in a Mark IV Spitfire with a single f 20 inch (0·51 m) camera I missed the last few dispersals on a German airfield. My flight commander, a most unsympathetic New Zealander, decreed that I should fly for the next week with a single f 36 inch (0·91 m) camera, which has a much smaller field than the f 20 inch (0·51 m), under the threat of instant dismissal from the squadron if I ever again missed so much as the German guard-room cat. For the next week I flew every target twice over and never again missed any part of any target.

Anyway, my later results showed that there was nothing basically wrong with the installation and purely photographic matters. It was only my flying that had to be improved.

It should be noted that the permanent fitting of a camera to an aircraft, as just described, requires clearance through P.F.A. Engineering in order to comply with the conditions of the C. of A. This is because they are concerned, as ever, about the all-up weight and its effect on the c. of g. So, if you decide to fit a vertical camera, keep it as far forward as possible and be prepared to do some calculations to justify your installation.

Stereo pair of vertical photographs of Stone Pier, Warsash

Vertical photographs have the advantage over obliques in that they can be flown and enlarged to an approximate scale so that measurements can be taken off them.

This is not to say that you can go into the air survey business overnight. That requires photogrammetric equipment costing hundreds of thousands of pounds, not to mention a ground staff of plotters and draughtsmen. If you are interested, or just do not believe me, go to any of the air survey firms who will be delighted to show you round. They may even let you play with the stereo plotter.

However your amateur efforts can be of enormous assistance to the many archeological and historical societies who rely heavily, and sometimes exclusively, on the work of unpaid enthusiasts. A folding pocket stereoscope costs little enough and will add enormously to the interest and to the value of your photography to the archeologist. It requires two consecutive photographs on both of which the object to be studied appears. Hence the requirement for a 60% overlap in your run of photographs.

This is just one suggestion of many more that one could think of for using your aircraft for more than just personal enjoyment.

I sometimes wish that I had not been brought up to the ethic that holds that pure self-gratification is sinful. That way I would enjoy flying my selfish little single-seater untroubled by a Calvinistic conscience that keeps telling me that so much delight is more than mortal man has any right to expect.

Appendix

U.S. Considerations

By Timothy R. V. Foster author of *The Aircraft Owner's Handbook* (1978). New York: Van Nostrand Reinhold.

Federal Aviation Regulations

The U.S. Government has assigned the responsibility for the control and regulation of civil aviation to the Federal Aviation Agency (FAA), which is a unit of the Department of Transportation (DOT). Its rules are spelled out in *Federal Aviation Regulations* (FARs). The FARs are issued in various *Parts* covering different subjects. The Parts that apply to the homebuilder are these:

Part	Subject
1	Definitions and abbreviations
21	Certification: products and parts
23	Airworthiness standards: normal, utility and acrobatic category aircraft
33	Airworthiness standards: aircraft engines
35	Airworthiness standards: propellers
39	Airworthiness directives
43	Maintenance, preventive maintenance, rebuilding and alteration
45	Identification and registration marking
47	Aircraft registration
49	Recording of aircraft titles and security documents
61	Certification: pilots and flight instructors
67	Medical standards and certification
91	General operating and flight rules

You can obtain these on a subscription basis from the Superintendent of Documents, US Government Printing Office, Washington, DC 20402.

Advisory Circulars

Advisory Circulars (ACs) are information issued by the FAA to inform the aviation public in a systematic way of non-regulatory information of interest. Some ACs are free, others are not. Three times a year the FAA issues a booklet called *Advisory Circular Checklist* which lists the status of both FARs and Advisory Circulars. In addition, the FAA issues AC 00–44 *Status of FARs* at regular intervals.

ACs are issued about various areas of interest and are numbered according to the pertinent FARs, as follows:

Subject Number	Subject Matter
00	General
20	Aircraft
40	Maintenance
60	Airmen
90	Air Traffic Control and general operations

If you want to be placed on an AC mailing list, make the request through: US Department of Transportation, Distribution Requirements Section M 482.3, Washington, DC 20590.

Separate mailing lists are maintained for the various areas of interest, so make sure you identify what you want. The best way to do this is to start with a current copy of the *Advisory Circular Checklist*, mentioned above. You can often pick these up at Flight Service Stations.

Here is a list of Advisory Circulars that should prove helpful to the homebuilder:

AC Number	Title
ACs that cost:	
AC 20–9	Personal Aircraft Inspection Handbook (out of print – being revised)
AC 43.13–1A	Acceptable Methods, Techniques and Practices – Aircraft Inspection and Repair (price $3·70)
AC 43.13–1A Chg 1	Change 1 to the above (price ·65¢)
AC 43.13–1A Chg 1	Change 2 to the above (price ·35¢)
AC 43.13–2A	Acceptable Methods, Techniques and Practices – Aircraft Alterations (price $2·75)
AC 91.23A	Pilot's Weight and Balance Handbook (price $2·30)

To obtain Advisory Circulars that cost, I suggest that first you get the latest copy of AC 00–2 – *Advisory Circular Checklist*, which, as I mentioned, is free. This will give the latest price and availability of ACs, as well as current ordering information. Then follow the instructions given therein. If you can't obtain the *Checklist* at your local Flight Service Station, you can get it, and all the other free ACs mentioned, from: Department of Transportation, Publications Section M-443.1, Washington, DC 20590.

AC Number	Title
ACs that are free:	
AC 00–2	Advisory Circular Checklist
AC 00–44	Status of Federal Aviation Regulations
AC 20–5D	Plane Sense
AC 20–27B	Certification and Operation of Amateur Built Aircraft
AC 20–28A	Nationally Advertised Construction Kits, Amateur-Built Aircraft
AC 20–32B	Carbon Monoxide (CO) Contamination in Aircraft – Detection and Prevention
AC 20–35B	Tie-Down Sense
AC 20–44	Glass Fiber Fabric for Aircraft Covering
AC 20–86	Aviation Education Through Building an Airplane
AC 21–12	Application for US Airworthiness Certificate FAA Form 8130–6
AC 21–13	Standard Airworthiness Certification of Surplus Military Aircraft and Aircraft Built From Spare and Surplus Parts
AC 43–5	Airworthiness Directives for General Aviation Aircraft
AC 43–9A	Maintenance Records: General Aviation Aircraft
AC 43–12	Preventive Maintenance
AC 43–16	General Aviation Airworthiness Alerts
AC 45–2	Identification and Registration Marking
AC 60–6A	Airplane Flight Manuals, Approved Manual Materials, Markings and Placards
AC 91–13B	Cold Weather Operation of Aircraft

Experimental Aircraft Certificates

The FAA allows various special purpose aircraft to be certified as experimental aircraft in accordance with FAR 21.191. Not all of these are homebuilts. For example, an aircraft undergoing research and development, or an aircraft used exclusively for air racing or exhibition flying may be certified under this rule. The key one, as far as this book is concerned, is 'for the purpose of operating an aircraft, the major portion of which has been fabricated and assembled by persons who undertook the construction project solely for their own education or recreation.' The important words here are *major portion*. This means that at least 51 per cent of the aircraft must have been built by the person or persons applying for the original certification. An example of how this has been interpreted recently is the stunning Christen Eagle aerobatic biplane. This is sold in multiple kit form, and one of the kits originally consisted of prefabricated wing ribs. The FAA stepped in and said that a person who bought the kits and assembled the aircraft was in fact building less than 50 per cent of it himself, and thus it could not be certificated as an amateur-built experimental aircraft. After some negotiating, Christen agreed to change

199

the kit so that the wing ribs have to be made up by the homebuilder. Thus at least 51 per cent of the aircraft is home-fabricated, and the requirements of the rule are met. You can still buy the wing ribs preassembled, but then the aircraft will probably have to be certificated in the *exhibition category* of FAR 21.191, which can place undesirable restrictions on its operation. In any event, it is the FAA Inspector who approves the aircraft who determines if the 51 per cent home-made requirement has been met.

No Formal Airworthiness Standards
Aircraft built by manufacturers receive type certificates, and must meet standards spelled out in FAR Part 23 *Airworthiness Standards: Normal, Utility, and Acrobatic Category Airplanes.* There are no such FAA airworthiness standards for experimental amateur-built aircraft. The FAA Inspector who examines the aircraft for the granting of the airworthiness certificate uses his own discretion and experience in approving the individual aircraft. This means that a design that is fairly conventional, using reasonably standard aircraft construction techniques, should have little difficulty in getting approval. Past experience and practices mean a lot. Untried methods, unusual systems or designs may mean that the Inspector will have to be shown to his own satisfaction that they will work.

Flight Restrictions
The Inspector may impose extra flight restrictions until it has been satisfactorily demonstrated that all is as it was expected to be. Any restrictions are designed primarily to protect the poor innocents who might be beneath the aircraft as it falls from the sky out of control. However, once the specified requirements have been met, most restrictions are removed. Only the FAA Inspector may lift these barriers, by the way. The restrictions start out by disallowing any passenger-carrying at all, and keeping the aircraft to flights over unpopulated areas within a certain distance from base. After a certain amount of time has been accumulated safely, the Inspector may remove the restrictions. However, one restriction is never lifted – the one that prohibits the aircraft from being used for carrying passengers or property for hire or reward.

Airworthiness Certificate Duration
Once the aircraft has been approved by an Inspector, an Experimental Airworthiness Certificate is issued. This is FAA Form 8130–7. They can be issued for various periods – even for as little as one flight. Once the minimum flight requirements have been met, the certificate is usually issued on a permanent basis, subject to the aircraft undergoing an annual 'condition inspection'. The key thing to remember about an airworthiness certificate is that *you must have one to fly an aircraft within the U.S.*

Repairman's Certificate

The FAA now allows a person who has built an aircraft successfully to apply for a *Repairman's Certificate*. This will be issued on application, using FAA Form 8310–2, provided that you can prove you built your airplane. The aircraft logbook should give enough evidence of this. Once you have this certificate, *which will be limited to the aircraft you built*, you are entitled to perform all maintenance on your aircraft, including the new annual *condition inspection* mentioned above. If you don't have the repairman certificate, the condition inspection must be performed by a qualified A & P mechanic or FAA Inspector.

The EAA

The Experimental Aircraft Association, the great guiding light of homebuilt aircraft in the U.S., simply must be joined forthwith if you are intending to build your own aircraft. They have so much experience and can help you in so many ways that any time spent not being a member is time wasted, once you've decided to commit your garage and self to aircraft manufacturing for the next few years. Their address is currently Box 229, Hales Corners, WI 53130, telephone 414-425-4860, however, they announced at the 1979 Oshkosh fly-in that they plan to move their headquarters to Oshkosh eventually, so check current sources (e.g., telephone information – Oshkosh 'Information' is 414-555-1212) for their new address and phone number. Membership cost $25 a year in late 1979, and that includes a subscription to the excellent magazine *Sport Aviation*.

EAA was started by Paul Poberezny in 1953, in Milwaukee, Wisconsin. It now has over 60 000 members and 600 local chapters. Its annual convention and fly-in, held at Oskosh every August, is the world's greatest air show for the true aviation enthusiast. About 25 000 members actually camp right at the airfield during the show. Throughout the week-long fly-in, over 10 000 aircraft visit, and about 300 000 people attend. During that period, air traffic at Oshkosh is three times heavier than at Chicago O'Hare, otherwise the world's busiest airport!

A big advantage of EAA is the local Chapter system – the equivalent to the PFA Strut Meetings in England. By joining a local Chapter, you'll be able to involve yourself much more meaningfully with other crazy people like yourself – whoever heard of building an airplane in a garage! At least you'll find yourself surrounded by people who have not only heard of it, they've *done* it and they're doing it *now*!

The FAA GADO and EMDO

The FAA Flight Standards Service operates numerous General Aviation District Offices (GADOs) and Engineering and Manufacturing District Offices (EMDOs) around the country. They administer the regulations within their respective areas. Both GADOs and EMDOs have Airworthiness Inspectors, and either variety is authorized to carry out inspection of amateur-built aircraft. After joining EAA, the next step in your stairway to the stars is to visit your local GADO or EMDO and meet with the Inspector you'll be getting to know quite well over the next few years. Talk to him or her and find out what their requirements are. What sort of notice do they need for an inspection appointment? How many inspections will they want?

Here is a list of GADOs with their telephone numbers:

FAA Region	Location	Telephone
Alaskan	Anchorage AK	907-276-3939
	Fairbanks AK	907-452-1276
	Juneau AK	907-789-0231
Central	Des Moines IA	515-284-4094
	Kansas City KS	913-281-3491
	Wichita KS	316-943-3244
	St Louis MO	314-425-7102
	Lincoln NE	402-471-5485
Eastern	Washington DC	202-628-1555
	Baltimore MD	301-761-2610
	Teterboro NJ	201-288-1745
	Albany NY	518-869-8482
	Farmingdale NY	516-691-3100
	Rochester NY	716-263-5880
	Allentown PA	215-264-2888
	New Cumberland PA	717-782-4528
	Philadelphia PA	215-597-9708
	Pittsburgh PA	412-461-7800
	Richmond VA	804-222-7494
	Charleston WV	304-343-4689
Great Lakes	Chicago IL	312-584-4490
	Springfield IL	217-525-4238
	Indianapolis IN	317-247-2491
	South Bend IN	219-232-5843
	Detroit MI	313-485-2250
	Grand Rapids MI	616-456-6427
	Minneapolis MN	612-725-3341
	Cincinnati OH	513-684-2183
	Cleveland OH	216-267-0220
	Columbus OH	614-469-7476
	Milwaukee WI	414-747-5531
New England	Portland ME	207-774-4484
	Boston MA	617-762-2436
	Westfield MA	413-568-3121
Northwest	Boise ID	208-384-1238
	Eugene OR	503-688-9721
	Portland OR	503-221-2104
	Seattle WA	206-767-2747
	Spokane WA	509-456-4618
Pacific	Honolulu, HI	808-847-0615
Rocky Mountain	Denver CO	303-466-7326
	Billings MT	406-245-6179

FAA Region	Location	Telephone
	Helena MT	406-449-5270
	Fargo ND	701-232-8949
	Rapid City SD	605-343-2403
	Salt Lake City UT	801-524-4247
	Casper WY	307-234-8959
Southern	Birmingham AL	205-254-1393
	Jacksonville FL	904-641-7311
	Miami FL	305-681-7431
	St Petersburg FL	813-531-1434
	Atlanta GA	404-221-6481
	Louisville KY	502-582-6116
	Jackson MS	601-969-4633
	Charlotte NC	704-392-3214
	Raleigh NC	919-755-4240
	West Columbia SC	803-765-5931
	Memphis TN	901-345-0600
	Nashville TN	615-251-5661
	San Juan PR	809-791-5050
Southwest	Little Rock AR	501-372-3437
	Lafayette LA	318-234-2321
	New Orleans LA	504-241-2506
	Shreveport LA	318-226-5379
	Albuquerque NM	505-247-0156
	Olkahoma City OK	405-789-5220
	Tulsa OK	918-835-7619
	Corpus Christi TX	512-884-9331
	Dallas TX	214-357-0142
	El Paso TX	915-778-6389
	Houston TX	713-643-6504
	Lubbock TX	806-762-0335
	San Antonio TX	512-824-9535
Western	Phoenix AZ	602-261-4763
	Fresno CA	209-487-5306
	Long Beach CA	213-426-7135
	Oakland CA	415-273-7155
	Ontario CA	714-984-2411
	Sacramento CA	916-440-3169
	San Diego CA	714-293-5280
	San Jose CA	408-275-7681
	Santa Monica CA	213-391-6701
	Van Nuys CA	213-997-3191
	Las Vegas NV	702-736-0666
	Reno NV	702-784-5321

Aircraft Logbook

You'll need an aircraft logbook as soon as you start your project. The EAA offers one – *Custom Aircraft Logbook* – specially designed for the homebuilder. In the logbook you'll record all the major stages of your building and flying progress. It is in here that the Inspector will certify what approvals have been given to date – e.g., 'OK to cover', 'OK to test fly'. This logbook is important evidence of compliance with inspection requirements should you ever move or should the FAA Inspectors change, and for obtaining your Repairman's Certificate.

Keep All Receipts

You must retain all the receipts for everything you buy in connection with the project, to establish ownership. You should record acquisitions and sources in the logbook. The FAA Inspector may ask to see them.

EAA Service and Maintenance Manual

The EAA publishes a preformatted *Service and Maintenance Manual* which has room for all kinds of entries relative to the construction and testing of the aircraft. This eventually becomes the airplane flight manual and is a very useful document. EAA suggests that it should contain information such as the following:

(a) Aircraft specifications and weight and balance
(b) Descriptions of all systems (electric, hydraulic, fuel, etc.)
(c) Lubrication procedures
(d) Pressures and electrical loads applicable to the various systems
(e) Tolerances and adjustments necessary for proper functioning of the airplane
(f) Methods of leveling, raising and towing
(g) Methods of balancing control surfaces
(h) Identification of primary and secondary structures
(i) Frequency and extent of inspections necessary for proper maintenance of the airplane.

Weight and Balance

The FAA publishes an Advisory Circular – AC 91–23, *Pilot's Weight and Balance Handbook* (for a small consideration). This contains recommended procedures for weighing and calculating the center of gravity of an aircraft. This is, of course, absolutely crucial to a safe operation, and must be *properly* completed before the first flight. Details of the calculations should be recorded. Mistakes can happen. I once did the preliminary test flying on a Volmer VJ–22 Sportsman, and after the first flight, in which I discovered very poor directional stability, we reweighed the aircraft and found a small error had been made in the calculations. The addition of 18 lbs of lead to the nose did wonders for its feel, but not much for its already-weak load carrying capability! Eventually the owner took the lead out and accepted the poor stability. Later he modified the aircraft aerodynamically and solved the problem.

Equipment List
You must make out a complete equipment list that includes such things as all the instruments, radios, electrical devices and so on, along with their weights. Any time anything is removed or added to the airplane, the equipment list and weight-and-balance data should be revised. Make sure that every entry and change is dated.

The EAA Designee
The EAA has a marvellous system of 'Designees' – highly qualified or experienced people who are there to help you. They are not official inspectors, and have no legal capacity, but they are a fine example of the dedication the people who build aircraft give to their chosen task. They are all volunteers. Time spent with a Designee will reduce embarrassing moments with the FAA Inspector. Your local EAA Chapter will put you in touch.

Cockpit Placards and Aircraft Instrument Markings
FAR 91.31 requires that all aircraft are marked and placarded according to the operating limitations for that aircraft, including such things as:
(a) Powerplant (RPM, manifold pressure, etc.)
(b) Airspeeds (Stall speed, normal operating speed, flap extension speed, etc.)
(c) Kinds of operation
(d) Fuel tank selectors and procedures for use, if required   .
(e) Flight manoeuvres (if the aircraft is non-aerobatic, it should state 'No acrobatic manoeuvres, including spins, approved'; if it is aerobatic, there should be a placard in full view of the pilot that states the approved manoeuvres and entry airspeed for each)
(f) Baggage compartment maximum load permitted
(g) Passenger warning: 'Passenger Warning – This aircraft is amateur built and does not comply with the Federal Safety Regulations of "Standard Aircraft" '
(h) Identification plate (required by FAR 45.11). This must be of fireproof material and must include the following:
   Builder's name and address
   Model designation
   Builder's serial number
   Date of manufacture
The EAA offers a suitable plate of this type.

Aircraft Registration
Federal registration requirements are spelled out in FAR Part 47. The first step in registering a homebuilt aircraft is to obtain the registration

number, which in the U.S.A. starts with the letter N, followed by up to five symbols, which may be all numbers (N12345), one to four numbers and a suffix letter (N2Y or N12X or N123A or N8251P), or one to three numbers and two suffix letters (N1AA or N23AA or N825TF). If you don't care what number you get, the FAA will assign one to you. However, you can apply for a custom number, which costs $10. When you are requesting a special number, give at least five choices, since the one you want may already be assigned.

To get a registration number, write a letter to: FAA Aircraft Registration Section, Box 25082, Oklahoma City, OK 73125, and request either any number, or a special number (in which case show your choices and enclose the $10 fee). Indicate in your letter that the aircraft is amateur-built and has not been previously registered anywhere. Enclose an affidavit of ownership as follows:

```
                    AFFIDAVIT OF OWNERSHIP

         Date _____

         U.S. Identification Number _____

         Builder's name _____

         Address _____

                 _____

         Model _____  Serial Number _____

         Class  (airplane. rotorcraft. glider, etc.)

         Type of engine installed (e.g. Reciprocating)

         Number of engines installed _____

         Make mode and serial number of each engine

         installed _____

         Built for land, water or amphibious operation

         Number of seats_____


         The above described aircraft was built from

         parts by the undersigned, and I am the owner.



                   _____

                   Signature of owner-builder


         [Notarization statement and notary signature]
```

FORM APPROVED OMB NO. 04-R0076

UNITED STATES OF AMERICA

DEPARTMENT OF TRANSPORTATION - FEDERAL AVIATION ADMINISTRATION

AIRCRAFT REGISTRATION APPLICATION

CERT. ISSUE DATE

UNITED STATES
REGISTRATION NUMBER **N**

AIRCRAFT MANUFACTURER & MODEL

AIRCRAFT SERIAL No.

FOR FAA USE ONLY

TYPE OF REGISTRATION (Check one box)

☐ I. Individual ☐ 2. Partnership ☐ 3. Corporation ☐ 4. Co-Owner ☐ 5. Gov't.

NAME OF APPLICANT (Person(s) shown on evidence of ownership. If individual, give last name, first name, and middle initial.)

ADDRESS (Permanent mailing address for first applicant listed.)

Number and street: _____

Rural Route: _____   P. O. Box: _____

CITY	STATE	ZIP CODE

☐ CHECK HERE IF YOU ARE ONLY REPORTING A CHANGE OF ADDRESS

ATTENTION! Read the following statement before signing this application.

A false or dishonest answer to any question in this application may be grounds for punishment by fine and/or imprisonment (U.S. Code, Title 18, Sec. 1001).

CERTIFICATION

I/WE CERTIFY that the above described aircraft (I) is owned by the undersigned applicant(s), who is/are citizen(s) of the United States as defined in Sec. 101(13) of the Federal Aviation Act of 1958; (2) is not registered under the laws of any foreign country; and (3) legal evidence of ownership is attached or has been filed with the Federal Aviation Administration.

NOTE: If executed for co-ownership all applicants must sign. Use reverse side if necessary.

	SIGNATURE	TITLE	DATE
EACH PART OF THIS APPLICATION MUST BE SIGNED IN INK	SIGNATURE	TITLE	DATE
	SIGNATURE	TITLE	DATE
	SIGNATURE	TITLE	DATE

NOTE: Pending receipt of the Certificate of Aircraft Registration, the aircraft may be operated for a period not in excess of 90 days, during which time the PINK copy of this application must be carried in the aircraft, together with an appropriate and current airworthiness certificate or a special flight permit.

AC FORM 8050-1 (8-76) (0052-00-628-9004)

208

If you bought a kit or parts, enclose a notarized copy of the bill of sale as well. This set of papers (letter, affidavit and bill of sale) will serve as legal documents and will substitute for FAA Form 8050–2 *Bill of Sale* which is normally completed for an existing airplane.

A couple of weeks later, you will receive a letter confirming the registration number that has been assigned, along with a blank FAA Form 8050–1 *Aircraft Registration Application*. Complete the form, retain the pink copy and return the green and white copies to the FAA Aircraft Registry. The pink copy will be your temporary Certificate of Registration and will allow you to fly the aircraft if you have a current certificate of airworthiness.

The Registration Certificate you eventually receive is good until you sell the aircraft, it is destroyed or scrapped, or you register it under the laws of a foreign country. It also will lapse thirty days after the death of the certificate holder.

If you change your address, you must notify the FAA Aircraft Registry within thirty days.

Aircraft registration marks must be displayed on the aircraft in accordance with FAR Part 45.23.

Getting Your Certificate of Airworthiness

Let's assume that you've built the aircraft, complied with all the requirements, got your 'N' number, painted it on properly, and you're ready for the actual C of A. To obtain this you must first arrange for the final look at the aircraft by the FAA Inspector. With your letter requesting this inspection, EAA recommends that you submit the following:

A statement giving the purpose for which the aircraft is to be used (e.g., recreation, testing, education, experimentation, etc.).

The estimated time or number of flights needed for the test flying (usually 50 hours for aircraft equipped with aircraft engines and 75 hours for aircraft equipped with non-aircraft type engines).

The areas over which the test flying will be carried out (this should be an area within about 25 miles of your base for day VFR operations, excluding airways and congested areas, but including any nearby airports).

A three-view drawing of the aircraft, or photos showing three views. Include with the drawing the following data:
Type of engine, HP, and type of propeller
Empty weight and maximum weight of aircraft
Number of seats installed and their arrangement with respect to each other
Whether single or dual controlled
Fuel and oil capacities
Maximum speed at which you intend to operate the aircraft.

Complete and forward FAA Form 8130–6 *Application for Airworthiness Certificate* with your letter (Advisory Circular AC 21–12 will help you fill this out). After the aircraft has passed its final inspection, you will receive an amateur-built 'Experimental' airworthiness certificate, along with a

Form Approved
Budget Bureau No. 04–R0058

DEPARTMENT OF TRANSPORTATION FEDERAL AVIATION ADMINISTRATION **APPLICATION FOR AIRWORTHINESS CERTIFICATE**	**INSTRUCTIONS**—Print or type. Do not write in shaded areas; these are for FAA use only. Submit original only to an authorized FAA Representative. If additional space is required, use an attachment. For special flight permits complete Sections II and VI or VII as applicable.

I. AIRCRAFT DESCRIPTION

1. REGISTRATION MARK	2. AIRCRAFT BUILDER'S NAME *(make)*	3. AIRCRAFT MODEL DESIGNATION	4. YR. MFG.	FAA CODING
5. AIRCRAFT SERIAL NO.	6. ENGINE BUILDER'S NAME *(make)*	7. ENGINE MODEL DESIGNATION		
8. NUMBER OF ENGINES	9. PROPELLER BUILDER'S NAME *(make)*	10. PROPELLER MODEL DESIGNATION	**11. AIRCRAFT IS** NEW / USED / IMPORT	

II. CERTIFICATION REQUESTED

APPLICATION IS HEREBY MADE FOR: *(Check applicable items)*

A	1	STANDARD AIRWORTHINESS CERT. *(Indicate category)*	NORMAL	UTILITY	ACROBATIC	TRANSPORT	GLIDER	BALLOON

B		SPECIAL AIRWORTHINESS CERTIFICATE *(Check appropriate items)*						
	2	LIMITED						
	5	PROVISIONAL *(Indicate class)*	1	CLASS I				
			2	CLASS II				
	3	RESTRICTED *(Indicate operation(s) to be conducted)*	1	AGRICULTURE & PEST CONTROL	2	AERIAL SURVEYING	3	AERIAL ADVERTISING
			4	FOREST *(Wild life conservation)*	5	PATROLLING	6	WEATHER CONTROL
			0	OTHER *(Specify)*				
	4	EXPERIMENTAL *(Indicate operation(s) to be conducted)*	1	RESEARCH AND DEVELOPMENT	2	AMATEUR BUILT	3	EXHIBITION
			4	RACING	5	CREW TRAINING	6	MKT. SURVEY
			0	TO SHOW COMPLIANCE WITH FAR				
	8	SPECIAL FLIGHT PERMIT *(Indicate operation to be conducted then complete Section VI or VII as applicable on reverse side)*	1	FERRY FLIGHT FOR REPAIRS, ALTERATIONS, MAINTENANCE OR STORAGE				
			2	EVACUATE FROM AREA OF IMPENDING DANGER				
			3	OPERATION IN EXCESS OF MAX. CERTIFICATED TAKE-OFF WEIGHT				
			4	DELIVERING OR EXPORT	5	PRODUCTION FLIGHT TESTING		

C	6	MULTIPLE AIRWORTHINESS CERTIFICATE *(Check appropriate Restricted Operation and Standard or Limited as applicable above)*

III. OWNER'S CERTIFICATION

A. REGISTERED OWNER *(As shown on Certificate of Aircraft Registration)* — IF DEALER, CHECK HERE ⟶

NAME	ADDRESS

B. AIRCRAFT CERTIFICATION BASIS *(Check applicable blocks and complete items as indicated)*

AIRCRAFT SPECIFICATION OR TYPE CERTIFICATION DATA SHEET *(Give No. and Revision No.)*	AIRWORTHINESS DIRECTIVES *(Check if all applicable AD's complied with and give latest AD No.)*
AIRCRAFT LISTING *(Give page No(s.))*	SUPPLEMENTAL TYPE CERTIFICATE *(List number of each STC incorporated)*

C. AIRCRAFT OPERATION AND MAINTENANCE RECORDS

CHECK IF RECORDS IN COMPLIANCE WITH FAR 91.173	TOTAL AIRFRAME HOURS—Enter for used aircraft only	3	EXPERIMENTAL ONLY—Enter hours flown since last certificate issued or renewed

D. CERTIFICATION—I hereby certify that I am the owner (or his agent) of the aircraft described above; that the aircraft is registered with the Federal Aviation Administration in accordance with Section 501 of the Federal Aviation Act of 1958, and applicable Federal Aviation Regulations; and that the aircraft has been inspected and is airworthy and eligible for the airworthiness certificate requested.

DATE OF APPLICATION	NAME AND TITLE *(Print or type)*	SIGNATURE

IV. INSPECTION AGENCY VERIFICATION

A. THE AIRCRAFT DESCRIBED ABOVE HAS BEEN INSPECTED AND FOUND AIRWORTHY BY: *(Complete this section only if FAR 21.183 (d) applies)*

2	FAR PART 121 OR 127 CERTIFICATE HOLDER *(Give Certificate No.)*	3	CERTIFICATED MECHANIC *(Give Certificate No.)*	6	CERTIFICATED REPAIR STATION *(Give Certificate No.)*
5	AIRCRAFT MANUFACTURER *(Give Name of Firm)*				

DATE	TITLE	SIGNATURE

V. FAA REPRESENTATIVE CERTIFICATION

(Check ALL applicable blocks) I find that the aircraft described in Section I or VII meets the requirements for: ☐ The certification requested, or 4 Amendment or modification of its current airworthiness certificate. Inspection for a special flight permit under Section VII was conducted by: ☐ FAA Inspector; certificate holder under ☐ FAR 65, ☐ FAR 121 or 127, or ☐ FAR 145.

DATE	DISTRICT OFFICE	4	DESIGNEE'S SIGNATURE AND NO.	1	FAA INSPECTOR'S SIGNATURE

FAA Form 8130–6 (7–70)

letter outlining the operating limitations applicable to the aircraft. These Special Airworthiness Operating Limitations must be displayed in the aircraft at all times.

<table>
<tr><td rowspan="6">VI. PRODUCTION FLIGHT TESTING</td><td colspan="4">A. MANUFACTURER</td></tr>
<tr><td colspan="2">NAME</td><td colspan="2">ADDRESS</td></tr>
<tr><td colspan="4">B. PRODUCTION BASIS (Check applicable item)</td></tr>
<tr><td></td><td colspan="3">PRODUCTION CERTIFICATE (Give production certificate number)</td></tr>
<tr><td></td><td colspan="3">TYPE CERTIFICATE ONLY</td></tr>
<tr><td></td><td colspan="3">APPROVED PRODUCTION INSPECTION SYSTEM</td></tr>
</table>

C. GIVE QUANTITY OF CERTIFICATES REQUIRED FOR OPERATING NEEDS:

DATE OF APPLICATION	NAME AND TITLE *(Print or type)*	SIGNATURE

VII. SPECIAL FLIGHT PERMIT PURPOSES OTHER THAN PRODUCTION FLIGHT TEST

A. DESCRIPTION OF AIRCRAFT

REGISTERED OWNER	ADDRESS
BUILDER *(Make)*	MODEL
SERIAL NUMBER	REGISTRATION MARK

B. DESCRIPTION OF FLIGHT

FROM	TO	
VIA	DEPARTURE DATE	DURATION

C. CREW REQUIRED TO OPERATE THE AIRCRAFT AND ITS EQUIPMENT

	PILOT		CO-PILOT		NAVIGATOR	OTHER *(Specify)*

D. THE AIRCRAFT DOES NOT MEET THE APPLICABLE AIRWORTHINESS REQUIREMENTS AS FOLLOWS:

E. THE FOLLOWING RESTRICTIONS ARE CONSIDERED NECESSARY FOR SAFE OPERATION *(Use attachment if necessary)*

F. **CERTIFICATION**—I hereby certify that I am the registered owner (or his agent) of the aircraft described above; that the aircraft is registered with the Federal Aviation Administration in accordance with Section 501 of the Federal Aviation Act of 1958, and applicable Federal Aviation Regulations; and that the aircraft has been inspected and is airworthy for the flight described.

DATE	NAME AND TITLE *(Print or type)*	SIGNATURE

VIII. AIRWORTHINESS DOCUMENTATION (FAA use only)

A. Operating Limitations and Markings in Compliance with FAR 91.31 as Applicable	G. Statement of Conformity, FAA Form 317 *(Attach when required)*
B. Current Operating Limitations Attached	H. Foreign Airworthiness Certification for Import Aircraft *(Attach when required)*
C. Data, Drawings, Photographs, etc. *(Attach when required)*	I. Previous Airworthiness Certificate Issued in Accordance with
D. Current Weight and Balance Information Available in Aircraft	FAR _____ CAR _____ *(Original attached)*
E. Major Repair and Alteration, FAA 337 *(Attach when required)*	J. Current Airworthiness Certificate Issued in Accordance with
F. This Inspection Recorded in Aircraft Records	FAR _____ *(Copy attached)*

Flight Testing

You must carry out the flight testing, in accordance with the operating limitations and within the designated flight-test area for the amount of time agreed upon by the Inspector. During this time, you must keep the aircraft logbook up-to-date, with all the data of each flight being recorded. Any problems or accidents should be particularly noted.

Amending Operating Limitations

When you have completed the flight testing required to your satisfaction, make an application to the FAA Inspector to have the limitations amended. Do this by letter, outlining what you have done, where the aircraft is based, and when it is available for inspection. You must also enclose another FAA Form 8130–6 *Application for Airworthiness Certificate*, which is also used to request amendments to limitations.

Keeping your C of A current

Your Experimental C of A is valid indefinitely (unless a shorter period was assigned by the Inspector), and it is kept current by the aircraft undergoing an annual *condition inspection* and your complying with any other requirements stipulated by the Inspector. If you hold a Repairman's Certificate, you may do the inspection yourself. The logbook should be signed out as follows: 'I certify that this aircraft has been inspected in accordance with the scope and detail of Appendix D of FAR Part 43 and found to be in condition for safe operation', and completed with the date of the inspection, the aircraft time in service, and the signature and certificate number of the person performing the inspection.

Who Can Fly Your Airplane?

A private or higher grade of certificate is required to fly a homebuilt aircraft solo initially. After the passenger-carrying restrictions have been lifted, it may be flown solo by the holder of a student permit, provided that a flight instructor has endorsed that the student may fly the aircraft. This means that the preliminary test flying *must* be carried out by the holder of at least a private pilot certificate.

Pilot certification requirements are spelled out in FAR Part 61. Flight rules are given in FAR Part 91.

Book Recommendations

I strongly suggest you obtain a copy of EAA's book *Custom Built Sport Aircraft Handbook – a guide to construction standards for the amateur aircraft builder*, and also *Sport Aircraft You Can Build*, which are available from EAA headquarters for $3·65 and $4·95, respectively. In addition, EAA publishes many other technical manuals on homebuilt construction techniques. Write to EAA for an order form that lists everything, with its current price: Experimental Aircraft Association, Box 229, Hales Corners, WI 53130. Telephone 414-425-4860.

Another group that offers many benefits to the private flyer in the U.S.A. is the Aircraft Owners and Pilots Association: AOPA, Box 5800, Washington, DC 20014. Telephone 301-654-0500.

Bibliography

P. F. A. Handbook. (1973) Popular Flying Association.

Civil Aircraft Inspection Procedures, Sections BL/6-25 Fabric Covering and BL/6-26 Doping. C.A.A.

Chris Morris 'Aircraft Covering Materials' *Popular Flying* (Mar–Apr 1976). P.F.A.

John Pothecary 'Be Your Own Test Pilot' *Popular Flying* (Mar–Apr 1974). P.F.A.

John Urmston *Birds and Fools Fly*. Vernon & Yates Ltd.

Birch & Bramson *Flight Briefing for Pilots* (4 Vols). Pitman.

Taylor, S. E. T. & Parmar, H. A. *Ground Studies for Pilots*. Crosby Lockwood Staples.

Aero Engineering (6 Vols) (1937) Newnes.

Bill Beatty *Flying the Evans V.P.* J. W. Beatty.

Judge (1943) *Elementary Handbook of Aircraft Engines*. Chapman & Hall.

Kermode (1941) *The Aeroplane Structure*. Pitman.

Taylor, M. J. H. (1977) *Jane's Pocket Book of Home-Built Aircraft*. Macdonald & Jane's.

Hoffman, R. J. *Engineering for the Custom Aircraft Builder*. E.A.A.

E.A.A.'s Aircraft Builder's Handbook E.A.A.

Airframe & Power-plant Mechanic's Handbook (3 Vols) F.A.A.

Haynes, J. H. (1973) *Volkswagen 1500 and 1600 Type 3 Owner's Workshop Manual*. J. H. Haynes & Co Ltd.

Macmillan, N. (1928) *The Art of Flying*. Duckworth.

Eric Clutton *Propeller Making for the Amateur*. Eric Clutton.

Bowers (1971) *Guide to Home-builts*. Modern Aircraft Series.

Air Navigation A.P. 1234 H.M. Stationery Office.

Taylor & Parmar *Aviation Law for Pilots*. Granada Technical.

Clive Canning *Charlie Mike Charlie*. C.J. Publications, Australia.

Index of aircraft types

General index